The Luckiest Orphans

The Luckiest Orphans

A History of the
Hebrew Orphan Asylum
of New York

Hyman Bogen

University of Illinois Press
Urbana and Chicago

To my sweet, precious Thelma, without whom this
book might never have been published

Library of Congress Cataloging-in-Publication Data

Bogen, Hyman, 1924–
The luckiest orphans : a history of the Hebrew Orphan
Asylum of New York / Hyman Bogen.
p.   cm.
Includes bibliographical references (p.) and index.
ISBN 0-252-01887-7 (cl)
1. Hebrew Orphan Asylum of New York. 2. Jewish orphan-
ages—New York (N.Y.)—History. I. Title.
HV995.N52H433 1992
362.7'32'08992407471—dc20   91–28913
                                                          CIP

Contents

Preface

The idea of writing a book about the Hebrew Orphan Asylum first occurred to me on the day it closed, September 20, 1941, while I was standing outside the dining room where a farewell dinner was in progress. In 1957 I prepared a questionnaire addressed to alumni asking them to describe their lives in the HOA and its later effects. To encourage more frankness in their answers, I asked them not to sign it. They returned nearly one hundred replies, five of which were from alumni who had grown up in the 1890s, the last decade of the Baar administration. I owe them a special debt because they provided a fairly complete, reliable, and vivid picture of life under the most rigorous circumstances any HOA child ever lived through. The questionnaire apparently released Louis Freund, Harry Gottheimer, Harold Greenberg, Jacob Gurkin, and Samuel Schwartzberg to write about their lives in the HOA for the first time, and they seemed eager and relieved to do so.

The alumni association in 1964 named me editor of its newsletter, which proved to be helpful because it kept me writing. In addition, I continued to learn more about the HOA from alumni who submitted letters, reminiscences, and photos.

Helene Weintraub of the Jewish Child Care Association gave me access to everything in its archive of HOA materials. From her I learned that the American Jewish Historical Society, in Waltham, Massachusetts, had an even greater store of HOA memorabilia, which it had acquired when the HOA closed.

Nathan Kaganoff, librarian of the American Jewish Historical Society, eased my research load by sending me a catalog of its HOA collection. I spent one long weekend there browsing through the material and met another helpful member of its staff, Bernard Wax, executive director, who later read the manuscript and offered advice and strong support. Kaganoff later referred me to Sylvan Dubow, a member of the Military Archives Division of the National Archives and Records in Washington, D.C., who also happened to be knowledgeable about American Jewish history.

Dubow was the single most helpful person in the early stages of my research on the book. He was familiar with a great many nineteenth-century sources, answered all of my questions promptly and thoroughly, sent me copies of documents I needed, and read my first chapter and offered perceptive suggestions for improving it. I cannot thank him enough for the wonderful support he gave me when I was getting started.

Five other research sources held special items that led me to visit them. The Jewish Division of the New York Public Library, for example, was the only one with a complete file of the *Jewish Messenger* and the *American Hebrew*. It also offered a great deal of material on the history of the New York Jewish community. Although many libraries had the *New York Times* on microfilm, it was more accessible and easier to read in the less hectic rooms of the New York Historical Society. Its files also contained the manuscript account of the Draft Riots I used in chapter 2. The Jewish Theological Seminary library had the only extant copies of *Young Israel*, the Jewish children's magazine published by the HOA. I found the biggest collection of books on child welfare and the only available copies of the annual reports of the State Board of Charities at the library of the Human Resources Administration. And I had to go to the Library of Congress for the issues of the *Mercantile Advertiser* that carried the notices on the founding of the Hebrew Benevolent Society.

I would like to extend my deepest gratitude to Pat Lewis. She believed in the book when no one else did. Her strong faith gave me the energy to continue working on it. Lucille Rankin Potts read the first chapter, praised it, and encouraged me to continue. Maurice Bernstein read two chapters and gave me useful advice and comments on them. I would further like to thank the University of Illinois Press staff, especially Karen Hewitt, who has provided constant guidance, support, and advice in preparing the manuscript for publication.

My only regret is that my beloved wife, Thelma, who was often my only moral support, did not live long enough to see the book itself, though she did know before she died that it would be published. Our life together coincided exactly with the long years it took to get the book written, find a publisher, and have it accepted. Without her it might never have happened.

E Pluribus Dis-Unum 1

To New Yorkers of 1822 who were aware of its existence, the tiny Jewish community of about five hundred souls represented one of the more exotic minorities in the city.[1] It had long been discreet about its own affairs, since its members generally kept to themselves and shunned publicity. That year, though, the community was agitated by a disagreement that momentarily divided it. Both sides argued their case in the *New York Mercantile Advertiser*, because no Jewish publication existed in which to air their views privately.

The first notice appeared on May 7:

COMMUNICATION
Charitable Institution—A society under the name of the *"Hebrew Benevolent Society of the City of New York"* has been formed, and Mr Daniel Jackson has been chosen President, and Mr Joseph Jackson, Treasurer. The object of this society is to ameliorate the condition of the unfortunate of the same faith, whether residents or non-residents of this city.

We are happy to find that the members of the house of "Israel" inhabiting this free country, and enjoying the blessings of civil and religious liberty, are alive to the finest feelings of humanity, in founding an institution which reflects honor on the projectors. —Native citizens, who feel an interest in the improvement of this too much neglected portion of the human family, are invited to join in aid of the society.

On the following day there was a reply—one might almost call it a rebuttal—in the form of a letter:

To the Editors of the *Mercantile Advertiser*:
It is proper that the public should know, that the majority of the Ancient Hebrew Families, and their descendants in this city, and many

who have emigrated from other countries, have no participation in the establishment of the Society, mentioned in the article in your paper yesterday, headed "Communication," and that they hold no intercourse with the persons, there named as President and Treasurer.

Every Editor throughout the United States, who may republish the "Communication," it is hoped will copy this letter.

An American

What seems evident from reading these items is that the "Ancient Hebrew Families" were embarrassed by the announcement of the new charitable society and wanted to be publicly disassociated from it. No doubt they resented the implication that they were not "alive to the finest feelings of humanity" and unwilling to "ameliorate the condition of the unfortunate of the same faith, whether residents or non-residents of this city."

These notices, whatever the overwhelmingly Christian readers of the *Mercantile Advertiser* might have thought of them, signaled an important change in the Jewish community. Daniel and Joseph Jackson, the founders of the new society, were Ashkenazim, Jews from central and eastern Europe; the self-styled Ancient Hebrew Families were Sephardim, Jews from Spain. Both groups professed the same faith but the conditions of the Diaspora had produced many differences between them. The Sephardim considered themselves the nobility of Israel because of the power and wealth they had acquired in Spain before their expulsion in 1492. They had also been the first Jews in America, having arrived in New Amsterdam in 1654. Given their aristocratic pretensions and their primacy as settlers, the Sephardim had always dominated the Ashkenazim, who arrived later, and expected them to accept their authority without question.

But the Ashkenazim living in New York in the early nineteenth century were beginning to feel restive under the Sephardim's dominance. It struck them as a paradox that while living together in the first free nation on earth the Sephardim ran the community as if it were a seventeenth-century European ghetto. Resentful at being treated as inferiors, the Ashkenazim wanted to run their own affairs. For years they had petitioned the Sephardim for the right to have their own synagogue rather than continue to worship at Shearith Israel, the oldest and only Jewish congregation in the city. They also wanted the right to provide for their own poor. The Sephardim, for their part, were tired of supporting every penniless Ashkenazic Jew that arrived in the city from Europe. They were prepared to help resident Jews but in the early 1820s they had apparently decided not to assist transients and nonresidents, as they had done for over 150 years. Because so many destitute Ashkenazim were entering or passing through the city, the problems of feeding and sheltering them had become burdensome. Still, they would not allow the Ashkenazim to care for their own.

In 1822 the Ashkenazim decided it was time to take matters into their own hands. Without obtaining the approval of the Sephardim, they formed their own charitable organization and provocatively advertised this step in the press. Naturally, the Sephardim were angry and they struck back with a letter that reads almost like a writ of excommunication, an attempt to kill off the newborn society with a crushing rejoinder. But their letter failed to accomplish its purpose. For the Ashkenazim the new society represented more than their first venture in self-help; it was their declaration of independence from the Sephardim.

Not a hint of this conflict, however, appears in the Hebrew Benevolent Society's own version of how it was founded. According to that version, it was the death in 1820 of a Jewish veteran of the American Revolution that eventually led to its organization. The soldier, who is never named, supposedly died penniless and friendless in New York Hospital that year. Some Jews learned of his death and began a collection to pay for a Jewish funeral and burial in a Jewish cemetery. They collected over $300, much more than was needed for this purpose. No one knew what to do with the considerable sum of money that remained after his burial, so it was placed in a bank for safekeeping. In 1822 the group that had initiated the collection decided to form a charitable society and use the money to help needy Jews in the city.[2]

It is a heartwarming story of patriotism, generosity, and religious unity—except that not a single "fact" in it can be documented. Indeed, it raises many questions. Why is the soldier never named? How could such a critical detail have been lost? Why was it necessary to make a collection to bury a Jewish veteran of the Revolution? One would have thought Shearith Israel would have felt obligated, if not honored, to provide the last rites for such a hero. Why was so much more money collected than was needed?

In fact the veteran story appears to be a myth. No expert on the American Revolution can identify the Jewish soldier, nor can documentary sources from the period confirm it. Shearith Israel, which operated the only Jewish cemetery at the time, reports that there were no male burials in 1820.[3] The society, unwilling to admit that it had been born in controversy, most likely made up the veteran story to save face. The Jewish community preferred to present a positive image to itself and the gentile public.

In the weeks after the exchange of notices in the *Mercantile Ad-*

vertiser, both sides appear to have sought and achieved a reconcilia-
tion. At the end of June 1822, the new society sent a formal letter to
Shearith Israel asking for its cooperation and was given a room in the
synagogue for its meetings. None were held that summer, though,
because the city was struck by a Yellow Fever epidemic in July. Thousands of panicky New Yorkers deserted their homes and fled the city.
During the crisis Shearith Israel closed its doors because it no longer
had a congregation. When the epidemic subsided, the congregation's
members returned to their homes and resumed worship. In November
the Hebrew Benevolent Society (HBS) held its first official meeting
in a basement room.

In 1825 the Ashkenazic members of Shearith Israel seceded from
the parent congregation and formed their own, B'nai Jeshurun. This
move had been brewing ever since the formation of the HBS. Indeed,
the leaders of the secession and the founders of the society were the
very same men. They took the society with them and made it an
affiliate of the new congregation for a number of years.[4]

Although one might have thought that the secession reflected the
declining influence of the Sephardim this was not the case; it actually
seems to have improved their touchy relationship with the Ashkenazim. One sign of improvement was that some leading Sephardim
began joining the HBS in the mid-1820s. So many eventually became members that when the society was incorporated by the state
legislature in 1832, it listed a number of prominent Sephardim as
officers.[5] Its anniversary dinners, then standard events for all societies, were huge, elegant social evenings catered in the biggest hotels
and attended by important civic guests.

The society's charitable works in the first decade of its existence
are not known, however, because its minutes for this period are lost.
Still, it is possible to reconstruct a reasonably accurate picture of its
charities from what is known about Jewish philanthropy in general
and from minutes published in the 1840s. Although it would later become concerned exclusively with the care of orphans and dependent
children, the HBS in the pre–Civil War period provided assistance
chiefly to families, widows and orphans, and immigrants. Its policy,
following a principle laid down by the Sephardim, was to help all Jews
regardless of national origin. The aid it furnished was then known as
outdoor relief—maintaining the poor in their own home by giving
them money, firewood, clothing, and, if possible, work.

Of all those in need, though, it was the immigrants who required
the most assistance and who made an ever-increasing drain on the
society's resources.[6] Jewish immigration, which had been negligible

for more than 150 years, began rising slowly in the 1820s, increased in the 1830s, and grew even faster in the 1840s. As that decade began, the Jewish community numbered about ten thousand, and it acquired new members at the rate of about five hundred a year.[7]

One consequence of this accelerating growth was a corresponding increase in the need for institutions—indoor relief, as it was called—to meet a number of special needs. These included a home for the indigent aged, an orphanage, and a hospital. In New York, as elsewhere in the nation, such institutions were being built in great numbers under civic, religious, or private auspices, and the city's Jewish community looked forward to the time when it would have its own facilities. As yet, though, it lacked both the financial and organizational resources to build them.

In 1842 the HBS elected as president the most distinguished Jew in America: Major Manuel Mordecai Noah. A Sephardi and a Philadelphian by birth, Noah was fifty-seven at the time and had enjoyed a long (and controversial) career as a public personality. No Jew in America had held so many public offices or had made a mark in so many professions. He had been a major of militia, American consul to Tunis, sheriff of New York, surveyor of the port, and was now an associate justice of the Court of Sessions. Noah had also been the first Jew to be elected a grand sachem of Tammany. Although fully involved in politics, he had found time to pursue two other careers simultaneously—journalism and playwriting. Of these, journalism had been his first and lifelong love. Since 1816, the year he came to New York, he had edited five dailies and was regarded by friends and rivals alike on Newspaper Row as the "Grand Mogul of the Editorial Tribe." During this same period he had written a number of successful plays and was, in fact, considered one of the most popular playwrights of his time.

Of all his accomplishments, though, Noah was best remembered in the Jewish community for an improbable scheme he had attempted to launch almost two decades earlier. In the fall of 1825 he had announced a plan to establish a Jewish colony on Grand Island, in the Niagara River, near Buffalo, and invited the Jews of the world to settle there. But no one heeded his call—indeed, he was ridiculed for being utopian—and the project died the day it was born. Still, his idea of Jewish nationhood did eventually find favor among his people and he is today regarded as one of the precursors of American Zionism.[8]

In naming Noah to lead the society its members may have felt that his considerable political skills would be used toward an urgent goal: unifying the society and the community as a whole. For the Jews of

New York in the 1840s had become a multinational, highly disorganized, quarrelsome body. Most were German Jews but there were also British, Dutch, Polish, French, and Bohemian Jews, all of whom were forming their own congregations and societies along national lines. None of the divisions that emerged was as sharp or as obvious as that between the Germans and the rest of the community. In emigrating to America, the German Jews had also brought with them the new Reform movement that had originated in their native land. Since all other groups in the community were still firmly Orthodox, the Germans became the unhappy target for a great deal of hostile, at times even violent, criticism.

As the city's leading Jewish charity, the HBS was particularly attractive to the most successful German Jews, and many of them joined it. Yet none felt at home among its largely Orthodox Sephardic membership. The fact that they were Reformers only partly explained the hostility they encountered; social considerations were also involved. To the Sephardim, the Germans were "aggressive" foreigners and uncultured parvenus—accusations that contained more bias than truth. If it was true that many German Jews had started their life as, in the Sephardic view, unseemly peddlers, it was also undeniable that some—the Seligman family, for example—had graduated into more respectable mercantile callings. As a result, they saw no reason to be treated patronizingly by the Sephardim. Nor would they consent to defer to them.

This simmering situation came to a head in 1844. That year the Germans in the HBS resigned and formed their own charity, which they imitatively named the German Hebrew Benevolent Society (GHBS). The new organization paid a compliment to its older rival by adopting most of its structure and operating procedures. It held its annual business meeting in the spring, hosted a fund-raising dinner in the fall, and established similar committees to investigate applicants and distribute relief. Its business, however, was conducted entirely in German, the only language used in its written records.

All this was no surprise. What did surprise and even anger the Jewish community was the Germans' announced policy to relieve only German Jews. Poor Jews of other nationalities would have to apply to the HBS for help. By insisting on the total Germanization of its charities, the new society had violated the ancient and hallowed principle that "all Israel is responsible for one another." As a result, they were criticized by many members in the community.[9]

Although the existence of two major competing charities was considered scandalous, a small number of Jews saw it as an opportunity.

These were the professional beggars, many of whom were applying for and receiving relief from both societies. This was fairly easy to do since neither gave the other access to its records; thus, none of the cheaters could ever be exposed. Partly as a result of the cheating, the expenses of both charities kept rising, compelling each to seek bigger contributions every year. A merger was the obvious solution to the problem but both organizations were too proud of their autonomy and status to even consider it.

Hopeful of changing this expensive and embarrassing situation, the community relentlessly pressured the societies for merger. In 1849 both organizations reluctantly agreed for the first time to hold a joint anniversary dinner. Under the influence of good food, strong wine, and conciliating talk, so everybody thought, the charities would forget their differences and amalgamate. Preparations for the dinner went forward with great care to avoid offending either society. By common consent, Major Noah, who was still president of the HBS, was chosen to preside at the affair. It was a point the Germans could concede without losing face. As a living monument, Noah was above internecine squabbles. Besides, as the Germans well knew, he had lately begun talking like a Reformer even though he had never shown any inclination to join the movement.

According to the *Asmonean*, the only English-Jewish newspaper of that period, "the greatest unanimity prevailed on the occasion"—an observation that makes one wonder what dinner the writer attended. For although the societies did get together, the enforced proximity did not lead them to the permanent embrace the community naively expected. The dinner's only success was financial: the collection came to $4,000. As a social event, it seems to have been rather less genteel than its planners envisioned, being marred by some shenanigans that are hinted at but not explained in the *Asmonean*'s guarded account. Its story blamed them on unnamed persons who "having no self-respect" disregarded "ought but their own momentary gratification." The phrase *momentary gratification* seems to have summed up whatever shocking sins were committed that night—probably drunkenness, for the meeting was held in a saloon.[10]

The following year the GHBS took what was for them an extraordinary—and presumably much lamented—step: they canceled their anniversary dinner to supposedly reduce "the great expenses of this institution."[11] Actually, there were no expenses to reduce; its treasury was exhausted. With one notable exception, all the other Jewish charities also canceled their anniversary dinner that year to disburse as much of their funds as possible for the relief of an exceptional number of needy immigrants who had arrived in late 1849 and early 1850. A great new wave of immigration had been triggered by grim economic conditions all over Europe and the failure of the liberal revolutions of 1848. Thousands of poor Jews plus a number of their revolutionary comrades fleeing hostile governments had arrived in New York without much more than the clothes on their backs.[12] The fact that many of them were German accounted for the drain on the GHBS's treasury; apparently fewer newcomers had applied to the HBS for assistance.

In that grim year of 1850, only the HBS remained solvent. It held its twenty-ninth annual dinner in its usual sumptuous style, as if nothing had changed in the past two years. Of the fifteen toasts offered that night one is worth noting: "The Hebrew Benevolent and Assistance Society of the City of New York—May we unite our means and our energies in erecting an Hospital and Asylum for the benefit of the poor and afflicted of our nation."[13] This marked the first public mention of these institutions as goals for the society.

The need for them was now greater than ever because the city's Jewish population, rising even faster in the 1850s than it had a decade earlier, now stood at sixteen thousand.[14] Under community pressure, all the societies, including the Young Men's Fuel Association, the Hebrew Assistance Society, and the Bachelor's Loan Society, agreed to send delegates to an ad hoc committee set up to consider plans for a hospital and an orphanage. Major Noah was appointed its chairman. The committee held its first meeting early in 1851 to discuss plans for both projects and prepare a report for distribution among the societies.

As might be expected, the meeting only served to demonstrate once again the quarrelsome state of Jewish communal affairs. Of all the groups represented, the Germans found themselves in the worst possible position. Although they had been the first to suggest a hospital—it had been set down as a goal in their constitution—they felt the committee would deny them the right to a major role in its establishment. Sephardic and English Jews on the committee were clearly determined to control its governing machinery and had the delegate strength to do so. All this made the Germans hesitant about committing their support. Despite their misgivings, they still offered to contribute their permanent fund to the projected hospital—something all the other societies refused to do.[15]

While the community mulled over the inconclusive outcome of its first meeting, the committee suffered an irreparable loss: Noah died in March of 1851. His funeral, the biggest ever held in the Jewish community, momentarily united all its bickering elements. But Noah's death seems to have taken the life out of the committee as well. Deprived of his leadership, its delegates lost their sense of purpose and had little heart to continue.[16]

When the HBS met in April, it considered the committee report with some "desultory remarks" and then quickly tabled it to see "what measures the other societies would adopt . . . and be governed accordingly."[17] The Germans played the same game. At a special June meeting called to deal with the report, they passed a number of mealy mouthed resolutions that seemed to suggest support for the committee while in effect denying it.[18]

So the buck-passing had begun and would continue all year. In October the Young Men's Hebrew Benevolent Association announced in its annual financial statement that it had established a permanent fund to be used toward the support of the hospital. Noting that the loss of Noah had "retarded the undertaking," it asked that "exertions toward so noble an object be resumed" and declared that they would be "the first to assist in its establishment."[19] No one seemed to be listening. By the end of the year the committee had practically ceased to function.

With things at an impasse, there now entered upon the scene a man who single-handedly took on the work of both major societies and nearly succeeded where they had thus far failed. He was Sampson Simson, a name that (to his eternal annoyance) was invariably misspelled as either Samson Simpson or Sampson Simpson. The Jewish community heard of his initiative for the first time when a small advertisement appeared in the *Asmonean* on January 16, 1852, announcing the "First Annual Ball" of the "Jews Hospital of the City of New York." Scheduled for February, its tickets were offered at five dollars apiece. Five men were listed as the hospital society's founders: President Sampson Simson, Secretary Benjamin Nathan, Treasurer Henry Hendricks, and Trustees John I. Hart and the Reverend S. M. Isaacs.

The announcement created a stir in the Jewish community, whose feelings were accurately reflected in an angry letter published on January 30 in the *Asmonean*. The writer, a member of the defunct Noah committee, obviously felt betrayed. "I am so sorry to say," he began, "that until I read the advertisement I was in perfect ignorance of there being any such Society in New York—and I feel vexed that I should have worked to get up such a concern when there already was one." What especially annoyed him was that he knew only two of the officers, Isaacs and Hart. Although one wonders why he had never heard of Nathan and Hendricks, both prominent Sephardic businessmen, it is easy to understand his ignorance about Simson.

In 1852 none but the oldest members of the community and a number of younger ones he had met recently knew who Simson was. By the end of the year, though, the entire Jewish community would know his name and be aware of his achievements. For Simson was the driving force behind the formation of the hospital society (and a new "Jews' Asylum for Widows and Orphans" that had not been so widely advertised). This burst of activity marked his sudden emergence as the community's leading philanthropist. In view of his age—seventy-two—and his temperament—he was a loner and an eccentric—it seemed to be a role for which he was totally unsuited. But Simson had always been an extraordinary fellow and the vigor he displayed at the end of his life was clearly foreshadowed by his earlier achievements.

A member of one of New York's oldest Jewish families, he was born in 1780 in Danbury, Connecticut, where his family was staying temporarily, having left the city when the British occupied it during the Revolution. He was the first Jew to graduate from Columbia University, one of the first Jewish lawyers in New York, and had been a confidential clerk to Aaron Burr during his term as vice-president. Simson served briefly in the War of 1812 and moved to Yonkers in 1815, where he farmed for pleasure until 1849, the year he returned to New York. To all who saw him then, he looked like a figure from the past—a Jewish Rip Van Winkle from the hills of Westchester. He wore old-fashioned knee breeches and buckles and carried a silver-topped cane, which he leaned upon when seated. His white hair was combed in wavy locks and he eyed everything through oversized spectacles. Despite his age, he walked in quick, short steps, like a man in a hurry.[20]

Simson seems to have spent much of his time seeking out and conferring with men who would listen to his ideas for a number of charitable institutions he had in mind. Few of the men he consulted were ready to follow him because he was an old man and his plans seemed much too ambitious for him to carry out. But Simson, who was wealthy and endowed with iron determination, dismissed all their arguments. In January of 1852, at a special meeting he called at Shearith Israel, he announced the simultaneous establishment of two institutions: the Jews' Hospital and the Jews' Asylum for Widows and Orphans. Both societies had the same group of eight men as officers, half of whom were native-born Sephardim and half immigrant English Ashkenazim. Simson planned to raise money for the hospital by enrolling members in its society at five dollars a year. What financial arrangements he had in mind for the orphan asylum have never been found.[21]

When the news about Simson's institutions was published, it was not, as we have seen, universally applauded in the community. His direct, single-handed approach had, in fact, ruffled a lot of feathers and there were angry demands for an explanation. All the societies were offended because they had been bypassed. The Noah committee, still feebly active, complained that it had been ignored. But the loudest and angriest cries came from the Germans. Their pet project had been usurped by yet *another* group—a new one they hadn't even heard about. If they were beginning to feel that conspiracies were being hatched against them, there was at least reality rather than paranoia to support their argument. For the truth was that the constitutions of both hospital and asylum societies had been deliberately rigged to exclude them.

Although spectacularly outdone by a septuagenarian loner, the two major charities reacted coolly, treating Simson as if he were a brilliant but transient phenomenon. The GHBS held its dinner in November and collected nearly $3,000. It put one-quarter of this sum aside as a possible contribution to the hospital building fund. No funds were allocated for the asylum, however.[22] The HBS assembled for its dinner a week after the Germans held theirs. As a conciliatory gesture, they invited the chief officers of the GHBS to attend—an offer they would later regret making. The evening apparently went well until it was time for the toast to "Our Sister Charities." Joseph Seligman, president of the GHBS, responded with a gaffe that probably made his hosts feel justified in calling the Germans boorish. Instead of praising the work of both societies, he dwelt only on the merits of his own. What was unpardonable, though, was that he had the chutzpah to solicit contributions from his hosts. Understandably, his words were greeted with "coolness," according to the *Asmonean*, which kindly labeled his blunder an "infelicity."

Editorializing on the outcome of the dinner, the *Asmonean* deplored the destructive squabbling that characterized the Jewish community at the time. "Competition is the life and soul of commercial undertakings," it observed, "rivalry is the bane of Jewish institutions. National jealousies and petty sectional spite at this day so divide the Hebrews of New York, that for any organized action, *truly great*, they are completely powerless." It was this anarchic state of affairs that made it easy for Simson to achieve so much alone.[23]

And Simson was moving at a headlong pace. In 1852 he donated two lots he owned on West 28th Street between Seventh and Eighth avenues as a site for Jews' Hospital (later renamed Mount Sinai Hospital). On Thanksgiving Day the next year he personally laid the new hospital's cornerstone. At the same time, his orphanage society bought two additional lots adjoining the hospital on its south side, which extended the site through to West 27th Street. As a result the hospital and orphanage would lie back to back, thus centralizing both institutions in one location. While plans for the asylum were being considered, a temporary office for it was set up at the Houston Street home of the Reverend Isaacs, a trustee of the society. No asylum was ever built, however, and no evidence exists to explain why.

With two institutions already to his credit, Simson in 1853 and 1854 organized two more: the North American Relief Society for the Aid of Indigent Jews in Jerusalem and the Jewish Theological Seminary and Scientific Institute of Yonkers.[24] That he had founded four organizations in three years was not as unusual as it might seem. Simson was simply the front-runner of a huge corps of charity organizers in his own community. From 1848 to 1860, when the Jews made up less than 5 percent of New York's population, ninety-three Jewish welfare societies were incorporated. Of these, the records show that sixty individuals had founded two societies apiece; seventeen had founded three apiece; and five had founded four apiece. The record-holder was a man credited with founding five charitable institutions. During this same period all other ethnic minorities in the city *put together* incorporated only ninety-six organizations, just three more than the numerically tiny Jewish community. The Irish and the Germans, the two biggest immigrant minorities who together made up almost half the city's population, each established thirteen societies.[25]

The creation of so many self-help organizations accelerated the adjustment of Jewish immigrants to American life. Still, the existence of so many autonomous, highly individualist societies made it all the more difficult to organize them into a cohesive community.

Simson died in January 1857, leaving behind an established and flourishing hospital but only the ghost of an asylum. The orphanage he planned seems never to have progressed beyond the drawing-board stage, probably because the community had been concentrating all its resources on building the hospital.[26] Now the orphanage loomed as the community's next priority need, yet it was clear that it would never be built so long as its two most important societies continued to reject a merger. The situation called for a Simson-like personality to step in and resolve the impasse. Fortunately, one was available and willing to assume the role—the Reverend Myer Samuel Isaacs.

Isaacs had been associated with Simson's hospital and orphanage projects, and he seems to have taken it upon himself to carry on his dead mentor's unfinished works. A native of Holland whose family had fled to England in 1814 to escape the invading French, he was one of five sons, four of whom, like himself, had become rabbis. For a number of years he had been the superintendent of a Jewish orphanage in London—an experience that seems to have made a lifelong impact on him. In 1839, when he was thirty-five years old, he emigrated to New York and, European rabbis being in great demand, was at once engaged by Congregation B'nai Jeshurun as its first hazan, or cantor, and preacher. Isaacs attracted instant attention because he was the first to preach in English in an Ashkenazic congregation in America. Apart from this minor innovation, though, he was in every other respect completely Orthodox. When a number of dissidents, mostly British, seceded from B'nai Jeshurun in 1847 to form their own congregation, Shaarey Tefila, Isaacs left with them and became their rabbi.

Shortly after Simson's death, Isaacs founded the *Jewish Messenger*, a biweekly English-language newspaper. In less than a year it became a weekly and acquired a great many readers. Isaacs was now in a position to exert his influence on the community from both press and pulpit.[27]

Near the end of his first year as editor of the *Messenger*, Isaacs opened a campaign to persuade the HBS and its German counterpart to merge. His crusade seems to have been motivated largely by the panic of 1857 and the depression that followed. Once again many immigrant Jews were out of work and forced to turn to charity for survival. "The calls on our benevolence will be beyond all precedent," Isaacs editorialized in early November. "A central board should be formed at once to mature a plan to relieve the distressed, ere it will be too late. The cry of the widow and the orphan is already on the ear. Israel, remember the poor."[28]

If the community's two major charitable societies heard the cry of the widow and the orphan, it wasn't reflected by any move on their part to heed Isaacs's words. A few weeks later, the rabbi-editor again urged a general meeting "of all the Israelites" in which there would be "no empty distinctions, no differences between American, English, German, or Pole."[29]

This time his plea was accepted, for both societies agreed to a meeting. Alas, plagued by the same old divisive squabbles, nothing came of it. Isaacs deplored its dismal outcome in an affecting editorial that summed up what had gone wrong. "Party lines should not be drawn so distinctly," he wrote. "A German society should not refuse to join in the good work because its president is not chosen president of the meeting. An American Jewish society should not allege, as a reason for their not cooperating with the others, that the greater part of those relieved would be Germans. It affords us much sorrow to be compelled to chronicle such a result so different from what we anticipated; yet such is the melancholy truth."[30] Throughout that winter and the following spring he wrote no more on the subject.

In April, Isaacs resumed his campaign for a merger. Taking an approach he knew would arouse his readers, he published a story about three Jewish half orphans who had been placed in a Christian home because their mother was too poor to support them.[31] Although it produced some comment from his readers, the story made no impact on the societies. Nevertheless, its implications were clear: an orphanage was needed to protect Jewish children from conversion. Stories about Jewish orphans who had been converted in Christian asylums were common in the Jewish community. (Similar stories about the deathbed conversions of dying Jews in hospitals had helped create a climate of support for Simson's Jews' Hospital.) This threat was magnified in the mind of the community by an event some months later that had an enormous impact on Jews everywhere. Indeed, it set the stage for the eventual merger of the two societies.

On June 23, 1858, papal troops acting on orders of Pope Pius IX appeared at the home of a Jewish family named Mortara, in Bologna, Italy, at ten o'clock at night and forcibly removed their six-year-old son, Edgar. The church justified the abduction on the ground that a former Catholic servant girl employed by the family had secretly had Edgar baptized four years earlier, when he was very ill and near death. Taken to Rome, the boy became a ward of the Pope and was converted to Catholicism. The incident created a sensation in Europe and became an overnight cause célèbre. Mass protest meetings were held in England. Napoleon III of France and Francis Joseph of Austria, both Catholic monarchs, wrote to Rome urging the release of the child. Sir Moses Montefiore, the British philanthropist, made a special trip to Rome to intercede personally in the case, but the Pope held firm against the pressure and would not return Edgar to his family.[32]

News of the Mortara case didn't reach New York until late September and it provided the city's press with the ammunition for an antipapal field day. Most Americans reacted to the incident with the same degree of indignation expressed by their European contemporaries. Understandably, the story had a special appeal for the Jewish community, and Isaacs gave it a great deal of space in the *Messenger* that fall and winter. His weekly was now the only Jewish newspaper in the city, the *Asmonean* having closed in June following the death of its publisher. Thus, Isaacs's influence in the community was greater than ever, and he was in a position to exert considerable pressure for any cause through the power of his editorials.

In mid-November, after devoting many columns to the Mortara case, he returned to the subject of merger in a two-part editorial headed "Amalgamation of Charitable Institutions." The effect produced by the first part was evident by the time the second part appeared a week later. In that issue was a small item announcing that a joint anniversary dinner of the HBS and the GHBS would be held on December 16, 1858.[33] As might be expected, the item said nothing about what had taken place to bring the societies together. But it seems quite clear that the conversion fears intensified in the community by the Mortara case had triggered such formidable pressures for merger that neither society could resist them.

In December the Jewish community staged a mass protest meeting on the Mortara case that attracted a crowd of two thousand persons, making it the biggest event of its kind ever held. In its organization, the rally attempted to present the image of a unified community—something it hadn't been able to do for decades. Its chair was a native Jew and its board of vice-presidents represented almost every congregation and sizeable national grouping. Isaacs, known to practically everybody because of his editorship of the *Messenger*, was named chair of the executive committee of the board of representatives. An immense success, the meeting and the harmony it demonstrated seemed a good omen for the joint dinner now two weeks away.[34]

Many participants from the Mortara rally also turned up at the dinner, which was held at a popular Broadway catering hall. Four hundred fifty guests attended and they were seated according to arrangements that seemed to have been even more carefully planned, if possible, than those for the unsuccessful 1849 joint dinner. Instead of the two main tables laid out then, which served only to emphasize the gulf between the two societies, there was now one long table on the dais set up for all the invited dignitaries. At its center were the two presiding officers, Philip J. Joachimsen, president of the HBS, and Joseph Seligman, president of the GHBS. Each was flanked by his own vice-president, both of whom also officiated as vice-chairmen of the dinner. To the right of the presiding officers were Mayor Daniel F.

Tiemann, a second gentile guest, and the Reverend Isaacs; they were balanced on the left side by the president of another Jewish charity and three rabbis, including the minister of Shearith Israel. Altogether there were ten rabbis at the dinner. Like the Mortara protest meeting, it was a gathering of the most distinguished members of the community.

With cordiality as the keynote, the dinner began auspiciously and without incident. After the opening prayer, given by a rabbi at the main table, the guests sat down to enjoy the banquet that had been prepared for them.

"The feast of reason," to quote the *Messenger*, got underway when the meal was done. Joachimsen was the first to speak, followed by Seligman. Each expressed more or less the same sentiments: congratulations to the societies on their merger and a request that their own members become part of the successor organization. One point both emphasized was an implicit acknowledgment of how costly their feuding had been: each society had been operating in the red for the past year. In short, it was either merge now or face the consequences.

The preliminaries out of the way, it was time for the toasting to begin; a modest ten had been scheduled. At the toast to charity—"the sweetest flower in the garland of virtues"—Isaacs rose to make the response. Presumably he had been given this honor in recognition of his role in bringing the societies to the dinner. In the collection that followed his remarks, the enormous sum of $10,000 was donated. When the treasurer of the dinner committee announced the amount, it produced the loudest and longest cheering of the evening.

If the extraordinary success of the collection represented the climax of the evening's serious business, Mayor Tiemann's speech was clearly the high point of its lighter, social side. A German immigrant who had made a fortune in paint manufacturing, he was serving his first year in office as the leader of a Reform administration. Tiemann's remarks, a conventional example of after-dinner political rhetoric, dwelt on all the themes familiar to that genre: civic pride, patriotism, religious tolerance, and ethnic pride. Concluding by "wishing success to the union of the two charitable associations," his honor, according to the *Messenger*, "hoped nothing would occur to mar the harmony of that union, so nobly cemented." Tiemann's final words were to prove more prophetic than he knew.

Another well-received speaker was the Reverend de Cordova of Shearith Israel, who responded to the toast to "The Ladies"—none of whom were present. His speech ended on the same note previously stressed by Tiemann. Pleading for "union in the common cause of charity," he urged the societies to relieve "the distressed without asking whether they are our countrymen or not; as long as they are poor, it is sufficient."[35]

As a rabbi began reciting the final benediction ending the meeting, the Orthodox, who included everybody in the Hebrew Benevolent Society, put on their yarmulkes, or skullcaps. But the Germans, holding to their Reform convictions, remained bareheaded. From the main table the Reverend de Cordova demanded that they cover their heads. Following the example of *their* rabbi, the Reverend Adler, the Germans refused. Indeed, they were surprised by the request because they had asked through their dinner committee representatives that such demands be omitted to avoid any unpleasantness.

Angered by the obstinacy of the Germans, the Orthodox Sephardim unloosed a broadside of colored handkerchiefs and napkins— many painted with pictures of animals—at the bared heads of the Germans. These were at once brushed off. A young Sephardi then arose and ordered Adler to put on a yarmulke. "I will make you cover up," he shouted and rushed to the dais. It was a foolish threat and he was not permitted to carry it out. A number of Germans quickly grabbed him and threw him out of the hall. The meeting's carefully built-up climate of unity seemed to be rapidly crumbling.

Somehow, despite the uproar, the benediction was concluded. The Reverend Adler now felt compelled to rise and make a short speech justifying the refusal of the Reformers to wear yarmulkes. He told the meeting that "one should not believe that charity has a greater virtue with or without covered heads." While he spoke, an Orthodox guest stood up and expressed his contempt for the Reform rabbi's words with a loud whistle. In a moment some Reformers surrounded him and began beating him with their fists. If Mayor Tiemann and other gentile guests hadn't intervened, the embattled whistler might have been badly mauled.

The wholly unexpected Tammany-style brawl that ended the dinner produced a terrible scandal in the Jewish community. It was spared any public embarrassment, though, because nothing about the yarmulke fight appeared in any city newspaper—including the *Messenger*. Although Isaacs published the most complete account of the affair, he omitted any mention of its shocking finale. The only story on the dinner that also described the yarmulke fight was published in January 1859 more than two hundred miles away—in a Baltimore German-language Reform journal named *Sinai*. Its editor, David Einhorn, treated the dinner as a victory for the Reformers and gloatingly pointed out that the GHBS had contributed two-thirds of the $10,000 collected that night.

The dinner was the last of its kind ever held. When committees from both societies met in April 1859 to plan their unification, the constitution they worked out for the new organization specifically prohibited the practice of holding anniversary dinners. Philip J. Joachimsen of the HBS was named president of the merged organization, whose assets totaled $25,000. A committee was set up to plan for the new orphanage as soon as possible.[36]

On December 15, 1859, a year after the anniversary dinner, trustees and guests of the society gave a testimonial to Joseph Seligman at his home on West 24th Street. It was presented by Joachimsen as a tribute to Seligman for his eight years of leadership and service to the GHBS in the cause of charity. In his reply, Seligman thanked them all and said he hoped that the union achieved the previous April would continue unbroken, like a perpetual "honeymoon." It was a pleasant, informal evening that came off without the least hostility shown between the former rivals.[37]

But the fact that it was Joachimsen who had made the conciliatory gesture of going to the party and personally honoring Seligman foreshadowed the immediate and long-range future of the society. Within the next few years, German Jews would assume leadership of the organization, provide most of its membership, and furnish the momentum for its philanthropic efforts. And the project that would absorb all their energies in the first months of 1860 was the establishment of an orphanage.

The Hero of
Lamartine Place 2

In April 1860, exactly a year after the merger, the HBS rented a four-story brick building at 1 Lamartine Place, in Chelsea, and opened the Hebrew Orphan Asylum (HOA).[1] Lamartine Place was just one block long and occupied the north side of what is now West 29th Street between Eighth and Ninth avenues. It consisted of twenty-eight identical row houses, with number 1 located a few yards from Eighth Avenue. Once a fashionable neighborhood, Chelsea had declined considerably after 1851, when the Hudson River Railroad began operating on Eleventh Avenue and attracted factories to the area. Shanties and tenements sprang up east of the tracks and their tenants, mostly Irish immigrant factory and railroad workers, were not welcomed by the community. Lamartine Place, a comparatively new development, was one of the few desirable sites remaining in Chelsea.[2]

The HOA was intended as a temporary home for a maximum of thirty orphans and half orphans of both sexes until a new and larger institution was built at a site the society was planning to buy uptown, at East 77th Street.[3] Samuel E. Hart, a Hebrew teacher, was engaged as the first superintendent, at an annual salary of $500. His wife, Hannah, assisted him. She had the title of matron, was in charge of the girls, and was paid $200 per annum.[4] Their four-year-old son, Morris, lived with them.

Almost all we know about the life of the children in the asylum's first few years comes from Henry Bauer, who was the seventh boy and the first full orphan admitted. At the age of nine, he was also the oldest boy and this advantage, he later admitted, turned him into a bully. In an interview published in the *American Hebrew* on April 18, 1910, he described the children's daily routine in two telegraphic sentences: "Get up, say your prayers, get your breakfast, go to school, come back, study your lessons, study Hebrew, get your supper, and go to bed. Very little play, very little play!"

According to Henry, the meals they ate were similarly monotonous: "Mush [boiled cornmeal] and milk, and hominy and milk, and mush and molasses, and rice and milk—and in the evening we had milk and bread." But his recollections do not entirely agree with the requirements for meals set forth in the society's minutes. True, the various grains and milk were prescribed for breakfast and supper but the Harts were also instructed to vary this diet with "either roast or stew with a vegetable for dinner" and "fruit or pie" for dessert on Saturday, the Jewish sabbath.[5] Was Henry's memory failing or was he deliberately making the food seem worse than it was for personal reasons? Did the Harts cheat the children by denying them meat and dessert and pocketing the extra money they cost? No one knows.

One of the first visitors to the new asylum was the ubiquitous Reverend Mr. Isaacs, who was there in mid-April, before any orphans had arrived, and again in October, when the home was caring for twenty-one children, or two-thirds of its capacity. Declaring himself "delighted with the appearance and progress of the orphans," Isaacs observed that they "seem to be a happy and intelligent family of children." Like a proud Jewish surrogate father, he noted that "several of the little fellows are remarkably bright." Then, in a somber concluding statement reflecting the lingering impact of the Mortara case, he reminded his readers that "some of them were rescued from Christian asylums, and imbibed their ideas, which have been happily effaced from their minds."[6]

These early visits by Isaacs were the first of many more he was to make regularly throughout his life, for he was one of the few non-society members of the community to take an active, personal interest in the care of the children. He became, in fact, the self-appointed inspector-general of the institution and the unofficial ombud for the orphans.

His occasional newspaper stories and the society's annual reports, first published in 1863, provide the only outside sources of information available about Lamartine Place. Both are notable for their total unconcern with the kind of life lived by the children. Many factual details are given—per capita costs, for example, averaged $100 a year for the first three years—but descriptive glimpses of any kind are lacking.[7]

Despite Isaacs's view that the Harts and the orphans were living together as a "happy" family, life in the asylum was not as rosy as he pictured it. To begin with, it was terribly overcrowded. Henry Bauer did not describe the sleeping arrangements in his interview but it seems likely that seven or eight children slept together in a bedroom. How they managed it—with cots, single or double beds, or pallets on the floor—is not known.

During their nonschool hours, they were restricted to the dining rooms, one for each sex. In them, they ate their meals, did their homework, were taught Hebrew lessons, and engaged in the "very little play" Henry complained about. Where the children went to relieve themselves is a mystery, since outside privies were not built until 1862. In addition, Henry remembered, "We never had the taste of clear water, no sir. I could never see the reason. We used to drink water on the sly out of the hydrants."

Understandably, some became runaways. But Henry was not among them. He had suffered so much before he was admitted to the orphanage—living with a Hebrew teacher on the Lower East Side who had beaten and starved him—that he found life there quite tolerable in spite of its rigid routine and the inevitable mush and milk for breakfast. Henry had his wild and prankish moments, though; it accounted for the nickname the Harts gave him, "Little Mischief." When he misbehaved, which was frequently, Hart would use a "black strap" to discipline him.[8]

The only times the orphans were allowed out of the home were to attend school or services at a synagogue during the high holy days, Rosh Hashanah and Yom Kippur, and such holidays as Passover, Purim, and Chanukah. Both presented problems. Although the school was only two blocks away, on West 28th Street near Ninth Avenue, getting the children there every day became a sortie into enemy territory because Irish gangs were always waiting for them. To protect the children, Hart himself, wearing a high hat and carrying a stout cane topped by a massive gold-plated knob, escorted the children to school in the morning and returned to take them back in the afternoon. As they marched in a column of twos, Hart scanned the street ahead of them, ready to use the cane on any rowdies who attempted to abuse his charges.[9]

Taking the children to synagogue for services was another kind of problem, a religious and political one. The Reverend Mr. Isaacs alluded to it in an item in the *Messenger* on October 4, 1861, reporting that the orphans had gone to "various synagogues" during the recent high holy days. The orphans were shuttled around because Hart was following the instructions of the trustees, who apparently were trying to mollify all the congregations represented in the merged but still far from harmonious HBS.

We do not know how many synagogues Hart took the orphans to but we can be certain that he didn't visit them all. There were about twenty-seven synagogues in existence in the early 1860s, all but two located below Canal Street. Traveling to any of them with twenty to thirty children was a nerve-racking responsibility. Even the two closest—Shearith Israel on 19th Street and Temple Emanu-El on 12th Street—involved long, troublesome walks through rough streets.[10]

Since none of the congregations were identical in the brand of Judaism they practiced and reflected social, cultural, and national differences as well, the effect on the children was undoubtedly very confusing, to say the least. At Shearith Israel, for example, they would have heard Orthodox liturgy read in Hebrew inside the synagogue and a good deal of Spanish spoken outside, in addition to English. But the Orthodox service there was not quite the same as the version used at Shaarey Tefila, where Isaacs gave his sermon in English. And Temple Emanu-El might have been even more bewildering, for there they would have sat through a Reform ritual conducted entirely in German, during which the congregants prayed bareheaded, without yarmulkes, and, more startling yet, the women were seated among the men. This problem was never resolved while the orphanage was on Lamartine Place or even when it moved uptown a few years later. As Isaacs complained in an editorial on October 7, 1864, there was no agreement on what "modes of worship" the orphans should be taught. He himself urged something he called "practical Judaism," whatever that was.

Most of the religious training the orphans received was taught by Hart, who Henry Bauer described as a stern, strict, Orthodox, and very pious "little man" who always wore a small velvet yarmulke. He held Friday night and Sabbath services in the home and made the boys lay on the required ritual garments.[11] What the girls did during the services is not known, since they could not take part in prayer. They might have been present as observers, like women in Orthodox synagogues. The home had been established chiefly to ensure that Jewish orphans were brought up in the Jewish faith and Hart's work was intended to support that goal.

In the fall of 1860, the state legislature in Albany approved a number of bills that assured the establishment of the asylum's permanent home. In November it authorized the Common Council of New York City to grant the society a tract of land on which to erect its new institution. The common council responded by appropriating a number of adjoining lots worth $20,000 on East 77th Street, near Third Avenue, and presenting them to the society.[12] Later that same month the legislature amended the society's original charter of 1832 and empowered it to accumulate a yearly income of $15,000; own capital of $250,000; receive any gift or bequest as well as property from estates; and have custody over orphans, half orphans, and indigent children no older than thirteen referred by the police or courts.[13]

While these legal actions proceeded in Albany, the children themselves had become the recipients of more tangible, immediate contributions from women in the Jewish community. In September, a number of women had organized the Ladies Sewing Society. Dues were three dollars a year, which went to buy cloth and other supplies. The women met once a week to make clothes for the orphans. Their output in the next few months was enormous: four hundred items of clothing, or enough to provide each of the twenty-eight children then living in the home with about fourteen garments apiece.[14]

The HOA's first few years coincided with the early years of the Civil War, but until July 1863 few echoes of that conflict were heard in Lamartine Place. That year, however, the war was to intrude with explosive impact on the lives of everybody living there and, for one terrifying hour, link the asylum with some illustrious neighbors and their celebrated friend. The neighbors were James Sloan Gibbons, his wife, Abby, and their three grown daughters, Sarah, Julia, and Lucy, who lived at 19 Lamartine Place. A Quaker who made a living as a banker and financial writer, Gibbons was also a lifelong Abolitionist whose reputation in the city as a radical antislavery advocate was second to that of Horace Greeley, the most famous journalist in America.[15] Greeley was an old and close friend of Gibbons and sometimes stayed overnight at his home.

The Gibbonses were the central members of a close-knit group on Lamartine Place that functioned like an extended family. Two doors east of them lived Abby's sister, Rachel, her husband, Samuel Brown, and their two children, Samuel and Sarah. The Samuel Sinclairs, cousins of Greeley, lived at number 26.[16] Another member of the group was Joseph H. Choate, a young married lawyer who was a frequent visitor. Choate had become acquainted with the family through their son, Willie, whom he had met when both were students at Harvard Law School. Willie had died in an accident at Harvard in 1854 and this tragic event had led to Choate's friendship with his family.[17]

With so many visitors coming and going, the Gibbons home was unquestionably the busiest one on the street. Among the callers, however, were occasional nocturnal guests who always arrived and departed in secrecy—runaway slaves headed for Canada. Their home was a station in the Underground Railway and secrecy was necessary because the Fugitive Slave Law of 1850 made it a crime to help escaping slaves. Another visitor who also came and left unobtrusively was John Brown, who spent an evening at their home in the fall of 1859. To Abby alone he confided his plans for the raid at Harpers Ferry and the slave uprising he hoped it would inspire.[18]

In March 1863 Congress passed a conscription act authorizing the draft of men between the ages of 20 and 45. One exemption written into the law, highly unpopular among the poor in Northern cities, permitted a conscript to escape military service by paying $300 to the federal government. Since few working men of draft age could afford this payment, they saw the exemption as a loophole for rich men to buy their way out of service. For a great many Northern workingmen already antagonized by the Emancipation Proclamation, which they felt would set free thousands of Negroes to compete for their jobs at lower wages, the draft law was the crowning insult. They were now going to be coerced into fighting a hated war whose outcome, if the Union won, would leave them worse off than before.

The first drawing of draft names by lottery in New York was held on July 11th, a Saturday. It attracted hundreds of men, all sullen and hostile, to the enrollment office at 46th Street and Third Avenue. None, however, attempted to interfere with the lottery. A total of 1,236 names were drawn; they were published in the newspapers that night.[19] As might be expected, there being so many more of them, poor men outnumbered rich men in the lists; but this fact was viewed by them as proof that the draft was dishonest and rigged against them. The city's copperheads and their allies worked hard through Saturday night and all day Sunday to stoke the seething resentment of the antiwar, antidraft sympathizers among the poor.

At dawn on Monday morning, July 13th—a hot, clear day—hundreds of men and women armed with metal, wood, or stone weapons left their Lower East Side homes and headed for the West Side. In the next few hours their numbers grew into a vast unruly mob that flowed uptown toward the enrollment office. They knocked down sixty telegraph poles and cut the wires connecting them before they reached the office at 47th Street and Third Avenue.

After milling about for an hour or so—waving anti-draft signs, singing drunkenly, cursing, and brandishing weapons—the mob suddenly erupted into violence. A pistol shot at about ten-thirty, according to some witnesses, seemed to be the signal for the assault. A shower of bricks and cobblestones flew toward the enrollment office, smashing almost every window in the building. The mob charged the doors and, after beating down the valiant but ineffectual resistance of police and military units assigned to protect it, poured into the office, destroyed the lottery machine, and set fire to the building, burning it to the ground. The Draft Riots—four of the most terrifying days New Yorkers have even had to live through—had begun.[20]

Its first goal achieved, the mob turned its attention to other targets: Negroes, Abolitionists, *Times* and *Tribune* reporters, police militia, the rich—more or less in that order. Negroes found in the streets were hunted down like animals and hanged from trees and lamp-posts, often with fires built under their bodies. That afternoon a mob burned down the colored orphanage on 45th Street and Fifth Avenue. Except for one girl, all the children were removed in time and taken to a nearby police station for safety. Among Abolitionists the one most wanted by the mob was—as everybody in the city knew—Horace Greeley. At almost the same time the colored orphanage was being burned, the mob was marching downtown to Printing House Square, near city hall, to attack the *Tribune* and kill Greeley. "We'll hang old Greeley to a sour apple tree," the rioters sang as they marched.[21]

The Gibbonses received a death threat on Monday. Inside the corner bakery that day a stranger told one of the servants that "Sinclair's house where Greeley lives" and the Gibbons home were to be burned that night. His threat so upset the girl that she broke into tears and ran back to the house empty-handed. Although disturbed by the news, James and Lucy, who were the only ones home, refused to believe the attack would take place; still, for the sake of caution, they decided to move some of their family heirlooms to the Brown home for safekeeping. Nothing happened that night, however, because a heavy summer rain at eleven o'clock drove everybody from the streets—including, the Gibbonses would learn the next day, the rioters who had planned to fire their home.[22]

Tuesday morning "was so quiet, so bright, and seemed so peaceful that I felt as if riots were impossible" that day, Lucy recalled in a memoir about the episode written in 1927. James left the house after breakfast to visit the Fifth Avenue Hotel to try to get police protection and perhaps obtain some news about the efforts being made to crush the riots. The hotel's telegraph line was linked to the police telegraph system and was kept busy sending and receiving messages about various riot actions in its vicinity.

Not long after her father was gone, Lucy greeted Julia joyously on her return, but they were interrupted with the news that earlier a passing stranger told one of their servants: "We didn't come to your house last night because it rained, but we are coming tonight." When

James returned he took out his pistol and sent Julia and Lucy down to the backyard for target practice. Julia did well with the pistol but Lucy fired the first shot accidentally while waiting for her father's instructions and the bullet went into the ground. Holding the pistol gingerly, she returned it to her father and suggested it might be safer for all of them if she didn't use it.[23]

By noon Tuesday everybody on Lamartine Place had a good deal to be worried about, for in their immediate vicinity the work of the rioters was becoming more visible and threatening. Early that morning, some gangs had begun building barricades all along Ninth Avenue. They were thrown up quickly with captured carriages and wagons, torn-up rails, telegraph poles, and debris from the streets. The longest of them stretched for nearly a mile along Ninth Avenue, from 24th Street to 41st Street. The barricades blocked access to the side streets and made it easy for the rioters to destroy any building at their leisure, without having to worry about interference from rescue forces. Mobs had already burned a feed store at 29th Street and Ninth Avenue and a Negro church at 30th Street and Eighth Avenue.[24]

Elsewhere in the city, the general picture that day—on the surface, at least—looked grim and discouraging. Hundreds of buildings had been burned, looted, or damaged; commerce, industry, and transportation in many sections of the city had come to a standstill; and hundreds, perhaps thousands, of New Yorkers had been killed or injured. But the fact that the mobs ruled the streets did not mean that they controlled the city. No key facilities—forts, armories, naval yards, munitions works, banks, or newspaper offices—had been captured. The credit for this achievement belonged to the police alone, the only force in the city with the training, discipline, and leadership to smash the rioters. Unfortunately, the number of police available for service totaled less than 1,000, perhaps 850 at most. They could count on some help from the militia, sailors and marines, and regulars guarding harbor fortifications, though many were poorly trained and led and performed ineffectively against the rioters. The pace and fury of the fighting was taking its toll of the force. Some policemen had been killed and almost all had been wounded; few had had any chance to rest or sleep or even to change their clothes. They were bone-weary and what kept them going was the knowledge that relief was coming. Troops had been ordered from the battlefields of Gettysburg and the first regiments were expected in the city late Wednesday night.[25]

At the Gibbons household, the strain produced by the stranger's threat was beginning to affect everyone. During the midafternoon

Julia and Lucy gathered some belongings and carried them over the rooftops to their Aunt Rachel's house. As they worked, they strained to pick up any unusual sounds that might herald the coming of the mob. "The dead silence was terrible," Lucy remembered. About four-thirty James decided he would go back to the Fifth Avenue Hotel to buy a newspaper and plead for police protection. He told the girls to go to Aunt Rachel's. He left the key with her after locking his own front door. Although he couldn't have known it then, it was the last time he would see his home intact.

At Rachel's the girls had tea and rested. It was nearly five o'clock. All at once the stillness was broken by an uproar and a clatter of hoof-beats. Two men on horseback waving swords and shouting "Greeley! Greeley!" come galloping down the street from Eighth Avenue. Trailing them was a man on foot, carrying an American flag. The trio appeared to be leading a mob of hundreds of men and women that followed the horsemen past the house to Ninth Avenue and then turned back. The riders pulled up at the Gibbons house and stationed themselves on either side of the front gate, facing the mob. The middle of the street was now crowded with rioters, with more streaming in from Eighth Avenue to join them. "Greeley! Gibbons! Greeley! Gibbons!," the mob chanted.[26]

The rioters opened their attack on the house with a barrage of bricks and paving stones that shattered every window and sent broken glass flying down to the street in a shower. Some men went through the gate and tried to force the door, but their efforts failed. A call went up for men with pickaxes and a few came forward. Before they reached the gate, however, a young man—whose name was Hyde, according to some newspaper accounts—unexpectedly ran inside the gates, mounted the stoop and bravely addressed the mob. Surprisingly, everyone paused momentarily to listen.

"I am a good Democrat," Hyde said, "and am bitterly opposed to the draft; but I do not wish to see private property destroyed. Mr. Greeley does not live here, and it is hard to see the private property of unoffending citizens destroyed. It is unjust to plunder and burn this residence simply because Mr. Greeley once boarded here." The mob was in no mood to listen to reason or logic. Cries were heard, accusing him of being a "damned Abolitionist" and a *Tribune* reporter. Hyde was seized, knocked to the ground, and beaten unconscious. He might have been stomped to death had not a stranger intervened and saved his life. His rescuer took the limp body to his residence nearby, where he was examined and—miraculously—found not to have a mortal wound.[27]

In the minute it took to make this rescue, the mob had broken down the door and about one hundred of them swarmed inside. They rampaged through it, smashing furniture, ripping draperies, and stealing everything they could carry. Others, remembering their comrades in the street, began throwing things out of the windows. Through the shutters in Rachel's house, Lucy saw "books falling like rain until they were heaped up and hid the fence." In front of the house, she recalled, "all was confusion, noise, and quarrelling." Soon smoke began to pour out of the gaping windows as fires were set inside.[28]

Many neighbors became alarmed when they saw smoke coming from the windows and one of them, a butcher named Wilson who lived at number 21, foolishly came out of his house to plead with the mob to stop the burning. It was a dangerous thing to do and almost cost him his life. Wilson was fifty years old and his graying, elderly appearance gave some rioters the idea that he was Greeley. The cry of "Greeley! Greeley!" was heard again, setting off a rush toward him. Wilson was thrown to the ground, beaten, and had the clothes almost torn from his limp body. He might have been killed as he lay on the ground unconscious had not his wife rushed out "with uplifted hands, and agony of voice truly pitiable to hear"—in the words of one newspaper story—and "implored the mob for heaven's sake to desist and not to kill her husband." Her "wild appeal caused a lull among the rioters." Three rioters came forward, gently lifted his body, and conveyed it back to his home.[29]

Around six o'clock Lamartine Place was cheered by an unexpected, thrilling sight—a detail of thirty police and fifty militia marching double-time into the street from Eighth Avenue. The police were members of the Broadway Squad, a special unit made up of the tallest men on the force. The mixed force—police armed with long locustwood clubs and soldiers with bayonets—made a "bold, steady charge" at the rioters, who outnumbered them at least five to one. For a moment, the rioters held their ground but then fell back as clubs crunched down on skulls and bayonets sliced into vulnerable parts. "Strewing the way with bodies as they went," the contingent broke the mob's resistance and sent it scattering. The rioters fled toward Ninth Avenue and the security of the barricades there. Both units now separated—a step which proved to be a tragic tactical mistake. The militia chased the rioters from the street and started clearing away the barricades while the police fought their way into the Gibbons home, intent on emptying it of rioters and arresting some as well. The sergeant in charge and a few others remained outside to grab those emerging from the house with loot.

While each unit went about its task, the mob, it seems, saw an opportunity to disrupt them both. Many rioters returned from the Eighth Avenue side of the street to harass the police outside the house. This appears to have taken place just as a number of rioters rushed out of the house and into the waiting arms—and locustwood clubs—of the sergeant's men. "Clubs and heads found a very intimate acquaintance" as the few police outside found themselves trapped in the middle of a growing melee.

Upon hearing the sounds of the renewed fighting, the militia returned from the barricades to help the police. And now, unhappily, a tragedy occurred. Unable to see the police and without waiting for orders from their leader, the soldiers raised their rifles and fired a volley in the direction of the house. Their fire not only killed and wounded a number of rioters but also hit about six policemen as well. All were wounded, one seriously. The rifle fire sent the rioters fleeing from the street in a rush, but both units had to return to their base.

When the contingent was gone, rioters slowly filtered back to the street to resume their looting at the Gibbons home, even though it offered little by now for them to destroy or carry away. At the Brown home, Julia and Lucy still felt it was dangerous to go out into the street. As the girls were musing among themselves about what to do the doorbell rang. Somebody called out to them not to answer it, but both girls recognized the voice outside requesting admission. They opened the door and Joseph H. Choate entered. Overjoyed to see him, the girls "threw themselves into my arms . . . almost swooning," Choate wrote to his mother some days later. His presence there was entirely accidental. He told them that he happened to be on 29th Street and Broadway around six and saw everybody on the street looking west, as though something was going on. Thinking at first that it might be trouble in the Negro quarter, he decided to investigate and kept walking west until he found the rioters outside the Gibbons home. Choate had gone inside the house to search for members of the family. Although he was obviously not one of them, the rioters ignored him. He said he had wrested some books from one youthful looter but then decided it was fruitless—indeed, dangerous—to interfere alone and decided to look for the girls at their aunt's.[30]

Choate wanted to leave at once but the girls persuaded him not to leave until they knew what had happened to their father. James turned up in a few minutes with a story similar to Choate's. At the Fifth Avenue Hotel, he had got in touch with the police and military authorities and had been told by both that they had no forces to spare. It was this discouraging news he was bringing back to the girls when he returned to Lamartine Place and found the rioters in possession of his home. Like Choate, he had passed among them unharmed as he went from floor to floor, depressed by the damage he saw but unable to do anything about it. None of the rioters gave him so much as a glance, so busy were they with looting, and none recognized him as the owner of the house. There being nothing he could do, he left and went on to Rachel's.

Choate went out to find a carriage and was back, in a few minutes, to announce that he had one waiting around the corner at Eighth Avenue. He told the Gibbonses that it was still too risky for them to go into the street. He had instead arranged for them to go over the rooftops and through the home of Samuel E. Hart at number 1. He had tried to get permission for their passage from homes nearer to theirs, but their neighbors had turned him down. The first house on the street was occupied by Jews, Choate said, and when he asked them to allow the Gibbonses to escape through it the gentleman who answered the doorbell replied, "We feel it a privilege to help people in so much trouble." Lucy would never forget his words even though she had heard them second-hand.[31]

Choate led the Gibbonses over the rooftops to the orphanage. Hart was waiting for them at the scuttle and invited them down into the house. They quickly passed through it and into the street, rounded the corner at Eighth Avenue, got into the waiting carriage, and went to the Choate home at East 21st Street.[32] The escape of the Gibbons family marked the end of the Draft Riots for the residents of Lamartine Place. When the carriage arrived, Choate's wife, Caroline, was there to greet them, as were five Negro refugees.

The entire family spent the summer with relatives, while James, Julia, and Lucy returned to Lamartine Place in the fall in an attempt to resume their life in the ruined house. They were welcomed back by Choate, who presented them with a gift of $2,750 collected by him from their friends and admirers. The money helped them to restore the home to something like its former condition, but living in it didn't seem the same any more. After a year the Gibbonses moved out, followed not long afterward by the Browns and Sinclairs.[33]

Hart had planned to leave sooner than any of them—by the end of July, in fact. But it took more than three months to find a replacement for him. Even then, he stayed on a while longer as a consultant to the new superintendent.[34] In mid-November the HOA would leave Lamartine Place and move uptown to East 77th Street.[35]

Although neither Hart nor the Gibbonses appear to have crossed paths again after their brief moment together during the riots, the incident at Lamartine Place did have an epilogue many years later. Lucy told the story of the burning of the house and the family's rescue at a meeting of the New York League of Unitarian Women many years later. When she came to the point at which she repeated Hart's reply to Choate—"We feel it a privilege to help people in so much trouble"—an elderly woman in the audience rose and said simply, with pride: "That was my husband." It was Hart's wife, Hannah, and her few words may have been the only public tribute he ever received for his generosity and courage on that turbulent July afternoon in the summer of 1863.[36]

Growing Pains in Yorkville 3

The new building at East 77th Street and Third Avenue was formally dedicated on November 5, 1863. About a thousand members of the Jewish community went uptown to view the opening day ceremonies in the asylum's lecture room on the main floor. Long before the ceremonies began the lecture room had filled to capacity, and there was some concern about the growing number of standees. At two o'clock, an hour late, the festivities got underway with a processional led by the officers of the HBS—plus little Henry Bauer carrying the Union flag. They were followed by a large troop of civic dignitaries and an even larger body of representatives from almost every congregation and charitable society in the Jewish community. The cortege marched to music provided by a full orchestra and the Temple Emanu-El choir.

When the marchers were seated, the building committee chair rose to present the keys to the orphanage to the organization's president, Benjamin I. Hart, a son of one of the society's founders. In his remarks, the chair proudly claimed that the society had established the first Jewish orphan asylum in the United States, though actually the first Jewish orphanage had opened in Philadelphia in 1855.[1] Hart's acceptance speech, self-congratulatory in tone, proudly noted that the society's membership had grown from eight hundred, when the building's cornerstone had been laid fourteen months earlier, to twelve hundred. And every new member, he declared, was good for an annual contribution of $100.

Although an elaborate program had been planned, some of it had to be dropped because of the massive crush produced by standees in the lecture room and others in the hall outside. To ease the overcrowding, the orchestra and choir were moved to an adjoining room, where they were followed by most of the standees. There, they were regaled by music and speeches by some of the minor dignitaries while the formal program continued in the lecture room.

Near nightfall, "the immense throng . . . dispersed highly pleased with the exercises that had taken place," the *Messenger* reported. What especially pleased the *Messenger*, apparently still haunted by memories of the infamous yarmulke fight at the 1858 joint dinner, was that no disturbance marred the dedication ceremonies. "Good will and good feeling reigned throughout, and everyone assembled found cause to congratulate himself that he had enjoyed the privilege of attending the inauguration of the first Jewish orphan asylum ever erected in this city," it concluded, in evident relief.

As most guests were departing, others were arriving to take part in the second and less formal half of the dedication program. The newcomers were members of the common council, then the city's chief legislative body. Their destination was a large room upstairs "where a bountiful collation had been prepared for them." Waiting to offer greetings were officers of the HBS, other municipal dignitaries, and reporters. One well-known official to whom the newcomers gravitated at once was the ebullient William Marcy Tweed, then a member of the board of supervisors and the Committee on Public Charities and Correction. A ubiquitous figure at political and social events held by immigrant groups, Tweed seems to have been as popular with the Jewish community as he was with all the others.

Refreshments were served in an empty dormitory, which was furnished with delights its future residents would never sample. Lined against a wall were tables "filled with choice edibles and various drinkables. . . . Above the din of the flashing knives and forks which were engaged in the dissecting of the various fowls, was heard the popping of the champagne bottles and the joyous laughter of the assembled guests." The politicians at this feast had good reason to be merry, for the spread they were enjoying with such audible gusto was apparently well earned. The common council had recently voted to grant the new orphanage a few city lots adjoining its western boundary. As a result, the orphanage now had title to the entire block on East 77th Street from Third Avenue to Lexington Avenue. Perhaps out of gratitude for this additional largesse from city hall, the HBS had invited its municipal benefactors to its private dedication day banquet.

What with toasts—fifteen were scheduled and many more were volunteered when the list was exhausted—and speeches, the dinner didn't break up until seven-thirty. As the guests left they were treated to a sight that doubtless made them stop and look up in admiration—the entire building had been illuminated and "presented a most beautiful appearance."

Illumination aside, the HOA had a solid elegance that commanded attention, according to the *Messenger*'s lengthy and detailed description. Its account, though not by-lined, was probably written by Isaacs himself. As an old orphanage superintendent, he was the only one in the Jewish community with the experience to qualify as a critic of new institutions. "A personal inspection of the building from cellar to skylight," he noted, "demonstrated that everything appears to have been done *well*, with a due regard to the nature of the building, and with a view to permanence. There is nothing of what is styled 'gingerbread work' about it. . . . Every appointment that could well be suggested we find there, and of the best. The arrangements for the laundry, dormitories, lavatories, school rooms, (a room for the refractory too, which doubtless will remain without occupants) apartments for the superintendent and subordinates, for committee meetings, visitors' reception, &c, &c, seem to be complete. There is a bewildering array of closets, bells and keys (of which there are some 684 to find in the matron's moderate key basket) dumb waiters, bathrooms, hot and cold water, and every 'modern improvement' and convenience that may well be expected."

Isaacs's stress on the "modern improvements" could not disguise the bleak fact that the new building was an orphanage, an institution planned as a home for two hundred young children. For along with the bathrooms, dumb waiters, and hot and cold water there was also a "room for the refractory," a detail Isaacs saw no reason to omit. Indeed, despite its interior splendors, the building resembled many orphanages of that period. It had a main section and two wings, one to house each sex. Though only three stories in height, its loft and central bell tower made it appear taller. The main floor was filled with offices, classrooms, a dining room, and a lecture room; dormitories were located on the second and third floors. The laundry, kitchen, boiler room, and storage rooms were in the basement and subcellar. The asylum measured 120 feet in length and 60 feet in depth. There was a good deal of open space around it, including a flower garden on its Third Avenue side, a court in front, a playground in the area facing Lexington Avenue so recently donated by the common council, and a long, narrow yard in back, where there were two outhouses. An iron railing bounded the asylum on three sides. The building itself cost $47,000, part of which was contributed by the state.[2]

In November the children at Lamartine Place plus a few others that were being boarded at other facilities—fifty-six in all—were taken uptown to their new home. They were accompanied by the Harts, who evidently had agreed to stay with the orphanage just long enough to help it get started at its new home. At the end of the year they resigned.[3]

In January the trustees chose his replacement, Dr. Max Grunbaum, a former Hebrew school principal, linguist, and scholar.[4] His annual salary was $750, $250 more than Hart received. A bachelor, he was assisted by Mr. and Mrs. Goodman, with the titles of warden and matron, plus some servants for cooking, cleaning, and other maintenance duties.

Dr. Grunbaum's superior academic training had obviously impressed the trustees, who were seeking someone better equipped to provide for the orphans' spiritual and religious needs than Hart may have been. Faithful to the goals set for him, the new superintendent had the children awakened by bells at five-thirty every morning during the year, got them dressed and washed promptly, and led them down to the basement playroom for prayers. Boys over thirteen were required to lay on the prayer shawls and read from prayer books while the younger boys formed a square around them and repeated the same prayers in Hebrew and English. At seven o'clock the breakfast bell signaled the end of the session. Where the girls were and what they did during this period is not known. Prayer meetings to celebrate the Sabbath were held on Friday night and Saturday morning for all the children, who assembled in either a school room or the lecture room on the main floor. Frequently singing alternated with the prayers, for Dr. Grunbaum had formed the children into a choir to keep the girls and younger children involved.[5]

Early in 1865 Dr. Grunbaum was faced with his first major crisis: the threat of a smallpox epidemic. Its first two victims were two sisters who had been admitted the previous December and fell sick soon afterward. When their illness was diagnosed as smallpox, they were taken to a special sick room on the third floor. This room, and a similar one for boys, had been designed with just such an emergency in mind, for they could be closed off from the dormitories and converted into isolation wards. Fear of an imminent epidemic spread after the girls were hospitalized and became intense when one of them died. Fortunately for everybody, though, her sister recovered and no new cases were reported.[6]

The smallpox victim of 1865 was the first recorded death in the HOA since it had opened five years earlier. It marred but did not spoil what was (and would remain) the most remarkable health record of any children's institution in the nation. Mortality rates for American children throughout the nineteenth century were extraordinarily high, averaging about 10 percent in institutions like poorhouses, workhouses, and orphanages. They fared even worse in the community at large. One study made in 1857 by the Association for Improving the Condition of the Poor, a city charity, found that the child mortality rate stood at 73 percent of the total number of deaths. According to another study, published in 1861, foreign-born children or those born to immigrant parents died at a rate eight times that of native-born children.[7] When the city's newly organized Metropolitan Board of Health produced its first, monumental report in 1867, its statistics were frightful: in American cities, one-third of all children died in their first year, and one-half died before they were five. Epidemic diseases—measles, smallpox, scarlet fever, diphtheria, tuberculosis, typhus, cholera—accounted for the overwhelming majority of these early deaths. The pestilential quality of urban life at the time, though, helped contribute to this high toll. Crowded tenements, garbage-strewn streets, contaminated food, unsafe water, and the inability of municipal authorities anywhere to enforce public health and sanitation standards created conditions that made it possible for an outbreak of disease to become an epidemic overnight. As usual, it was the poor who suffered most and their dead, especially children, increased the mortality statistics.

Because they were isolated from the community, children in institutions were often spared from epidemics raging outside. But when one struck inside, it frequently spread faster and caused more fatalities in less time than it did in the community. In addition, there were epidemic diseases that, though seldom fatal, left their victims permanently crippled. Ophthalmia, for example, was endemic in many institutions. An eye disease, it produced either partial or total blindness. Another scourge of asylums, and often a fatal one, was dysentery, an infection of the lower intestinal tract producing pain, fever, and severe diarrhea.[8]

If the HOA seemed to be miraculously immune from the health problems that beset other institutions, there were some perfectly rational reasons to explain it. One was the wisdom of the building committee, which approved the idea of providing isolation wards. Another was its requirement that all new applicants pass a medical examination. This usually—though not always, as the case of the two sisters with smallpox had shown—served to prevent the admission of children with contagious diseases. A third reason was the extraordinary role of Mount Sinai Hospital. Although few children needed hospital care in the early days, the hospital had always provided it to them on the same basis it did to all poor patients—free. But in 1871, going one step further, it signed an agreement with the HOA guaranteeing free hospital care to all children who needed it.[9] But the fourth and most important reason for the home's remarkable health record was that it enjoyed the services of the most famous children's doctor in the city and the man who is regarded by medical historians as the founder of pediatrics in America: Dr. Abraham Jacobi.

A German Jew, he had agreed to become the asylum's chief consulting physician before it opened. Medicine was actually his second career and he was a great deal more successful at it than he had been in his first, which was revolution. In 1848, then an eighteen-year-old university student, Jacobi had taken part in the revolution that shook his native land that year. Even after receiving his medical degree from Bonn University in 1851, Jacobi still preferred working at revolution to practicing medicine. But that year the authorities arrested him for high treason. Sentenced to jail for a long term, he escaped in 1853 with the help of a friendly warden. Then, following what had already become a familiar path taken by many of his revolutionary comrades (including Carl Schurz, who remained a lifelong friend), he set out for America. Upon arriving in New York he went into private practice and achieved immediate success by pioneering a new medical specialty, children's diseases. In 1854 he won the attention of the American medical profession by his invention of the laryngoscope, an instrument for examining the vocal cords. Three years later he was invited to lecture on pediatrics at the College of Physicians and Surgeons of New York—an appointment that is considered the starting point of clinical and scientific pediatrics in America.

As Jacobi's reputation grew so did his work schedule. By 1865 he was maintaining a furious professional pace that made his former career as a revolutionary seem almost lethargic by comparison. Besides his own practice, centered around a pediatrics clinic he had established in 1862, he was also teaching at the University of the City of New York, making occasional appearances at other clinics and hospitals, and somehow finding time to look after the orphans at the HOA.[10] Presumably he took a keen professional interest in the children there because of the opportunity they offered for research. Not only were they a group who were always available for observation but their membership remained fairly constant for years at a time. Simply by being there, the orphans helped contribute to the accumulation of new knowledge and new techniques in pediatrics.

Unfortunately for the asylum, not all the men it chose to look after the orphans were of the same caliber as Dr. Jacobi. One clear impression that emerges in reading about Dr. Grunbaum's regime is that he was a bungling administrator. A hint of this appears in a story in the *Messenger* on March 23, 1866, in which Isaacs reported receiving complaints about the asylum's "domestic economy," or management. He didn't specify what the complaints were or who made·them but he did note that the trustees would correct "whatever abuses may be brought to their attention." Whether any abuses were uncovered cannot be determined because the *Messenger* said no more about the subject.

Isaacs was far less reticent in the fall, when Dr. Grunbaum committed a blunder that led the rabbi-editor to write an angry editorial. What angered him was the poor judgment the superintendent showed in a conflict that arose between the orphans' secular education and their religious training. That fall, the first day of school coincided with the first day of Rosh Hashanah, the Jewish New Year and one of the holiest days in Judaism. Without consulting the trustees, Dr. Grunbaum sent the children off to school instead of taking them to services. His excuse was that the children were eager to attend in order to register and thus not lose their place in class.

Yet, as Isaacs pointed out in a editorial, "It was quite unnecessary for the children to attend school at all on the holy-days. A note addressed to the Principal could have accomplished the same purpose." Dr. Grunbaum's faux pas provided Isaacs with another opportunity to harp on a favorite theme: the HOA'S need for "a synagogue and regular service." As at Lamartine Place, the orphans were still being taken to different synagogues for services. In the same editorial, though, Isaacs touched on another, more ominous, theme that presumably worried Dr. Grunbaum: he suggested that the orphanage "be placed in the charge of a competent Superintendent, who is a consistent Israelite and not only a philosopher."[11] It was the last phrase that probably drew the most blood and was not entirely justified. Dr. Grunbaum was attempting to supervise the asylum practically single-handed and finding it a desperate responsibility as admissions continued to grow. With the kind of publicity he was getting from Isaacs, though, his days as superintendent were clearly numbered.

A week later, however, Isaacs wrote about an event held at the asylum that seemed to put Dr. Grunbaum in a happier light. The previous Sunday there had been an examination of the orphans held in the presence of the trustees and (as Isaacs complained) a "sparse . . . attendance of visitors." Dr. Grunbaum "addressed the audience, pointing out his system of instruction, the difficulties under which he had labored, and the results that might be expected." He seemed to be

apologizing in advance for what might turn out to be a poor performance, for as Isaacs observed, "the examination had been hurriedly
prepared." Dr. Grunbaum then proceeded to examine the more advanced boys in Hebrew grammar, Bible history, and the geography
of Palestine and tested others in German as well as English. At the
end of the session, prizes were distributed to the best students by
the chairman of the society's board of governors. Pleased—perhaps
unexpectedly—by the performance, Isaacs praised Dr. Grunbaum for
being "an excellent teacher."[12]

While Isaacs was satisfied with the outcome of the examination,
he still found room for complaint in other aspects of asylum life.
For example, there was a note of sad irony in his observation that
the community, which had been so eager to see the home built, paid
no attention to the orphans who had been placed there. Apart from
officers of the society, members of the Ladies Sewing Society, and
parents, few others went uptown to spend any time with the children.

Another situation that Isaacs brought to light was the need to apprentice the older boys. Residents were supposed to be discharged at
thirteen, but there were at least half a dozen boys in this age group
whom the board of governors were unable to place with families. No
such problem had come up with the older girls, who found ready acceptance in Jewish homes as domestics. In touching on this matter,
Isaacs had hit upon a major issue in the care of the orphans: their
future after discharge. It made no sense to rescue orphans, provide
them with shelter and care, and then discharge them with no way of
making a living.

Predictably, Isaacs continued to be critical about the HOA's failure to provide its own religious training for the orphans. His solution was simple: convert a room into a synagogue. A synagogue had
not been included when the building was being designed because of
the intense conflict between the Orthodox and Reform factions. The
HBS would not have permitted Orthodox services in the asylum; on
the other hand, the community might have terminated its support
if the orphans were being trained exclusively in Reform principles.
By requiring the superintendent to take the orphans to various synagogues for services, the society presumably prevented this issue from
coming to a head.

The most incongruous detail in Isaacs's comments about the state
of the HOA was the item that "three fine cows, pastured in the adjoining lot, furnish pure milk daily." But he had mentioned it for a very
good reason: it assured the community that the asylum was not using
swill milk. This was the name given to milk produced by cows who

had been fed swill, the waste product of the fermentation process, obtained from distilleries or to milk adulterated by such additives as magnesia, chalk, and plaster of paris. Swill milk could usually be identified by its thin texture and slightly bluish tinge. Despite its uninviting appearance, it sold well because it was cheaper than pasture milk bought from farms outside the city. Cows that produced swill milk were kept in stalls on the Upper West Side, above Fourteenth Street, since pastures were already scarce in lower Manhattan. Tethered in foul surroundings where they received no exercise whatever, the cows often became ulcerated and diseased, but this did not deter their owners from selling their milk to unsuspecting citizens. Milk then was sold out of buckets carried in open carts that roamed the streets. In 1857 one newspaper estimated that two-thirds of the milk sold in the city came from distillery dairies. Although the milk that came from outside the city was likely to be a lot purer, this did not always mean that its vendors were necessarily more honest. As one writer explained in the 1850s, 91,000 quarts of milk entering the city daily were "by some miraculous process" increased to 120,000 quarts by the time they reached the market. In this case, of course, the miraculous ingredient was water. Thus, when New Yorkers went out to buy milk they frequently faced a kind of Hobson's choice between a cheap contaminated product or an expensive diluted one.[13]

In December 1867 Dr. Grunbaum resigned. From the evidence available, one gets the impression that this resignation was not voluntary. Isaacs, for example, announced it in the *Messenger* with a terse item that lacked the usual conventional phrases suggesting that Dr. Grunbaum was leaving for riper opportunities elsewhere. The new superintendent—the third in eight years—was Louis Schnabel, another pedagogue. Born in Moravia and educated at the University of Vienna, he moved in 1854 to Paris, where he became principal of a Jewish girls' school for a number of years. During this period he developed an interest in journalism and contributed many articles to Jewish newspapers. In 1869 Schnabel emigrated to America and settled in New York.[14] Presumably his education and teaching experience impressed the HBS and led to his appointment as superintendent.

Schnabel had his own ideas for improving the administration of the orphanage and, with the society's approval, began working on them months before he took office. Changes were desperately needed because the asylum during Dr. Grunbaum's regime had grown from a small home to a congregate institution. Although planned for a capacity of 200, it actually could shelter no more than 150. The building had been designed with two identical wings to provide for an equal number of male and female admissions. As it turned out, though, boys outnumbered girls by a two to one ratio, and this probably led to changes in the sleeping arrangements that required a reduction in total occupancy. The *Messenger* on October 11, 1867, reported that the society was considering adding a new wing, expected to cost $50,000.

What this overcrowding meant in administrative terms was that Grunbaum, assisted only by the warden, was supervising 150 children—an impossible responsibility from any point of view. It was clear that these children could not be shepherded about like an extended family, as the Harts had done at Lamartine Place. The time had come to establish administrative machinery—regulations, lines of authority, channels of communication—for the operation of the HOA as an *institution*.

Schnabel, however, seems to have been well aware of what the home needed. In December, a month before he officially assumed office, he completed the project he had started that fall and presented it to the society as his blueprint for the future operation of the HOA. Titled "Rules and Regulations for the Internal Management of the Hebrew Orphan Asylum," it was a four-and-a-half-page document outlining the duties of the superintendent, assistant superintendent, governess, warden, matron, and assistant matron. At the time Schnabel was preparing the new rules, the positions of assistant superintendent and governess didn't exist; he included them because he knew the asylum intended to create them for his regime. Appended to the rules and regulations were two additional items covering visitors: "By-Laws Relating to the Relatives and Friends of the Orphans" and "General Rules." Schnabel's rules were adopted by the board of governors in December and included by them in the 1868 annual report.

Schnabel further indicated some of the major improvements that had been achieved in "but four months." Schnabel's writing tells us a good deal about what had gone wrong under Dr. Grunbaum's administration. For one thing, he seems to have been permissive in supervising the children's meals. Schnabel was more firm. "The dining room arrangements," he declared, "have been entirely changed; the presence of myself, with my assistant and of the Governess, at the head of each table, have contributed largely toward the decorum and demeanor of the pupils." Another change he introduced, however, was the first of many depersonalizing steps: "Every inmate has received a number, which is marked on every article belonging to him or her. The value of this arrangement can scarcely be overestimated, a child feeling himself the sole proprietor of any garment, book, &c., will naturally have the '*amour propre*' to keep it carefully." Numbering also prevented the spread of skin diseases because children received only their own garments back from the laundry. A third improvement dealt with visitors, who apparently had been responsible for "many disturbances." Schnabel resolved this problem by "upholding strictly and to the letter the rules regulating visits from relatives of the orphans."

Important as these accomplishments were, however, the new superintendent was proudest of the new religious instruction: "Regular Divine service is held in the House. I feel the greatest satisfaction in being able to state that during service the children behave so exemplarily, and with such devotion, that the seed of our holy religion, I hope, will be implanted into their youthful hearts so as to bear fruit in after life."

One can be certain that the services he conducted—in a lecture room converted to a synagogue—were Reform. Schnabel, however, was not qualified to provide any religious training since he was not ordained. No one seems to have challenged him on this point. Besides, he had given himself the authority under "Duties of the Superintendent," Rule 9, which stated that "he shall commence and close each day with family worship, the prayers being in part Hebrew and part English, to be offered in a reverential manner." Prayers in English were an established Reform innovation, and the phrase *in a reverential manner* was an obvious thrust at the Orthodox, whose undisciplined services were regarded as disorderly by the German Jews.

Schnabel attempted to broaden the children's religious training by inviting outside speakers to present sermons. One such guest speaker in 1869 was a nineteen-year-old Columbia University student preparing for a career in the rabbinate and thus to follow in his father's footsteps. His name was Felix Adler and his father, rabbi at Temple Emanu-El, was the man who had led the Reform contingent at the merger dinner of 1858. Adler gave three sermons on Jewish martyrs in Spain.[15]

Although new to the HOA, the imposition of written rules was a standard practice in many orphanages. It was under Schnabel's regime that life in the home began to assume the regimented quality that would characterize it until the day it closed, more than seventy years later. The duties of the assistant superintendent, who was hired to supervise the boys, spells out their daily routine. He was expected to maintain "a general supervision" over his charges and "keep a roll of their names"; see that they were "up betimes in the morning, and that they were properly and cleanly dressed before proceeding to prayers"; escort them "to and from public school, and assist them at their studies, watch them at their play, and instruct them as the Superintendent may direct"; be present at the "children's meals, and at their meetings with relatives"; call the roll before retiring to bed"; and be present at the children's prayers. The duties of the governess were practically identical to those of the assistant superintendent, with one exception: she was required to "designate the larger girls each in turn to do housework, so that all may have an equal chance in pursuing their education." The "education" the HOA had in mind for them was training as domestics, the only occupation then considered suitable for orphan girls.

Although the assistant superintendent and the governess were responsible for the supervision for the residents, the person who actually did the work for them was the warden, whose role was a mixed one. He was not only in charge of the workers in the kitchen, laundry, and basement but also spent a great deal of his time supervising the children. He was expected to rouse them from bed every morning, see that they washed and dressed and took a weekly bath, and was required to be present at their meals, prayers, and meetings with relatives. What was unusual about his duties, however, was that he worked with both sexes. In fact, he was permitted to associate with the girls on the most intimate terms. When they took their weekly bath it was the warden—not the governess—who personally supervised them. He was allowed to enter their dormitories every morning to rouse them from bed and get them into the washroom and toilet. Since there were about a dozen or more girls thirteen or fourteen years old, the warden was in a highly sensitive as well as potentially corrupting position. How he used his power depended on the kind of person he was. And what we know about the wardens in the HOA suggests that they were a degraded, abusive, and invariably sadistic lot. Fortunately for the orphans, the position of warden was a shortlived one; it was to be abolished within a decade.

Schnabel's inclusion of an entire section to bylaws dealing with visitors suggested that the problem had gotten out of hand during Dr. Grunbaum's administration. Visitors were turning up any time it suited them and their presence was always disruptive. To establish the HOA's authority in this area, Schnabel decreed that relatives and friends could visit only on the first Sunday of every month from two to four o'clock. However, his bylaws did allow one humane exception: extended visits by relatives when their children were dangerously ill. Another rule prohibited visitors from giving candy, fruit, and money to the children although it allowed them to turn these over to the superintendent for distribution later on. In some cases, though, the food was not distributed because it was either contaminated or spoiled. Rather than risk sickness or an epidemic, Schnabel ordered such food to be destroyed. His reason for collecting the money was probably simple security: the children had no place to keep it and stealing was rampant, especially among the boys. Schnabel also forbid the children to leave the premises to visit relatives or friends except on special occasions and then only with his consent or the consent of the board of governors.

The final section of his administrative code was devoted to general rules, a catch-all category. Residents could not be sent on errands or leave the premises except by special permission of the superintendent. In addition, they were required to maintain "a strict marching order" while going from one room to another. (The "strict marching order" Schnabel referred to was not the humiliating lockstep, an American invention. Then used by all penitentiaries, the lockstep required the marchers to line up behind one another as close as possible, and move in mechanical unison, in a step combining a march and a shuffle.) Except for the superintendent, employees were forbidden to accept any gifts donated to the orphans or the home. And the final rule was not a rule at all but an admonition. "The government of the children," it declared, "is to be based on mildness blended with firmness. Punishment should always be administered in moderation and in perfect temper and self-command. For punishment of serious transgressions, the advice of the Superintendent shall be taken."[16] A caution against the use of excessive force in maintaining discipline, one wonders how closely it was followed by Schnabel's subordinates. Still, it was expedient to have it on paper and included as part of the annual report.

Because they read so well and sounded so progressive in their day—few then believed in "mildness" or "moderation" in dealing with children, let alone orphans—Schnabel's rules were favorably received by the Jewish community. Also pleased, Isaacs reprinted them in full in the August 7 *Messenger*.

While the HOA struggled to cope with its growing pains, its parent organization was undergoing similar stresses. In the post–Civil War years the HBS had recruited a great many more members. By 1867 it had nearly four thousand on its rolls, a tenfold increase since the merger in 1859.[17] It was the largest Jewish charitable organization in America and quite possibly the largest charity in existence at the time. Samuel S. Cohen, its president, retired from office in 1867 after serving two years and his departure led to an unbelievably fierce contest for a successor.

In "the largest vote ever polled in a Jewish society" in the city until that time, 1,140 ballots were counted; the winner was a man named Joseph Fatman. But the extraordinary number of votes was only part of the election story; the total would have been at least 25 percent higher had not three hundred members angrily left without voting. They did so because of the crush on the polls that Sunday and the miserable arrangements for voting. The society's election bylaws required the polls to be open only four hours, but when this period had expired by two-thirty that afternoon, the number of members still waiting to vote was so great that the voting period was extended to five o'clock. Even then, getting into the polling room was no easy matter. "There were several instances of severe contusion," the *Messenger* reported, "and at least one black eye, while some stout members were laboring under serious difficulties and not a few fainted for air." So great was the crush that police had to be called to keep the crowds in line. Thereafter, the voting proceeded "steadily and always with perfect good humor." In the street, "electioneering, posters, circulars . . . were in full play," the *Messenger* happily noted, "and the Orphan Asylum was not unlike Tammany Hall in its palmy days."

It is clear that a power struggle was taking place, and the issue at stake seems to have been the religious education of the children. As the *Messenger* put it, this was "a sacred duty whose importance cannot be over-rated, and we hope our confidence is not unreasonable when we accept the assurances of the Trustees, whatever their personal views, that the laws of the Society will be sacredly maintained."[18] Apparently the issue was not the principle of reform itself —German Jews, after all, dominated the society—but how much reform should be permitted. There seems to have been a difference of opinion on this point within the society, with the trustees wanting more reform and the majority of members less. The members won, but their victory was a temporary one. The HOA would adopt more and more Reform practices as the years went on, until in 1911 it took the ultimate step of abandoning kashruth, the kosher dietary laws.[19]

A year after the most turbulent election in its history the HBS was, paradoxically, afflicted by almost total apathy. To get its members to the polls that year a special drive had to be undertaken. Of the 1,200 who voted, only 64 stayed for the election for the board of governors, which supervised the asylum's operations. And the situation worsened in 1869, when the society couldn't raise a quorum of two hundred for its annual meeting. Why had interest died so precipitately? Boredom with organizational business, according to the

Messenger, which quoted a member it had overheard leaving one session as saying, "We really cannot attend these dry meetings."[20]

At the HOA, Schnabel was also having his own problems, the most troublesome being slow turnover. While admissions grew year by year, discharges were not keeping pace; the asylum had become like a funnel with a clogged tube. The situation was first brought to the attention of the society in 1867. In his president's report that year, Samuel S. Cohen broached a subject of "vital importance": that of "placing our orphan boys, when they become of an age that forbids their retention in the Asylum." That age was thirteen, the year of bar mitzvah, when a Jewish male acquires the responsibilities of adulthood. Cohen pointed out that in the May 1866–April 1867 period there had been seventy-one admissions but only twenty-four discharges. He argued that "unless effective ways and means are devised and adopted for placing and providing homes for boys over age, there must necessarily be an end to admissions."[21] Boys were a special problem because they were much harder to place with Jewish families, who preferred girls because they could work as domestics.

In other institutions, boys were discharged either by giving them out for adoption or binding them out as apprentices. Of the two, the second method was more common. But the HBS, which tried to follow the same system, had little success with it. Few Jewish families were willing to adopt Jewish boys and far fewer still were in a position to accept them as apprentices. Although some Christian families were willing to apprentice boys from the HOA, the society refused their offer. Its board of directors had decided unanimously that no boy should be placed in the position of having to work on the Jewish Sabbath.[22]

Another idea other asylums had tried was to send orphan boys to farmers in the South and the West, and the HBS had made a few such placements with Jewish farmers. But since Jewish farmers were scarce and hard to locate, this could not be viewed as a long-range solution to the problem.[23]

By 1868 the number of overage children had grown to fifteen— fourteen boys and a girl between the ages of fourteen and sixteen. That summer discharges rose slightly, an improvement directly traceable to a B'nai Brith convention held in the city. A group from the organization visited the HOA and some among them were persuaded to take seven boys. A year later there were sixteen overage boys waiting for discharge. Not far behind them were fifty-one others between eleven and thirteen, and the 1869 annual report projected an estimate of sixty in this group by 1870 if none were placed by then.

The problem of unplaceable overage children was compounded by yet another situation that the home was just beginning to recognize: more and more single parents were using it as a boarding school. They were finding it easier to leave their children at the asylum and pay it for their maintenance rather than caring for their own children. In some cases, the *Messenger* indignantly reported, the parent involved was "fully able to attend to their wants" but preferred having the orphanage do their work for them. The view that many parents were dumping their children on the asylum was borne out by its own statistics: only 15 percent of the inmates were full orphans and this total was slowly shrinking.

Early in 1869 the HOA decided to set up an industrial school on the premises, teach the older boys trades, and thus equip them to earn a living without having to be either adopted or apprenticed. Shoemaking was chosen as the trade most suitable for launching the project. In May of that year the asylum engaged a master shoemaker and set up a shop for him in the basement. Six boys, all volunteers, were assigned to the shop as its first apprentices; two more were added in August, followed by another two in October.

Because they were working, the ten apprentices enjoyed special privileges. They were also paid from twenty-five cents to a dollar a week, the amount depending on the "industry and behaviour" each demonstrated at work. Most of the money was withheld and banked for the boys so that they would have some savings when they were discharged. The money for the allowances came from an appropriation of $20 a month from the society, which wanted to encourage the boys in their chosen trade.

The shoe factory's goals were modest at first: to make and mend shoes for the residents and also produce some for the poor recommended by the society's charity committee. When their training was more advanced, the boys began to make shoes for paying customers, who flocked to the shop in ever increasing numbers. Attracting them was easy because the shop could undersell any similar establishment in the city. Business was so good that it was able to show a profit of $244 at the end of its first year of operation, in April 1870. Thus what had begun as a training program to help the older boys become self-supporting had become surprisingly lucrative. Naturally the society was pleased and said so in its annual report.[24]

With the shoe shop successfully launched, the HOA began thinking about a second trade that would enable still more older boys to "earn their honest bread by their honest labor." The idea for it came from Schnabel. When Jesse Seligman, a society officer, was considering a gift for the orphans in honor of his son Henry's bar mitzvah, he consulted the superintendent, who suggested a printing establishment. Seligman thought it a splendid idea. Schnabel ordered a steam press, a number of fonts, furniture, and supplies and had it all installed in a basement playroom, near the shoe shop. The bill came to just over $1,000 and Seligman paid it.

On June 10, 1870, the Hebrew Orphan Asylum Printing Establishment, staffed by a master printer and seven apprentices, formally opened for business. Because he had so much faith in the new enterprise, Schnabel did not ask the society for a grant of funds to get it started, as had been the case with the shoe shop. Instead, he took a loan of $400 the first month and later took another loan, nearly $750, from the shoe shop. Within a few months the print shop fully justified Schnabel's high expectations by attracting an enormous volume of orders. Demand for its services was so insistent that the HOA decided in October to buy a second press, more fonts, and more supplies. This additional investment cost $1474, a heavy debt for an infant business to write off.[25]

Although proud of its thriving experiment in vocational training, the home soon became unhappy with the location of the shops. Not only did they deprive the residents of playroom space but they also made a lot of noise, which disrupted other activities. In addition, the customers who came to both shops were a disturbing element; too many behaved like tourists once they were inside. Late in 1870 the society decided that a separate building was needed and ordered the construction of a four-story factory on East 76th Street, just behind the main building. It was designed to provide dormitories, a dining room, and classrooms as well as shops so that the boys would live where they worked.

The society now approved another project: having the print shop publish an illustrated monthly children's magazine. This was Jesse Seligman's idea. The profits it made, he told the society, would be used for the benefit of the industrial school alone. Children's magazines were a post–Civil War innovation, and a number of successful ones were in circulation. However, none were published under Jewish auspices for Jewish children—a gap Seligman felt should be filled. As a result, the first Jewish children's magazine in America was born— *Young Israel*. Its editor was Schnabel, who had been a writer on Jewish subjects during his Paris years. Though it meant extra work for him, he eagerly accepted the assignment.

Starting a new magazine was an expensive and chancy venture, and Seligman sought to ensure its success by obtaining the services of a well-known writer whose name would attract subscriptions. He already had such a person in mind—Horatio Alger, the young Harvard graduate who was then tutoring his children. An old family friend and a rising star among writers of children's stories, Alger had achieved success in the field after his novel *Ragged Dick* appeared in book form in 1868. Invited to contribute an article for the first issue, Alger surprised Seligman and delighted Schnabel by offering to write its main story.

The first issue of *Young Israel*, published entirely in English, appeared in January 1871. It was a forty-eight-page edition filled with stories, articles, poems, puzzles, and illustrations and sold for three dollars a subscription. Except for the binding, it was wholly the product of the HOA's print shop. Alger's contribution was a novel whose title seemed meant as advice to the inmates who had printed it— *Paddle Your Own Canoe*, serialized in twelve monthly issues.[26] As expected, Alger's contribution had a magical effect on subscriptions, which flowed into the print shop's office at a gratifying rate.

Despite what was to become a long association (eight years) with *Young Israel*, Alger rarely visited the asylum, even though he loved being with children. He preferred the Newsboys Lodging House, where it was easier to mix with the boys and listen to their stories of life on the streets. Many of their hard-luck tales were used by him as plot ideas for his novels.[27] And though most of his young fictional heros were orphans, he spared them the rigors of an orphanage childhood for purely literary reasons. No boy, after all, could conceivably improve his status in an orphanage, where any adventure was likely to end with punishment rather than with the kind of reward that led to a bright career.

Throughout 1871 Schnabel's reputation soared. The industrial school was an immense success, earning him the complete confidence of the society. His standing with the Reverend Mr. Isaacs, the asylum's most vigilant critic, was, if possible, even higher. On March 3 that year a letter writer to the *Messenger* reported that "within [the asylum] there is everything to praise" and "nothing to condemn, even if fault-finding be the visitor's object." Schnabel clearly was headed for lifetime tenure as superintendent, provided he intended to stay. Thus far he had not given the society any reason to believe he had other plans for his future.

From the society's point of view, the well-ordered and smoothly functioning administration of the HOA by Schnabel couldn't have been accomplished at a more propitious moment in its history. For as the year was ending a golden milestone loomed for the Hebrew Benevolent and Orphan Asylum Society (to use the name it adopted in 1870)—its fiftieth anniversary. The celebration of this event took place on April 11, 1872, at the Academy of Music on Fourteenth Street. That evening every seat in the theater was filled, and the guests of honor—"these tender flowers of humanity," to quote the *Messenger*—were the orphans themselves. Scrubbed and neatly dressed for the occasion, they sat up front near the stage. Their role in the exercises that night was, apart from being on display for the audience, entirely musical; they either sang alone as a group or led the house in singing. Between songs they listened to several speeches, including—inevitably—one in German. It was the first time that an American Jewish society had celebrated its fiftieth anniversary, a theme emphasized by every speaker. To prove the society's right to call itself ancient, its president, Myer Stern, produced a relic—Rowland Davies, Sr., the sole surviving member of the small group of men who had founded the HBS in 1822. Stern also gave his audience some figures to savor. One was that the society had distributed more than $1 million in charity since its founding. Another was that the income from dues in 1871 had totalled more than $40,000, the highest ever collected.[28] Self-congratulation—clearly earned—was the mood of the evening. Though no figures exist to support the claim, it seems quite likely that the HBS was the biggest organization of its kind in the nation.

The only sour note was the news, not announced until after the celebration, that Schnabel had resigned. The society knew about his planned resignation a few weeks before the anniversary. Ironically, the success of *Young Israel* was largely responsible for his decision to leave. Editing it seems to have aroused an apparently latent ambition for a career in journalism and he wanted more time to pursue it. Hoping not to lose his services entirely, the society allowed him to remain as editor of the magazine so long as it continued to be printed in the asylum print shop and a share of the profits went to the industrial school.[29] In addition to editing *Young Israel*, Schnabel had a second enterprise in mind: opening a private boarding school for boys. It was the kind of work for which his experience in the HOA had been ideal training.

Once again the orphanage was faced with the recurrent problem of finding a replacement, one who would stay. It was more like a crisis than a problem, for Schnabel had taken the assistant superintendent with him when he left. So far no superintendent had lasted more than four years in the job, and each time the search for a successor took longer. There was something about supervising an orphanage that seemed to discourage the best applicants. Although a boarding school had much in common with an orphanage, there was an important difference that made men like Schnabel and Hart prefer one to the other. That difference was the quality of life. Living in a nineteenth-century orphanage was an intensely melancholy experience, a mean burden that few could tolerate for long. As we shall see, it was a burden that no asylum could escape.

The Unhomelike Homes 4

The orphanage was not an American invention but Americans in the second quarter of the nineteenth century behaved as if they had acquired exclusive rights to the patent. Relatively rare until the Jacksonian period, the orphanage in the 1830s achieved sudden and widespread popularity as an institution for the care of dependent children. The upshot was the first great wave of asylum building. By 1851 there were seventy-one orphanages in the United States, more than a third of them—twenty-seven—in New York State alone. All were established under private auspices by philanthropists and charitable societies (largely religious) who saw them as an enlightened alternative to existing systems of caring for the poor. To the builders, the worst form of care was that provided by public almshouses, where little children were thrown together with a highly mixed lot of adult paupers, including the aged, widowed, mentally ill, retarded, disabled, homeless, and unemployed. Because almshouses were frequently mismanaged and exploited by corrupt politicians, they were the target of numerous investigations by legislative committees and concerned citizens. However their reports may have differed on other aspects of almshouse care, they were invariably unanimous on one point: the children in them should be removed and raised elsewhere. But this recommendation was generally ignored by officials and voters alike.

To the charity reformers who opposed the almshouse as an institution in which to raise children, the orphanage seemed to offer a golden opportunity. They eagerly accepted on faith the prevailing liberal ideology that supervising the upbringing of children in a different kind of institution would be immensely beneficial, indeed therapeutic. In their utopian vision, the orphanage would nurture its residents in a kind of moral hothouse; that is, it would provide a protective, rehabilitative environment free of corrupting influences in which routine, discipline, and regimentation would shape children into shining models for society to admire and emulate. That the children involved were simply exchanging one form of incarceration (admittedly evil) for another (presumably benign) was an idea that apparently never occurred to them.

Although their idealistic supporters may not have realized it, their noble experiment in child saving had already failed by the time of the Civil War. With rare exceptions orphanages had become purely custodial institutions where the children lived in overcrowded dormitories, were marginally clothed and fed, and nominally educated. In some instances they were taught a trade, though it was often a menial one. Routine, discipline, and regimentation had become ends in themselves because no asylum could do without them and still survive as an administrative entity. The needs of the residents had to be subordinated to the needs of the institution. Every home started out (like the Hebrew Orphan Asylum) with a small group of orphans who functioned for awhile like a large family; but as admissions increased it developed into a monstrous establishment resembling a children's prison. In the process the residents were transformed into robots, their natural spontaneity extinguished by years of enforced conformity.[1]

As might be expected, the failure of the orphanages did not escape the notice of critics. The most outspoken and controversial among them was Charles Loring Brace, a Protestant minister and founder of the Children's Aid Society, in 1853. Brace was opposed to any long-term institutional care for children, whether in the public almshouse or the private orphanage. Foster care was the alternative he favored, and he was a pioneer in this movement at a time when public opinion strongly supported institutional care. A prophet with few followers at first, his new organization would in the next half-century take thousands of children from the streets and *place*—not indenture— them on western farms. They were transported out of the cities on the so-called orphan trains. At every step, waiting farmers picked the children they wanted. If either the child or the foster parents became dissatisfied with the arrangement, each could (in theory) terminate it without the necessity for legal proceedings. Though the plan seemed sound Brace too attracted a great deal of criticism because he did not take the religion of the children into account in finding homes for them, nor did he follow up on them afterward to see what care they were receiving.

Brace was particularly scornful of the claim made by orphanage authorities that their graduates would make better citizens because of their institutional training. It was the other way around, he insisted. *"The longer he is in the asylum, the less likely he is to do well in outside life."* [2] A considerably harsher judgment on asylum graduates was rendered by Ambrose Bierce in *The Devil's Dictionary*. In his definition of "Orphan" he wrote: "When young the orphan is commonly sent to an asylum, where by careful cultivation of its rudimentary sense of locality it is taught to know its place. It is then instructed in the arts of dependence and servitude and eventually turned loose to prey upon the world as a bootblack or scullery maid." [3]

One big weakness of the orphanage system (as the HOA had already learned) was its fixed capacity. There were always more children applying for admission than any asylum had room for; and there was no way it could expand without adding a new wing or a new building. This of course took time, at least a year. In the interim, the best it could do was to allow a certain amount of overcrowding, which usually created additional problems.

This weakness became more apparent in the early 1850s, when New York City for the first time in its history experienced a new and disturbing phenomenon: the emergence of a large floating population of vagrant children who lived in the streets and survived by their wits and reflexes. Seldom numbering less than ten thousand in any year, this army was almost entirely foreign-born and included orphans, half orphans, runaways, drifters, waifs. Because of their nomadic life they were known as street arabs. They eked out a chancy living as newsboys, bootblacks, flowergirls, streetsweepers, peddlers, musicians, gamblers, pickpockets, beggars, pimps, prostitutes. Almost all were illiterate and most were clothed in rags. At night they slept in whatever shelter was available: doorways, tenement cellars, shanties, stairwells, printing office lobbies. To New Yorkers they represented a threat to civic order and public safety, and there was always talk of placing them in institutions. But the city would have needed at least a dozen more homes to care for them. Even if these existed it is doubtful whether many of these children would have willingly gone to them.

In 1854 Charles Loring Brace established a new kind of facility planned especially for homeless children—the Newsboys Lodging House. For six cents a night, boys could get a bed and bath. This seems to have been what many of them wanted, for in its first year the lodging house was used by thousands of homeless children. Encouraged by their response, Brace opened more lodging houses and eventually had six in operation, including one for girls. He also added evening schools, reading and music rooms, and kitchens where cheap, wholesome meals were sold. Although lodging houses were institutional in nature, they actually operated more like private clubs with an open membership, for the children who used them could come and go as they pleased.[4] Brace's innovation wasn't the answer to the city's juvenile vagrancy problem by any means, but it did supplement the work of the orphanages.

Unhappily for the city, though, the Civil War helped worsen the situation. It orphaned thousands of children all over America and was directly responsible for the nation's second great wave of asylum building. In 1866, eight states established homes exclusively for war orphans—the first time such institutions were built under public auspices. States were compelled to take this unusual step because almshouses and orphanages everywhere were terribly overcrowded, creating a desperate situation. In New York State, for example, the number of children in almshouses increased by more than three hundred percent one year after the war, with war orphans accounting for almost all the new admissions. Only one orphanage in New York City was available for war orphans, the Union Home for Soldiers' and Sailors' Orphans, on 151st Street and Boulevard Avenue. It filled quickly and had to turn away all others. Soon many more children joined the ranks of the street arabs. Their number was further augmented by thousands from the broken families of penniless immigrants who arrived in the new migrations that began after the war. Always a problem, juvenile vagrancy had now become a plague.

New Yorkers were fond of saying that for every social ill there was a charity organized to ameliorate or eliminate it. If one could measure the size of the problem by the number of charities working to relieve it, then surely the dependent child represented the single most important problem confronting the city. Aware of its magnitude, the private charities made a greater effort than ever to deal with it—by building more asylums, of course. By the end of the 1860s there were nearly two dozen orphanages in operation. New York, in fact, had more children's institutions—orphanages and others—than any city in the United States.[5] This proliferation, though, was not always greeted with approval. Some citizens believed that there were too many asylums in existence, and suggested that many be merged since they all more or less provided the same services. Their argument had merit, for the dependent child was being cared for not as an individual but as a member of a special category according to need, condition, and status. Although such separation made some sense for groups like the sick and the disabled, it made none whatever for the great majority of dependent children who required the same kind of care regardless of how they came to need it.

In the winter of 1869, when public interest in these institutions was growing, the *New York Times* sent a reporter out to visit them. His story, published on Sunday, December 5, 1869, provides a capsule history of the institutional care given to orphans:

> In a City like New York, there are constantly many hundreds of children who are left in destitute circumstances, without parents, and dependent on public charity for a substitute for a home. The few who are actually adopted into good families are the only ones who know what a real home is. The rest, or such of them as are not left to take the perilous chances of the world or with friends of doubtful character, are cared for in the Orphan Asylums. These are, at best poor substitutes for home; but in most cases everything is done which can be done by a few teachers and nurses for a collection of a hundred or more children gathered into one establishment.
>
> An Orphan Asylum is, in fact, a sort of boarding school, with no home to look back or forward to; no holidays or vacations, with delightful visits of parents and friends; but year after year of the strange, unnatural school life, to end in most cases with an apprenticeship to a trade, or an indenture to service. Still, the meek sisters of the Catholic faith, or the kind Protestant teachers and nurses, give the children careful instruction, and their lot is far better than if even these unhomelike homes were not provided for them.
>
> In or near the City of New-York there are twelve of these institutions, supported for the most part by private donations and subscriptions, with occasional assistance from the Legislature. The general management is much the same in all. On entering one of these establishments, the visitor ordinarily finds himself in a large hall, with a staircase ascending to the upper part of the building. Near the entrance is a reception room, and the office and private rooms of the Superintendent, generally well carpeted and furnished, and having a very comfortable appearance. The family, teachers, &c., have rooms in the immediate vicinity of the stairway, very similar to those of any private residence, while the children are always disposed of in large apartments accommodating fifty or more. If boys and girls are admitted to the same institution, they are generally put into opposite wings of the great building. To begin at the bottom of the house, the dining-rooms are in the basement, and invariably large, cheerless apartments, furnished with rough tables and rude seats. Nothing is done to make this department attractive except the periodical providing of "plain and substantial" food. This is not as it should be. The school rooms appear to differ in no particular from those of an ordinary board school, having the same ranks of little desks, with an unusual uniformity of

neat pinafores behind them, however, the same somber blackboards and mysterious charts and gloves, and the same prim teachers. In the dormitories are row after row of little beds, with uniform covers, and generally in the corner a large couch for an attendant, who puts the little urchins in bed and keeps all frightful things away by sleeping in the same room. A large room on each side of the building, vacant of anything in the shape of gymnastic apparatus or "plaything," is called the playroom, from the fact that the children are periodically turned loose therein to amuse themselves as best they can. At most asylums there is also a yard with playgrounds of moderate size for the fine weather. The older girls are taught to sew, and most of the clothing is made in the establishment, while the boys are employed in light work about the house or the grounds, but seldom taught any regular trade or branch of labor. In fact, they are generally too young for that, being retained in the asylum only until the age of fourteen. On leaving, unless they have friends to whom they may be prudently returned, they are provided with situations, and in most cases indentured until such time as they shall become of age. There are constantly more applications for children from persons wishing to take them into service than can be provided for.

THE NEW-YORK ORPHAN ASYLUM

About the year 1806 Mrs. GRAHAM, Mrs. HOFFMAN and several other benevolent ladies formed an association called the Orphan Asylum Society of the City of New-York and begun the good of [sic] providing homes for these unfortunate waifs. Their labor and their means increased upon their hands, and in 1835 they erected the main building of their present edifice, the two wings being added in 1855. It is situated on the Hudson River at Seventy-fifth street, quite retired from the general trade and travel of the streets, and past its western windows glide the boats and steamers on the lordly river. The building itself is a dark brown structure, with a somewhat gloomy and monastic appearance, with large arched windows made up of small diamond panes. The two wings stand at right angles with the main building, and as one passes between their dark walls it has a somewhat chilling effect, but this is immediately dispelled on reaching the pleasant rooms within, and the cheering presence of the Superintendent, M. C.C. Pell. There are now about 160 boys and girls in this institution. It is under the direction of fourteen ladies, with Mrs. JOHN ANTHON at their head. In former times, Mrs. BETHUNE and Mrs. HAMILTON took great interest in this Asylum, and did much to promote its welfare. It is supported mainly by private donations and subscriptions. Its grounds formerly extended over nine acres, but one-half the land has recently been sold for the sum of $300,000, and a new site, comprising fifty-seven acres, purchased up the Hudson, in Westchester County, between Yonkers and Hastings. New buildings will soon be erected upon this land, and the present site will be swallowed up by the encroaching City. . . .

THE COLORED ORPHAN ASYLUM

The same vicissitudes of life occur to white and black alike, and if the latter are bereft of parents in childhood they are hardly ever in circumstances which render the aid of others unnecessary. In none of the asylums into which white orphans are taken is a colored child ever seen. A number of years ago, however, an asylum was established especially for colored orphans. The officers and the matron and teachers are white, and the institution is supported in a great measure by the contributions of white citizens. This asylum was formerly located on Fifth-avenue, but at the time of the riot, in 1863, the prejudice of the mob found vent in meanly setting it on fire. The children were for the time being sent to the Almshouse on Randall's Island, and afterward removed to a temporary home on One Hundred and Fifty-first-street. Within the last three years, however, a new building has been erected on the banks of the Hudson, at One Hundred and Forty-third-street. It has a high situation, overlooking the river, and is surrounded with the rural scenes which still render that portion of the island a place of retirement and of quiet. In front runs the Bloomingdale road, now called Broadway, and between the house and the river the Boulevard is at present in the course of construction. The building is a substantial structure of brick, well arranged and very neat in appearance. There are five schools in the building, and 273 children are at present in charge of the institution. On Sunday, a preacher sent by the City Mission, talks to them in the morning, and in the afternoon there is a Sunday school. This institution, like the others, depends mainly on private benevolence for support, and is generally in need of funds. . . .

THE HEBREW ORPHAN AND HALF ORPHAN ASYLUM

The Israelites, who have for many years formed a large element of our population, have not been neglectful of the unfortunate children among their people. As early as 1822 a Hebrew Benevolent Society was formed for general charitable purposes, which, at a later date, became the Hebrew Benevolent and Orphan Asylum Society, and included within its scope the establishment and maintenance of an asylum both for orphans and half-orphans, who are left in destitute circumstances. A building was erected in 1862, corner of Seventy-seventh-street and Third avenue which combines all the best improvements in this department of architecture. Inside it is one of the most elegant buildings of its kind in the City, and unlike some of the others it has halls and apartments comfortably heated. There are a main building and two wings, the entire front measuring 120 feet and depth 60 feet. There are about 160 children cared for in this institution, and they are an intelligent and cheerful assembly of boys and girls. One of its peculiarities is, that it is rather a home for the children than a boarding school, and they are all sent to the public schools in the neighborhood, the instructions at home being of a religious character only. An attendant accompanies the children to school and they are always punctual and regular. An industrial feature has been introduced and a shoe shop for boys is already in operation and has been attended with marked success. The Superintendent of the Asylum, MR. LOUIS SCHNABEL, gives his personal attention to its welfare and has great interest in the results. He is constantly in receipt of letters from children who have left the institution and are doing well for themselves in practical life.

In reading this story one cannot escape the pervasive sense of monotony the reporter felt as he carried out a dismal assignment. Visiting one orphanage may have been an experience, touring twelve seems to have been a trial. Yet his bad experience could have been nothing compared with the experience of the children. Rightly, the reporter does not delude himself or his readers into believing that asylums are a substitute for real homes. In an apt phrase, he labels them "unhomelike homes." It was a judgment that applied to even the best of them.

The article further indicates that the number of homeless children in all twelve homes is slightly over two thousand. Though this seems like a great many children, it actually represents less than a quarter of those sheltered by the newsboys lodging houses. On December 20, 1868, the *Times* reported that 8,599 additional children used them in the year 1867–68. But even this total is not accurate, for it does not include the figures for the populations of ten other homes the reporter did not visit.

Another fact that merits attention is that almost all the orphanages were administered by women. Nuns ran the Catholic homes and "benevolent ladies" ran the Protestant homes. Managing asylums, it seems, was considered women's work—a fact that may help explain why institutions like the HOA had trouble finding male superintendents.

Third, almost every asylum had money problems, for the cost of maintaining a child grew every year. Most of them depended on "private donations and subscriptions" while only a favored few had private endowments. Some were receiving state and city funds, a practice that would become general in the next decade. The orphanage that received the biggest appropriation was the Colored Orphan Asylum, which was granted $25,000 by the state legislature in 1869. Its status was unique and deserves more discussion.

Until the Colored Orphan Asylum was established, colored orphans in the city fared worse than any other homeless children. No white asylum would accept them and their own people lacked the means to build one. In 1833 two white women, named Anna H. Shotwell and Mary Murray, began organizing a society for their relief. By 1836 they had collected $2,000 and had recruited a board of twenty-two women and an advisory committee of five men. But because no one would lease them a building their new institution was nearly doomed. After three months of heroic but frustrating effort, the women finally decided to buy a house on Twelfth Street and convert it. When the building became overcrowded the orphanage moved uptown to a new site on 44th Street and Fifth Avenue. Draft rioters burned it down in July of 1863. At its next location on 143d and Broadway its directors had to cope with rising admissions while operating under the threat of imminent financial crisis. Of all the asylums in the city, it was and would always remain the poorest, an orphaned institution struggling to survive.

Though he visited the Leake and Watts Orphan Asylum, the Orphans' Home of the Protestant Episcopal Church, the Protestant Half Orphan Asylum, the Wartburg Orphan Farm School, and several Catholic orphanages, he failed to visit ten others, probably because he was unaware of their existence. Five were Protestant, four were Catholic, and one was nonsectarian, the Union Home and School. Among the Protestant asylums the most unusual was the Sheltering Arms, with one hundred children, on 110th Street. It had been founded in 1864 to care for a special class of children: those deserted by either parent or left alone because both parents were sick. Two things about its operation made it unique. Though managed by Protestants, it admitted children of all faiths and was supported by contributions from all religious groups. Second, the new building it would occupy in 1870 (its second) had been designed in decentralized fashion with four separate cottage units, each of which—equipped with its own dining room, playroom, washroom, and dormitory—could function like a family household. Borrowed from the Germans, the cottage idea would attract more and more attention from charitable organizations toward the end of the century. The House of Mercy, founded in 1854 by a minister's wife and managed by the sisterhood of St. Mary's Episcopal Church, stood at 86th Street and the Hudson River. It cared for about fifty "fallen women"—a fairly flexible category in those days—between the ages of twelve and twenty. Another Episcopal home was St. Barnabas House, on Mulberry Street, founded in 1865. Planned as a refuge for homeless women applying directly from the streets, it also offered convalescent care for homeless or destitute women discharged from the hospital who needed a temporary home. Judging from St. Barnabas's own statistics, most guests didn't tarry long enough to get used to it. In 1869 it cared for 2,150 women who stayed an average of three and one-fifth days. Only one small group of special guests were kept on longer than any others: sixteen homeless children who lived there as regular residents.

Two of the Protestant asylums were almost brand new, having opened in 1868. They were the Shepherd's Fold, on 28th Street, and the Women's Aid Society and Home for Training Young Girls, on 13th Street. Another example of the way homes of that period selected special groups to shelter, the Shepherd's Fold admitted children from the ages of one to fifteen who had been left practically, if not actually, orphaned as the result of alcoholism, desertion, and crime. The fifty children it cared for had been rejected by other homes because they were not genuine orphans. The Woman's Aid Society and Home for Training Young Girls had begun its career in charity some years earlier under another, shorter name: the Women's Evangelical Mission. In this phase it was an institutional scavenger specializing in human salvage—rescuing and reforming young girls who had been abused in public institutions, chiefly the almshouse. In 1858, however, for reasons that cannot be determined today, it changed into a genteel institution that trained orphaned, friendless and abused young girls as domestics. The smallest of the Protestant homes, it accommodated thirty girls.

Among the four unvisited Catholic orphanages, the newest was the New York Foundling Asylum, on East 68th Street, which opened in October 1869. Foundlings were one orphan group that had been neglected by other asylums; thus the new home helped fill yet another gap in the care of dependent children. Before its establishment, infanticide was a common crime in the city. Every month 100 to 150 dead babies were found in various places—empty barrels or crates, vacant lots, or floating in the rivers. This number declined by 90 percent after the foundling home opened. By April 1871 it had received nearly two thousand babies, 62 percent of whom later died. Although the nuns who ran the home farmed out some babies to healthy women to nurse for ten dollars a month, they refused to allow any of them to be adopted, even by the best Catholic families. An order of French nuns known as the Sisters of the Holy Cross operated the Orphan Asylum of St. Vincent de Paul, on West 26th Street. They cared for a total of two hundred boys and girls, a polyglot group who came from a dozen countries and had to be taught English along with their catechism. Like almost every other home in the city, St. Vincent de Paul was expanding and planned to move into a new building on West 39th Street that would accommodate four hundred children. Another order of French nuns operated the House of the Good Shepherd, on 90th Street and the East River, which carried out its work in great secrecy. Few outsiders were permitted inside its two buildings and visitors spoke to the Lady Superior through an iron-grated ceiling. Its facilities were vast even by the oversized standards of Catholic institutions, for it not only cared for 700 children but had room for 150 more. It was a house of correction for "ruined women," many of them sent there by the courts. Its residents were divided into four classes, depending less on age than on their crimes and potential for improvement. Each group lived separate from the other, and its members were not permitted to communicate with those of another group. The majority were adolescent girls, who were taught hand and machine sewing, embroidery, handicrafts, and laundry work. A few girls who had escaped from the home told doleful stories about its discipline and food, but no one could get inside to investigate. The Roman Catholic Protectory was perhaps the only Catholic home in the city managed by laity, a group called the Christian Brothers. It was located in West Farms, the Bronx, and it had been organized to save Catholic children from the influence of Protestantism, which prevailed in all public institutions. Its residents, mostly Irish, ranged in age from five to seventeen and almost all—girls included—were either vagrants or criminals who had been committed by the courts. The protectory's original plan had been to keep its children for a short period and then apprentice them, but it soon gave up this arrangement and denounced the apprenticeship system as a "great evil." Through experience it had found that the undisciplined children it had received were unsuited by education and temperament to work as apprentices. It also found that the crafters who engaged dependent children as apprentices invariably overworked them, neglected their education, and scrimped on their food and clothing. As a result, it stopped apprenticing its residents and bought a large farm in the Bronx. There, its boys were taught farming, baking, tailoring, shoemaking and printing while the girls were taught only one trade, skirt-making. In its first seven years, the protectory had cared for more than thirty-five hundred children.

The Union Home and School for the Maintenance and Instruction of the Children of Our Volunteer Soldiers and Sailors—that was its original, full name—was the only non-sectarian asylum in the city and admitted Christian children of any denomination. It had been organized in upstate Delaware County by some patriotic women in May 1861, was incorporated the following year, and moved to New York City in 1868. That year, it bought a three-story mansion at 151st Street and Boulevard Avenue and planned to convert it into an orphanage for 350 children. For various reasons beyond its control, however, the building would not be ready for occupancy until June 1870. In those days, charity fairs were the standard social events held to raise money for philanthropic institutions. And the Union Home and School, to use the abbreviated name it soon acquired, could offer one celebrity figure on its letterhead that gave it an edge in attracting donations from wealthy contributors—its president was Mrs. Ulysses S. Grant.[6]

The number of residents in the ten institutions the *Times* reporter did not visit came to about two thousand. If we add this figure to the ten thousand previously counted as the combined census for the twelve asylums he did visit and the newsboys lodging houses, the grand total for all the children cared for by the city's private homes and charitable societies came to around twelve thousand. But this statistic did not include all the homeless and dependent children in the city by any means, for it was estimated that there was one child at large in the streets for every child in a home. In fact, since statistics for this period are incomplete and unreliable, there is no way of knowing how many needy children were roaming about at any time in the decades before the turn of the century.

The greatest single source for the growth in the number of dependent children was, of course, the heavy and continual flow of immigration. Such children were part of the human wreckage left behind after every new wave of migration had spent itself. Beginning in the 1870s, though, the city became the port of entry for yet another great migration, the hundreds of thousands of Jews from eastern Europe and Russia. Although many moved inland, most settled in New York. Inevitably the hardships they faced as foreigners struggling to survive in a new land helped break up and destroy thousands of families. Their children became the innocent and suffering casualties of that collective tragedy. Many of them would find their way to the HOA, the only Jewish orphanage in existence. But their number would soon grow too great for one home to absorb and the need for more institutions became evident. Thus, in the 1870s, the city would begin to acquire even more asylums—Jewish ones, this time. In one way or another, all of them—including the Jewish homes that would be established in other cities throughout America—would model themselves after the Hebrew Orphan Asylum of the city of New York.

An Orphan's Lot

Mr. and Mrs. Jacob Cohen, the new superintendent and matron, "come from Cleveland with good credentials," the *Messenger* reported on May 3, 1872, after the couple assumed direction of the HOA. Cohen's "good credentials" consisted of his previous employment as a Hebrew teacher at the Cleveland Jewish Orphan Asylum. This made him the only superintendent who had worked in an American orphanage before his appointment. The orphanage he took over in 1872 was now bigger than most Protestant homes and would soon overtake the smaller Catholic homes. As of April that year there were 167 residents, 119 boys and 48 girls. Ninety-nine were half orphans, 80 of them fatherless. Two-thirds were native-born, one-third foreign-born, all from Europe. Among the foreign-born, ten had come from Russia and their presence in the home reflected a trend. The first Russian-Jewish immigrants had arrived in the city in 1870. The children's ages ranged from five to eighteen, with most falling within the ten to fourteen range. Except for nine who were kept home because of illness or poor health, 55 attended primary school held inside the HOA, 79 went to public school outside, and 24 worked as apprentices in the industrial school. In the fiscal year ending April 1872, the HOA had spent more than $25,000, or about $200 on each child. The cost of caring for a child had doubled in a decade.[1]

In June Cohen took part in a testimonial honoring Louis Schnabel organized by the older boys and the apprentices. Schnabel received some embossed resolutions and heard himself praised in a number of laudatory, emotional speeches. He responded to them "in his quiet but impressive manner," the *Messenger* observed. Adding its own testimonial to that of the children, the paper noted: "It must be admitted that for such a difficult position, a man as able and as zealous in the education of the youth as was Mr. Schnabel is rarely found."[2] What the testimonial clearly established was that the children were still loyal to their former superintendent. This bond presumably made it harder for Cohen to win them over. And since Schnabel was staying on as principal of the industrial school, Cohen was not given the same responsibilities. Instead, he ran the home while Schnabel managed the shops. This division of authority was made to avoid the awkward situation of having Schnabel supervised by Cohen. Still, both men apparently got along well together, at least for the first two years.

Eighteen seventy-three began badly for everybody connected with the asylum except Myer Stern, its president. In March Cohen lost his eldest son, aged twenty, who died after being run down by a Third Avenue horsecar.[3] At the society's annual meeting, Stern announced the unhappy news that membership and contributions had fallen off considerably the past year, a decline attributed to the depression then in progress. For Stern, himself, though, all the prospects were pleasing. The *Messenger* in its story on the annual meeting praised his performance on the podium and declared him to be "the best chairman this Society has yet produced."[4] In May, Stern, who had many friends in and out of city hall, was appointed one of three commissioners in the Department of Charities and Correction by the new Reform mayor, William F. Havemeyer. His salary was $16,500. The department had an annual budget of about a third of a million dollars and cared for nearly ten thousand persons in twenty-five welfare and correctional institutions.[5] The new commissioner, who was still running his own fur goods business, continued as president of the orphanage. If there was a conflict of interest here, no one said so publicly.

Not long after his appointment, Commissioner Stern invited the mayor, comptroller, and some common council members to the HOA. They were escorted through the main building and the industrial school and left trailing words of praise for the institution.[6] Stern regarded it as one of the high moments of his career in private charity.

Had he devoted more time to his duties as president, Stern might have learned that conditions at the orphanage had been slowly deteriorating under Cohen's administration. That summer, the apprentices at the industrial school struck twice in a week in protest against the terrible meals they were fed. The first strike occurred when Schnabel was in his office; he put it down at once. The second took place when he was downtown on an errand. In each instance the complaint was the same: the food was inedible because it was poorly cooked, full of bugs, and lacked variety. Schnabel tried to pacify them even though he agreed with their complaints. Since the apprentices were fed the same food as the residents, Schnabel went to Cohen and suggested he improve the meals. Cohen listened but did nothing, so Schnabel took the apprentices' complaints to the board of governors. They agreed the meals could be improved, but they passed the buck by suggesting he see Cohen. Schnabel soon found that even the food at the staff table was getting worse and he began taking more of his dinners at a downtown restaurant. The matter simmered through the summer of 1873 and into the spring of 1874.[7]

In the main house, though, the residents found that one area of their lives did improve slightly during Cohen's regime: they were permitted some moments of play. Play was a luxury the orphans rarely enjoyed since the board of governors apparently believed that recreation and entertainment would distract them from the serious business of preparing to earn a living in a hard world. Thus, the budget had no allowance for such extravagances as toys, athletic equipment, or musical instruments. It was one thing to rescue the children, so the thinking went, but quite another to spoil them in the process. Still, they desperately needed some relief from the stupefying sameness of their clockwork existence. The sole redeeming feature of Cohen's regime was that it was the first to recognize this need and attempt to provide for it.

Under Schnabel about the only regularly scheduled recreational activity had been walks in nearby Central Park. They filled many empty hours on weekends when the children had little to do. The only other events that added some variety to their lives were the donations made by wealthy members on special occasions like bar mitzvahs and Jewish holidays. Most were treats of one kind or another—ice cream, cakes, fruits, even special dinners. For example, in June 1872 one member treated the children and staff to a catered banquet on the feast day of Shavuoth—the fifth time this donor had provided a free dinner.[8] Summer, when the days were long and the children restive, had always been a time when the need for recreation was greatest. The orphanage, however, could think of little better to offer than more hours of religious education. It had no summer program to speak of beyond permitting occasional play and organizing more walks in Central Park.

In the summer of 1873 this situation began to change. Prodded by the Jewish community the orphanage arranged a new activity: an all-day excursion in late June to Oriental Park, on the north shore of Long Island. Alas, when the day came, drenching rains washed out the trip. For consolation, the children ate the picnic food, which had already been prepared. At the next scheduled outing date—July 3—the day was hot and sunny. That morning the orphans plus an even larger contingent of poor children from the city's Hebrew Free Schools—about 450 in all—boarded a barge at an East River dock for the trip to Oriental Park. The boys were dressed in "neat brown suits and caps" and the girls wore "light calico dresses, white aprons, and straw hats." They were serenaded aboard the barge by the 71st Regimental Band, which also accompanied them to the park.

As the barge headed upriver, sandwiches and milk were passed out to all on board. At eleven, cheered on by its impatient passengers, the barge docked at Oriental Park. Sandwiches and lemonade were served after the children had disembarked. Baseballs and footballs were given to the boys while the girls, shrieking and squealing all the way, ran to the swings. Around two there was a Punch and Judy show and—for the girls only—dancing. The outing ended at four, when the children were rounded up and brought back to the dock for the trip home. To sweeten the inevitably anticlimactic ride back to Manhattan, ice cream and cake were served. They returned home a little after six, while it was still daylight. It may have been the happiest day any of them could remember since their admission to the HOA.

Because the excursion was considered an immense success, another was scheduled in early August—a Hudson River cruise to Excelsior Grove, opposite Yonkers. Bigger than the first in every respect, it involved 750 children from three institutions: the HOA, the Hebrew Free Schools, and the Union Home. Two paddlewheel steamers were hired to transport this army of children, and the arrangements for picking them up required the precise timing of a military operation. First to embark were the two hundred children of the Hebrew Free Schools; not long after dawn they boarded a steamer at a downtown dock. While they steamed upriver, the children from the HOA were hurrying north to 151st Street to rendezvous with the Union Home at a nearby dock. When the two steamers (the first had picked up the second en route) docked there at eight that morning, they were greeted by a thrilling sight. Awaiting them on the pier were two large formations of about 450 children from the HOA and the Union Home. Between them stood the Union Home's brass band, blaring out Civil War marches. It was an emotional moment and the Hebrew Free School children broke out into spontaneous cheering.

Throughout the excursion all three groups got along remarkably well, particularly those from the two orphanages. So well, indeed, that many friendships were formed. To renew these friendships, the Union Home children, accompanied by their band, paid a social call at the Hebrew Orphan Asylum near the end of the month. The HOA repaid this courtesy by visiting the Union Home in October.[9]

About the only tangible result of this mutual exchange seems to have been a decision by the HOA to organize its own brass band. Children's brass bands were rare in the city—indeed throughout the country—and the asylum's trustees seem to have been enchanted by the Union Home's musicians. Using their own money, the trustees bought instruments for a brass band of twenty, had the asylum recruit the boys for it, and hired a musician to train them. After rehearsing all winter, the band made its debut at the annual meeting in April. Their playing delighted the society and helped ease the boredom of the meeting. None were more pleased than the trustees; their investment had yielded entertaining dividends.

Although the band's music soothed the society, it had no such effect on some disenchanted members of the community who were present at the meeting. Among the most critical was a man named Katzenberg, who belonged to the Committee of Fifteen. Formed in January, the committee and the HOA were jointly organizing a new agency to be known as the United Hebrew Charities. The UHC would soon assume responsibility for such problems as relief, unemployment, medical care, maternity care, free burial, and immigration, leaving the orphanage free to care exclusively for children. Katzenberg had a number of complaints: the children were not as advanced in public school as they used to be; they were being trained as printers and shoemakers but not as teachers and bookkeepers; and their religious education was inadequate. He also demanded to know why there had not been a public examination for years. Attempting to appease him, a member of the school committee rose to announce that an examination would be held soon, without giving a date.[10]

The next month the orphanage staged a performance by the residents that was labeled an "Exhibition," presumably in answer to Katzenberg's criticisms. Because it was advertised as a "literary and musical feast," a large audience came to see it. What they were served, though, was a tasteless cultural repast. It consisted of martial music by the brass band and numerous recitations, including such gems of elocution (perhaps reflecting Cohen's taste) as "The Whiskers" and "The Rhyming Apothecary." Although their efforts were dutifully, if unenthusiastically, applauded, many in the audience were not amused. One dissatisfied spectator complained in the *Messenger* about the "unhappy choice of pieces delivered by the boys," suitable only for a "Bowery audience." Isaacs was more blunt. "The exercises would have given pleasure," he wrote, in the same issue, "but for the singular absence of any indication that the institution is Jewish and the orphans of Hebrew parentage. This is a serious error."

Another warning signal was sounded in August in a letter in the *Messenger* under the headline "Is This True?" "While much attention is paid to the training of a brass band," the writer commented sarcastically, "little is taught to remind [the children] of their duties and hopes as Jews."[11] Although under community fire for months now, the governors ignored the sniping going on around them.

Their reluctance to act led another member of the community to do their work for them. He was the Reverend Raphael deCordova Lewin, a Reform rabbi who also happened to be the editor of a radical Reform monthly, the *New Era*. Since the winter of 1873 the magazine had been published in the HOA's print shop. Lewin lived a few blocks away and was there almost every day, working on the *New Era*. Schnabel got to know him well as did the boys in the print shop.

One August morning around ten o'clock Lewin visited the asylum, as usual, but went to the main house instead of to the industrial school. He was looking for Cohen, whom he found in a classroom. The class was ending and Cohen was sending the boys off to take a bath. Lewin told him he had come to examine the children. Startled by the request, and, hoping to put him off, Cohen told the visitor to return in the afternoon. To his immense chagrin, Lewin did come back in the afternoon and renewed his request. Nervous now, Cohen was very reluctant to carry out his earlier promise. Lewin assured him he was a friend of the institution and had come to determine for himself the truth or falsity of recent reports about the neglected religious training of the children. If he found the reports were wrong, he told Cohen, he would defend the HOA; but if they were true he "would take such measures" as he thought best "in correcting the abuses." Cohen apparently found this talk more alarming than assuring; he told Lewin to come back in three months. Lewin wouldn't go and stated he intended to hold just "a cursory examination." Grudgingly, Cohen finally yielded.

The results of the examination were published in the September 1874 *New Era* under the headline "SERIOUS CHARGES AGAINST THE HEBREW ORPHAN ASYLUM OF NEW YORK." In his article, Lewin charged the "internal management" (meaning Cohen) with "greatly" neglecting the religious training of the orphans and serving such poor food to the apprentices in the industrial school "as to create general discontent."

Lewin was appalled by the residents' monumental ignorance about even the most basic tenets of Judaism: "Of the 173 boys and girls not one was able to recite the ten commandments in English, much less in Hebrew." No children had been taught any night prayers. Religious instruction was given only to those over ten, and then only on Saturdays. Yarmulkes were not worn during services and Temple Emanu-El's ritual was used exclusively. As a Reformer, Lewin did not object to the last two practices. Still, he did not want to see Judaism reformed to the point of extinction; he drew the line when he found that "no prayer-book was used at all" during services.

To support his charge about the poor food served the apprentices, Lewin spelled out their daily "bill of fare": breakfast "consists of bread and butter and a fearful liquid which is dignified by the name of coffee, and nothing more, except occasionally hominy." Dinner was "some beef, of a very inferior quality, and which is always cooked in one especial way; one kind of vegetable, and sometimes, though not often, a salad, and nothing more." Soup used to be served before dinner, Lewin noted, but the apprentices had requested that it be discontinued, "it being to their mind unfit for use." Supper was like breakfast, consisting of "bread and butter again, with occasionally an apple, and some more liquid, this time known as tea, but which for color, thickness, and taste bears close relationship to the morning's coffee."

Lewin reported being told that Sunday dinner was "a trifle better, for this is the exhibition day, when the asylum is turned into a menagerie, and visitors drop in 'to see the animals feed.'" And the Sabbath dinner was "in this Jewish asylum worse if possible than on the ordinary weekdays." So abominable was the food, Lewin claimed, that the apprentices "are constantly grumbling, and many of them spend their little pocket money to satisfy the demands of an appetite which is honestly earned by diligent and hard work."

In concluding his exposé, the crusading editor touched on the question of motivation and asserted that his was purely professional —"the interest of the asylum, and the spiritual and physical benefit of its inmates." Perhaps. But the timing of the article suggests that its real target was not so much Cohen as Stern, the HOA's president. Stern had been having a great deal of trouble in his first year in office as a commissioner of charities and correction. Lewin's charges, in fact, could not have come at a more inopportune moment in his career.

Stern's political benefactor, Mayor Havemeyer, had become, almost overnight, the most controversial and unpopular mayor in the history of municipal politics. Although he had won handily in 1872 as the candidate of the Republicans and Reform Democrats, Havemeyer within six months had succeeded in antagonizing nearly the entire city—the press, his political supporters, and the electorate. In February 1874, a year after he took office, he was totally friendless with no one supporting his acts, policies, or leadership. Most of his term was taken up in heated wrangles with the board of aldermen over his many questionable appointments.[12]

One such appointment was Stern's. His difficulties had begun in April 1874, after a grand jury accused him and a fellow commissioner of paying a merchant named Louis Sternbach a higher price for cloth than could have been paid elsewhere and in addition throwing Sternbach three-quarters of their department's annual business in dry goods. Although Stern and his colleague offered the lame defense that the required bidding procedure was too slow and complex, the case against them was not pursued by the city. The grand jury would not indict and the district attorney refused to take any action.[13]

In September (when Lewin's exposé appeared) Stern became the target of new charges. He was accused of not having properly written up his department's cashbooks and of having evaded the law specifying contract bidding, a revival of the previous accusation. Stern admitted a delay in writing up the cashbooks but defended his purchasing practices by insisting that the department bought all its dry goods on the "open market." But this defense fell flat when it turned out that the open market he meant consisted entirely of three merchants: Louis Sternbach, now revealed to be his brother-in-law, and Mayor Havemeyer's son and son-in-law. The smell of hanky-panky grew stronger when it developed that the department's purchasing clerk, Moses Goodkind, was also a relative of Stern's. Despite the new evidence, the grand jury and the district attorney again refused to indict, and the charges were dropped a second time.[14]

With its president under attack for his behavior in public office and the orphanage he headed facing charges of mismanagement, the HBS found itself experiencing the worst moment of its entire career as a charitable institution. What made the situation even more embarrassing was the fact that Moses Goodkind was a trustee and Louis Sternbach was a member.

Though unable to do much about Stern's personal predicament, the orphanage felt compelled to respond to Lewin's charges. In late September the officers met and passed two contradictory resolutions. The first branded the *New Era*'s allegations "false and malicious" and motivated by "private animosity and malice" against Stern; the second announced that a committee of ten members "outside this

Board" together with the board of governors and the industrial school and education committees would be appointed to investigate "the truth or falsity" of the charges.

Lewin at once pointed out the glaring inconsistency of the resolutions. He also criticized the way in which the investigative body had been loaded to insure a whitewash. For although the board was to select a committee of ten outside of its own members, they would all be outvoted by the thirteen members of the three other committees, whose loyalty to the orphanage was unquestioned. When this plan was attacked—not only by Lewin but by others in the community—the committee of ten decided it would manage the investigation alone.

The committee began its work in October by calling an inquiry. Its members first decided not to let Lewin appear as a witness, but changed its mind, apparently fearful of the enormous criticism this omission would produce. Held in the HOA, the inquiry was closed to the public, including the press. Four sessions were held, and they were conducted a good deal like regular courtroom trials. Every witness was sworn by the committee chair, then underwent direct examination and cross-examination. Lewin was given the right to call and examine his own witnesses and cross-examine those called by the committee, though he was not allowed to object to anything.

Lewin was the first witness to appear. His direct testimony consisted of a summary of the main points in his article. For the next hour or so, he was subjected to a bullying cross-examination by the committee chairman, much of it an attempt to learn whether his informants had been employees or residents. Citing journalistic privilege, he refused to inform on his sources. Also, many questions about his educational and religious qualifications for testing the children boomeranged. Lewin was not only an ordained rabbi but he had been a principal of public schools in the United States and the West Indies.

Second to testify was David Levy, a former resident and teacher who taught Hebrew to the older children and elementary school subjects to the younger ones. Asked whether he also provided religious instruction, he answered that this was done solely by Jacob Cohen. Under cross-examination he admitted to some "occasional differences" with his superior. He and Cohen had had "words" when he found his fiancée, Mary Bernstein, a resident, weeping as the result of "Mr. Cohen's ill-treatment of her."[15] His testimony further helped substantiate Lewin's charges about the lack of religious training.

David Levy's brother, Edward, also a teacher, followed him on the stand. Unlike his brother, who had been tentative in suggesting his dislike of Cohen, Edward was open and blunt in expressing his feelings. "I do not like Mr. Cohen," he told the committee. Cohen, he testified, was "rough," treated his assistants "very ungentlemanly," answered them "abruptly," and gave "no satisfaction" when complaints were brought to him. In addition, he charged that Cohen was very poor at religious instruction. The children told him that "they couldn't understand the [religious] instruction given to them." Edward concluded by declaring that Lewin had "written the truth."

The next witness, Jacob Katz, a twenty-year-old Russian immigrant and skilled compositor who earned four dollars a week, plus room, board, and clothing, complained of getting the same meals every day and of finding many "bugs" in the food. The quantity of food was not the issue, he stated, but its quality, which was neither good enough nor properly cooked. Beef was usually boiled until white, the potatoes were rotten, poultry was served only on Jewish holidays, cake was rare and seen only once or twice a month at Sabbath breakfasts, the coffee was often burnt while the tea was invariably bitter; only the bread was both edible and plentiful all the time. Despite a long, badgering cross-examination, Katz would not change his testimony.

Schnabel was the last of Lewin's witnesses. His appearance there, testifying against his employers, angered the committee. In cross-examining him the committee's interrogators tried to insinuate the idea that the food has always been poor, even when he had been superintendent. But Schnabel rebutted them by pointing out that there had never been any complaints about the food during his administration. His questioners also implied that he had been disloyal to the HOA by not tipping Cohen or the governors about the publication of Lewin's charges. Schnabel's integrity on the stand—he would not answer questions he considered improper—both baffled and infuriated the committee. They couldn't understand why, as a trusted and obedient official, he was opposing them.

The HOA's first witness was Dr. Lassar Stern, the attending physician. As expected, he praised the food and declared the children to be "very healthy." His proof: "there had been no death in the asylum for three years." But the committee's pleasure at finally hearing favorable testimony from a witness soon faded. Midway through Lewin's cross-examination the doctor inexplicably turned toward the committee chairman and told him that the coffee and tea bought were "very inferior" and "bought too cheap." Such unexpected charges caused the committee to squirm in its seats. They squirmed even more when their chairman openly admitted that he bought the coffee and tea cheaply, though claiming they were worth "much more." It was an unexpected triumph for Lewin, who had only argued that the food was poorly prepared.

The last witness called was Jacob Cohen, and his appearance was welcomed, for different reasons, by both sides. The orphanage saw him as their last hope of salvaging what had become a losing case while Lewin was eager for a confrontation he was sure he would win. On the stand, Cohen's strategy consisted of presenting his own version of conditions in the orphanage and denying Lewin's attempts to refute it. For the most part it worked. But Cohen became rattled for the first time when questioned about his qualifications for superintendent. It then developed that he was only a public school graduate and had received only a nominal religious education. Indeed, he had been in the clothing business before he went to work at the Cleveland Jewish orphanage. When Lewin demanded to know how many times Cohen had "failed in the clothing business," the entire committee jumped to its feet to shout him down.

In later testimony, Cohen claimed that the orphanage's food was not only better than that served at the Cleveland orphanage he came from but several notches above the food he had sampled at Protestant and Catholic orphanages in the city. Then, as if to explain the residents' seemingly gourmet palate, he made the most astonishing statement heard at the inquiry: "I have found that orphan children are more fastidious about their food than the children of rich people."

Although the apprentices' behavior was not an issue relevant to the inquiry, the committee unexpectedly introduced it into the questioning. Cohen called them "wild and reckless" and said he had been "especially careful" not to permit them in the main house. What the committee was doing was transparent: building a case against Schnabel as a lax disciplinarian.

When Cohen left the stand, the inquiry was over.[16] Had an impartial jury been present, Lewin would easily have won his case. The committee knew this and so indulged in a charade to provide some positive testimony for the record. It called two of its own members to testify; both claimed the food was "excellent" and as good as that served in their own homes. Then a third member rose spontaneously to make a brief speech arguing that the apprentices, a "willful" group, were still leaving food uneaten even though several months had gone by since the *New Era* article had appeared.

The committee took a month to prepare its report but would not release it. During this period Jacob Katz was quietly dismissed and left without a protest. In November the committee leaked highlights from its report to the *Messenger*. Their point was that Lewin's charges had not been proven. While grateful for the inside information, Isaacs suggested it would be best for all concerned if the full report were released. But he lost his temper when the committee sat on its report through December. In an angry editorial published on January 1, 1885, he observed that since the committee had taken the trouble to hold an investigation it should release its report. Though rebuked, the committee still was reluctant to publish.

Yet, that same week, it took a harsh step it did not want publicized: it fired Schnabel—and on just four days' notice. Schnabel retaliated by writing a sharply worded open letter to the trustees, a copy of which he sent to the *Messenger*. In it he denounced his dismissal as "arbitrary, unjust and indefensible" and challenged the committee to produce the evidence against him.[17] Forced to defend its decision, the committee finally released its report, which was published in the *Messenger*.

As Lewin expected, the report denied all the charges, including some he had never made. Its opening section depicted the orphanage as the very model of a model Jewish institution. The religious instruction given there, it claimed, was of the "highest and most impressive character." As for the food, "a variety of substantial dishes is served regularly to the inmates," which were "of a quality equal, if not superior, to that used in other well-governed institutions of this class."

After these complimentary passages, the report took a sudden critical turn and professed to find "grave abuses" in the management of the industrial school. Charging its principal (without naming him) with failure to discipline the apprentices, it indirectly recommended his dismissal (a step it had already taken) for "incompetency." Cohen was praised for having "faithfully" performed his duties while Lewin was admonished for offering "hearsay evidence." The report concluded by recommending public examinations twice a year "to avoid a future attempt on the part of anyone to mislead the public."[18]

After Lewin read the report, he dashed off a letter to the *Messenger* labeling it a whitewash and promising to write his own report. His version, twenty-four pages long, included the full text of the inquiry and appeared in the February 1875 *New Era*. Half of it was devoted to a point-by-point refutation of the report. Based on the actual testimony given by the witnesses, he showed how the report had distorted, falsified, or ignored the real facts. He deplored the unwarranted dismissal of Schnabel and Katz, whom he regarded as scapegoats. Noting how the committee had complimented Cohen, he offered a private view of the superintendent's performance given him by an inside authority. "One of the directors frankly told us," he wrote, "that the Board knew perfectly well that Mr. Cohen was not the right man in the right place, but that he had been retained in office simply because of the difficulty of obtaining a suitable person." As additional supporting evidence, Lewin appended four letters, two from former print shop foremen, the third from a former apprentice, and the last a petition signed by all the apprentices attesting to the "entire truth" of his charges about the food.[19]

Lewin's rebuttal enabled him to have the last word in his dispute with the investigating committee. It also marked the end of his involvement with the orphanage. He had achieved his purpose— that of "being the means of making things better." But the price of his victory was excessive and its consequences perverse, for it had resulted in the unjustified dismissal of two competent, innocent employees and the unmerited retention of the one official who should have been fired.

Although no one knows what happened to Jacob Katz—presumably he found work in another printing establishment—Louis Schnabel suffered only a slight, temporary setback. Shortly after his dismissal he was appointed principal of the preparatory school of the Hebrew Union College, a Reform rabbinical institution. Subsequently he undertook a private tutorial assignment which earned him a minor, though secure, footnote in American-Jewish history: he taught Hebrew to Emma Lazarus, the Sephardic Jewish poet whose verse appears on the base of the Statue of Liberty.[20] Meyer Stern was reelected president of the asylum in April despite an editorial in the *Messenger* recommending that a new slate of officers be nominated.[21] Apparently his colleagues did not want to add to his troubles. Stern had lost his job as commissioner in December, a few weeks after Mayor Havemeyer had died suddenly of apoplexy. Jacob Cohen continued as superintendent through the rest of the year (unaware that the governors had quietly begun a search for a successor).

What effect these events had on the orphans is difficult to determine. True, their religious education had improved and their meals (which seldom satisfied them anyway) were slightly better. Yet their lives as a whole remained largely unchanged. Still, the attention they were now receiving from the Jewish community had led to some unexpected benefits—chiefly, more entertainment.

In February 1875, Rabbi Gotheil of Temple Emanu-El staged a cultural evening (his second in a row) on a Saturday night. After supper all the residents (except the very youngest, who had been put to bed early) gathered in the main floor meeting room. Rabbi Gotheil welcomed them with a brief speech outlining the evening's program. First to perform was an elderly member of the society, David Leventritt, who offered serious and comic recitations. He was followed by two male singers, another rabbi, and a female concert artist. The asylum's own brass band was next and presented such selections as "Yankee Doodle" and "Watch on the Rhine." And the orphans participated by singing a number of choruses.

Dancing filled the entire second half of the program, but only the girls and the male guests were permitted to dance together; the boys were excluded for fear of sexual activity between the boys and girls. During the dancing some of the governors present heard a commotion from the dormitory upstairs. Looking up, they saw the youngest orphans mimicking the dancers by prancing about in their nightgowns on the staircase landing. All were shooed off to bed.

Rabbi Gotheil's entertainment was considered a success by everybody present. The orphanage was pleased because the visitors had all commented favorably on the appearance and conduct of the children. Two months later, during Purim, the Rabbi and his entourage returned to present another Saturday night entertainment similar to the previous two.[22] From then on, in fact, amusements of this sort became a more or less regular activity and the residents welcomed them.

Yet, if the administrators thought that the few hours of recreation and entertainment they occasionally arranged for the children brightened their lives to any measurable extent they were deluding themselves. True, the children accepted them eagerly, but a little cynically, too. When visitors came, they willingly played the role of the grateful orphans in return for the goodies they knew would be forthcoming. Still, no amusements, no cake and ice cream treats, no catered banquets meant much more to them than a diversion, a transitory pleasure. For the real essence of their lives was, simply, survival. To outsiders, survival might not have seemed an issue, for the children were obviously being fed, clothed, and sheltered. But a good deal more happened inside an orphanage's walls than even the most perceptive of visitors might have imagined. Even Lewin, the journalist-crusader, had seen only a small part of it. In fact, there is a documentary picture of that life still extant which suggests that Lewin had exposed just the tip of the iceberg. It is an undated, incomplete, anonymous memoir:

> After donning a blue jeans Blouse and a pair of Duck pants I became a full fledged witness of the inside happenings and history of the "Old House" as it is now called.
> Like most institutions where gathered true blue American Youth

hazing was the rule, it was practiced in two distinct forms, Muscular and *Food Promises* for a period of time on *Honor*, which I will explain briefly, both classes of hazing was the result of a niggardly policy for personal gains and the brutal instinct of the Warden. I speak knowingly on the subject. The boys looked upon their detention here as incarceration from the manner of the Warden's acts and addresses, and not as a Benevolent Institution, and so when any boy would tell tales or carry news to the Warden even when called for, he received physical punishment for same, every day for a week when the chance was given, and I may say here to the credit and honor of the boys that few committed this act and others incurred punishment in almost air tight closets rather than betray their comrades.

The Food Promise Hazing was carried out thus wise. A boy more muscular although younger would watch for his prey and then pounce upon him, claim an imaginary wrong or insult on the part of the weaker and pummel him several successive days and then discontinue on the promise that the weaker one would give to the stronger, his pie every Saturday for three months, or half the good things his poor relatives would bring him on visiting day, which was looked to as the bright green oasis of their desert lives and the sun on this particular day moved westward much too rapid for the bereft boys and their friends, as for myself I never expected anyone to visit me and was therefore disinterested except for the sight I witnessed which gave me an inkling of what human nature was.

All the boys knew I was alone and many took pains to look me up, take me to the lecture room and introduce me to their relatives with one object in view, that I should also share in some of the good things received by others more fortunate. Time and again I know of cases where a boy had a pie contract, he begged for an extension lapse for the time being, giving for a reason that not having pie for some time that he be granted to eat it himself that Saturday and he would give in exchange his portion of milk in the evening. This so far, relates to the hazing part, but this Interstate Commerce of Food reached further in its evil effect and here is where I wish to qualify my statement of the niggardly policy for personal gains on the part of the Warden. I feel sure that the boys were not gluttons but that they were underfed and poorly at that. The best evidence of this is that necessity being the mother of invention, the stronger boys invented a ruse to obtain more food, and to get it, part of the weaker boys' portions was the salient point, a test of the survival of the fittest, it is a fact that this was general among the stronger boys. We as boys believed then and believe now that the Warden made it a point to give as *little* and get as *much* out of it as human endurance at so early a stage could stand and benevolent hands continue to give.

There are a few of us living when we chance to get together who rehearse the story of hairbreadth escapes in robbing the breadbasket

when being delivered by the baker and placed in the basement vesti-
bule without being guarded for a few moments, how it was taken in
the outhouse and eaten there, how we reached through the iron barred
window of the scullery and took soup bones and the same bone went
through three different hands to be licked off and a perfect lustre put
to it, and this trick was performed at the table during meal time, it
was a stereotyped request to one another, "Give me the bone after you,
please."

We received our portion morning and evening of one-sixth of a loaf
of Rye bread, the loaf being the size of one selling at the present time
of five cents, and a bowl of milk diluted with water, at noon the bill of
fare varied, Irish stew of uncertain stamina one day and rice another,
extras on Saturday with Pie added, but the King day was Sunday, when
the Board of Trustees met, and I confess that some of us went in training for the event and it did not take much preparation either as we
were on a rigid training diet right along.

Let me say here that some of the weaklings, poor fellows, when
the chance offered, sneaked in the dining room after meal time and on
their hands and knees crawled under the tables picking up the stray
crumbs, even from the cracks in the floor. I am almost ashamed to relate that the swill barrel was not overlooked and what was the result,
underfed, poorly fed and the swill barrel attacked. Look up your records
and they will bear me out, how many were spared from the general
attack of scurvy and itch and sore eyes, in the year 1866, in your institution? How many could you give a clean bill of health so that they
could attend Public School No. 53, and how were they treated during their isolation, almost nude, being covered by an oily salve, from
below the chin to the soles of the feet, which was put on coat after coat
twice a day for weeks, not being allowed to wash, the floor became like
polished glass over which their bowls and bread was thrown to them
while sitting down in a row. The large pail of Milk and Water was left
standing near the door for someone to get and distribute the contents,
directly outside in the Hall and the Bed touching the doors of the Pest
Room which was on the third floor facing 3rd Avenue slept two girls,
Ida Cohen and Bertha Meyers, endangered by contagion, placed there
as a punishment for wetting their beds. The cries of these poor girls
could be heard in the early morning as they were beaten by the Warden
for a fault which their physical condition only was responsible.

There were several cases of this sort among the boys, Louis Phillip-
son . . . I believe was a victim; he was taken time and again from his
bed in the early morning, placed in the bath and the cold shower turned
on him, being threatened if he moved with a rawhide by the Warden,
his screams could be heard all over the building and it was only when
his cries became faint that he was released but not before he received
a few welts from the rawhide. And another, David Levy, a weak, frail

lad, whose speech was a trifle louder than a whisper was beaten with a rawhide every morning for months and then placed in the shower bath. This boy became so cowed and timid at the approach of the smallest boy that he was nicknamed "The Lady" and "Sissy." He became subject to intermittent fever until his friends took him and after being in their care became a strong and powerful athlete; the last time I met him, about three years ago, he desired to meet some of the boys who teased him in his melancholy days.

Another case, that of Nathan Hamburger, a well behaved, gentle, and as I remember him, a *pretty* boy, this boy stood the shower, the rawhide, and the Warden's fists, but the crowning deed came one day when it was rumored that he was to complain of his treatment. Alas it was unlucky Friday, school had been dismissed and he came to meet his punishment; it was two o'clock when he was locked in a hall closet in the basement where there was positively no ventilation except the keyhole. The closet measured about 18 inches in depth, about 30 inches wide and 6½ feet high. He was forgotten that evening and overlooked in the morning. He was not at the breakfast table, and was thought of only when the change of clothing took place about 9:30 when I mentioned the fact of his clothing being uncalled for.

At this the Warden turned deathly pale and several boys followed to see him release the poor fellow. As a boy I read the story of the Russian Nun Barbara Abryck, the inhumanity of her prosecutors and the shocking sight she presented when discovered; it was paled along-side the *sight* this boy presented when dragged from the hole in the wall. He was unconscious, drenched, and soiled with the purgings of his bowels. For the first time I saw this man quail with fear and begged that not a word be said. The boy was carried upstairs, revived, put in a warm bath and placed in a bed where he remained for several days, received the best of care from Miss Betty Lichtenstein, sister-in-law to the Warden, who was indeed a ministering angel to all the children.

Saturdays, after breakfast was devoted to outfitting and many a poor boy dreaded the moment when he faced the Warden presenting a pair of worn out shoes. These shoes of the cheapest sort were meant to wear well by resting and not to exercise in: the shoes would be taken from the hands of the boy and his head was the objective point, the boys being convinced that the heels at least were solid and getting an idea of the language used in the Volunteer Fire Department of which the amiable and genial Warden was once a member.

It was in this Shoe Department that the Warden picked up what knowledge he had to enable him to when he left the Asylum to set up in the Shoe business. I mean to convey by this that in looking up the cheapest stock and the worst he could buy give him both experience and a fund, infer from this what you please. . . .

This Warden who had previously been a waiter at the St. Nicholas

Hotel ought to have had *some* sense of propriety, but it was well known
and talked of among the older boys that he spent a pleasant hour or
two in the girls bath room while they were bathing and their ages
were from 11 to 14, the younger ones being bathed separately by the
older ones.

There also existed a line of punishment for both Boys and Girls to
be deprived of certain meals, but in most cases the victim was cared for
by his friends, they putting by a trifle for him at the risk of being themselves punished by imprisonment. There were many cases of brutal and
inhuman treatment which the lapse of time has somewhat obliterated
as to the cause and name of the sufferer, but may at some future time
obtain the information from the actors themselves.[23]

The period of this memoir seems to have been the mid-1860s to
the early 1870s, or during the Grunbaum and Cohen administrations. None of their names, however, appear in the narrative, which
is dominated by the cruel figure of the warden, presumably Goodman. After the orphanage moved to its 77th Street site and began to
admit many more children, the superintendent spent less time with
them. Although he continued to give the orders, it was the warden
who carried them out; he was the adult who ruled the dormitories.

Whatever it may be as literature, this anonymous recollection
represents a vividly accurate record of orphanage life. In it are reflected, in capsule form, all the nuances of life: the morning terrors
of the rawhide beating and the cold shower, the code against complaining or snitching, the stronger boys preying on the weaker ones,
the use of pie as a trading currency, the harsh punishment administered to bed wetters, the self-sacrificing nobility of children saving
crumbs from their own meager meals for friends under punishment,
the cheap shoes bought for the children by the greedy, cheating warden, the boy locked in a closet overnight who is found unconscious
in the morning. Though there is no way now to verify the incidents
described in it, they all bear the unmistakable ring of truth. Anyone
who has ever lived in an orphanage will recognize this at once. And
what is sad to relate is that seventy-five years later, in the third decade
of the twentieth century, some practices similar to those mentioned
here still existed.

The Right Man in the Right Place 6

Myer Stern decided not to run for a third term as president in 1876. Grateful for this sacrifice, the orphanage in October gave him a testimonial dinner at which he was presented with an inscribed watch and United States bonds worth $5,000.[1] It is not clear where the money to buy the watch and the bonds had come from, but it was the most expensive farewell given to an outgoing president. He was later elected a trustee and served until his death in 1899.

His successor, who assumed office in May, was Jesse Seligman, whose older brother Joseph was a past president of the society. Cohen had left a few months earlier, presumably by dismissal since no explanation for his departure was ever offered publicly. The HOA advertised for a new superintendent but experienced extraordinary difficulty in finding suitable candidates in the city.[2] Eventually, the search was extended far beyond the city and ended in New Orleans, the home of Dr. Hermann J. Baar.[3] Compared to Cohen, the failed clothing salesman and failed Hebrew teacher, the new superintendent was a brilliant jewel, in many ways overqualified for the job.[4]

Dr. Baar was fifty-one at the time—the oldest man ever to take the job of superintendent. Questions were raised in the Jewish community about the ability of a man approaching old age to manage an orphanage of more than two hundred children. Although justified, the questions reflected an apprehension that had no basis in fact. Dr. Baar was far from senile and his maturity was, if anything, an asset to the home, for it virtually guaranteed that he would not be looking for more rewarding opportunities elsewhere.

The new superintendent—the fifth in sixteen years—is the first whose life can be reconstructed almost in its entirety from various sources. And it was the kind of life that was fascinating enough to have served as an inspiration to any orphan steeped in self-pity.

He was living proof of what intelligence, industry, determination, and courage could accomplish against the most discouraging circumstances. Dr. Baar was born in 1826 in the village of Stadthagen, near Hanover, in Lower Saxony. His childhood was clouded by two successive tragedies—the death of his father when he was seven and the death of his mother three years later. Though fully orphaned at ten, he fared better than many contemporaries in the same position, for two uncles came forward to care for him.

Young Baar received his primary education in Stadthagen and was hoping to attend the *gymnasium,* or high school, in Hanover.[5] According to a dramatic story he often told the HOA's children, he lacked the money to pay for his studies and obtained it through a daring gamble. His teacher, who considered him an excellent student, advised him to seek a scholarship from the reigning nobleman in the principality, Prince George William of Schaumberg-Lippe.

It was an idea with little hope of success, for Baar was Jewish, an orphan, unknown to the prince, and without influential friends at court. Yet so great was his ambition for an education that he decided to go alone to the prince and plead his case in person. This part of the plan was the most foolhardy part of all. It was winter, the prince lived many miles away, and he had no idea whether, if he got there, the prince would agree to see him. Furthermore, having no money for coaches, the fourteen-year-old Baar planned to walk the entire distance.

Early one Saturday morning he started on his journey in freezing weather. Lacking an overcoat, he wore his Sabbath suit and a shawl around his neck. All day and through the night Baar trudged on without food or sleep. Not long after dawn Sunday morning, stupefied from exhaustion, he staggered into the prince's estate and knocked at the door. When a male servant opened it, he collapsed on the threshold—frozen, weak, half-starved. He was taken to the kitchen, warmed at the fire, and served his first meal in twenty-four hours. Revived and refreshed, he then explained why he had come to see the prince. That one so young should have come so far and endured such hardships for the sake of an education astonished the servant. He promised to get the boy an audience with the prince.

In the afternoon he was shown into the library, where an old, grey-haired man with a kind-looking face sat at a large table piled high with manuscripts and books. The prince motioned Baar to be seated but for a very long time he said nothing and just stared at him, studying his face. Finally he smiled and said, "What can I do for you?" It was the moment Baar had been hoping for ever since he had decided to make the difficult journey. He spoke for about fifteen minutes, explaining his intense ambition for a higher education and a professional career. When he finished, the prince asked a few questions and then rose. Extending his hand to the boy, he said, "I will help you. Go home. You will hear from me." Baar thanked him and left for home. The prince kept his word. Baar enrolled at the *gymnasium* at Hanover in the fall of 1841—the beginning of a long and successful academic career.[6]

This happy-ending story cannot be verified. Indeed, Baar may have invented it himself for it was the kind of inspirational fairy tale that would go over well with orphans. German records in Hanover reveal that the only relationship between Baar's family and Prince George William of Schaumberg-Lippe was that of debtor to creditor. His family received two mortgages from the prince, one in 1834 and another in 1838.[7] Some of this money may have been used to send young Hermann to school at Hanover.

Baar completed his schooling there in the spring of 1844. In November he was hired as a teacher by the Jacobson School in Seesen, a small city south of Hanover. The Jacobson School proved to be the kind of liberal haven Baar needed to nourish his awakening pedagogic talents. It had been established decades earlier as a private school for Jewish boys who were barred from German schools by law or quota systems. Because it employed a first-rate faculty, the school had acquired some local fame as a center of learning and attracted a growing number of Christian students.

On joining the faculty, Baar had to sign a contract specifying his duties and the remuneration he would receive. As a teacher or reader, he was required to spend from twenty-five to thirty hours a week at teaching, correct his students' work, train students in decorum, supervise them at their morning and evening prayers in conjunction with the house father, conduct inspections of the school during the week, aid in the children's growth by individualizing their lessons, and contribute to the growth and strength of the school. In addition, he was expected to serve as cantor at the Reform temple on the school grounds. His pay for these services was 100 thaler a year in four installments plus free housing and board.

The contract was subject to immediate termination upon the written notice of either party every half-year, at Easter and Michaelmas, but neither party ever found cause to use this escape clause. Baar, then eighteen, stayed for five years, possibly the five most valuable years of his life.[8] For the first time ever, he enjoyed security, stability, and the sense of status that comes with authority and responsibility.

It also gave him his first experience of living with a large group in a position of respect and power. Baar thus acquired a foretaste of institutional life, a prelude to his career, forty years distant, in the HOA.

In October 1849, when he was twenty-three years old, he made what was probably a very difficult decision: to leave the school to pursue a doctorate at the University of Göttingen. He was admitted there that winter on the basis of a "diploma from Seesen," according to the university's records. He stayed at Göttingen for three years, until the summer of 1852, when he left without graduating. His departure cannot be explained by anything in his records from Göttingen. He never received a doctorate degree; instead, he was awarded a "Certificate of Completion," whose significance is not known. Was it the equivalent of a doctorate given only to Jewish students who had completed the formal requirements for the degree but were ineligible, under law, for a diploma? Perhaps. Without a degree he was not entitled to call himself a doctor, though he did so throughout his life.

Still, he had as much education as he needed. At Göttingen he had studied German history, literature, and philosophy; Bible history; theology; theory of primary school; psychology and mental illness; English grammar; and Shakespeare's *Hamlet, Macbeth,* and *King Lear.*[9] In one way or another, he would manage to put all his education to some use during his lifetime.

Ironically, his first professional employment after leaving Göttingen was at the Jacobson School, which appointed him a governor and a teacher. Presumably he returned in triumph, a shining example for students to emulate. Yet, he may have felt some sadness as well because he didn't stay long, only three years.[10] Around 1855, when he was twenty-nine, he emigrated to England. Why he left his homeland is something he never seems to have discussed afterward. Most likely he had applied to many German schools and colleges and was rejected by all because he was Jewish. In Germany, Jewish teachers were even less welcome than Jewish students.

Dr. Baar's first few years in England were spent as a footloose scholar, and just where, when, and how long he worked in various cities are vague in the records. One story has it that England's Chief Rabbi Adler recommended him as a private tutor to the Rothschilds and arranged an interview for him. Having no money for a ride, he walked and arrived too late; another candidate had beaten him to the job.[11] (Dr. Baar as superintendent would retell this story again and again to stress the need for punctuality.) But if the Rothschilds didn't want him, other families did. He is said to have been the tutor to a wealthy family named Lewis, in Brighton. In the late 1850s, he settled in Liverpool, where he developed a lucrative private practice in coaching languages and modern classics. At the same time he became a member of Liverpool's Old Hebrew Congregation, known as the Seel Street Synagogue.

Because of his reputation as a man of learning, the young professor was asked by the worshippers in 1859 to deliver a charity sermon on behalf of the Jews of Morocco, then suffering intense persecution. His sermon was so well received that he was invited to preach there on other occasions. And the more sermons he delivered the more he found himself drawn to the pulpit as a profession. A somewhat similar feeling was taking hold in the congregation, whose members were increasingly attracted to the rhetorical talents of the German-Jewish academic living among them. A few years earlier Jews had been admitted to Parliament for the first time, and Jews everywhere in England were experiencing a sense of pride over their emancipation from second-class status. Caught up in this movement, the Jewish community of Liverpool was looking for someone with a university education to lead them. Dr. Baar seemed the ideal candidate for this assignment. In 1860 the congregation formally invited him to become its rabbi, and thus leader of the community as well. Though it meant, among other things, a loss of income, he accepted the position and embarked on a new career.

One of Dr. Baar's contemporaries, writing about him over fifty years later, described him as possessing "a winning personality, a fine presence and the muscular physique of a blond Teuton, with barely a trace of his Semitic origin." Not looking Jewish seems to have been especially helpful to him during his Liverpool days. Once he began preaching on a regular basis, his sermons became very popular—so much so that even gentiles were attracted to the synagogue. Among them was a wealthy Quaker woman who attended almost as faithfully as a congregant.[12]

Dr. Baar's room in town soon become a literary salon where he held occasional symposia on various subjects. These gatherings were frequently attended by local celebrities in the fields of literature, music, drama, and journalism. In 1861 he received formal recognition of his own status as a local celebrity: he was elected a member of the Historic Society of Lancashire and Cheshire. It was a singular honor for he was not only a foreigner but a Jew to boot, and one who spoke in an unmistakable German accent. But the new member was tactful. At the society's meetings, he seldom presented papers dealing with German culture; he concentrated instead on Shakespeare, which endeared him to them all the more.[13]

Dr. Baar might have remained permanently in Liverpool if he had not contracted a severe throat infection in 1867 after conducting a burial service over an open grave in terribly bad weather. Confined to bed by the worsening infection, which all but destroyed his voice, he found it impossible to carry out his rabbinical duties and eventually resigned.

Even after he recovered, months afterward, his speech was never the same. Although he could have returned to his position at the synagogue, he decided to seek a new career elsewhere. The next few years appear to have been a transitional period during which he tried a number of new activities. For example, he is said to have opened his own school in Brussels, an enterprise that failed. According to another unverified account, he came to America in 1867 and was chaplain at Mount Sinai Hospital in New York until early 1868.

What is definite, though, is that early in 1868 he had been elected lecturer (or preacher) to the Hebrew Congregation in Washington, D.C. Expected there that fall, he did not arrive—through some unknown delay—until the following year. As at Liverpool and despite a rather unpleasing pulpit voice, the congregation took an immediate liking to him. In 1870 they renewed his contract and raised his salary to $2,000—an extraordinary wage at the time for a cleric of any faith.

But Dr. Baar didn't stay long in Washington. He had had the bad luck to come at a time when the congregation was racked by the Orthodox-Reform controversy. Its officers, ultra-Reform in their practices, had introduced such radical changes as an organ and a choir, among others. Outraged by them, thirty-five dissidents left in the early summer of 1870 to form their own, more conservative, congregation. Unhappy over the split and none too pleased with the radical reforms as well, Dr. Baar resigned shortly afterward.[14]

While looking for a new position, he made the most of his stay in the capital by working hard at a new career—journalism. Most of his literary output consisted of papers and sermons rewritten in the form of essays, and he had no trouble getting them published. In July, for example, the *Washington Chronicle* published an essay of his titled "On the Term 'Gentleman.'" In it, he told how he had written in the album of a boy attending a school where he had once taught the advice: "My young friend, fear God and become a gentleman." A few weeks later the *Washington Sunday Herald* carried another of his essays, "Beethoven and the Germans," which praised the cultural achievements of his compatriots. It also digressed from its theme long enough to comment briefly on a noncultural event then in progress in which his native land was involved—the Franco-Prussian War. He argued that it had been instigated by Napoleon III, who had forced the war on the Germans. In late August, evidently seeking a wider audience for his work, he had an essay published in the *Messenger*, his first appearance in print in New York. A discussion of egotism, it was titled "Talking of Self." Since his pieces were generally preachy in tone, they were ideal for Sunday editions, and their readers, mostly Christian, probably had no idea that their author was Jewish.[15]

Later that year Dr. Baar was appointed professor of German and Hebrew at a private school in New Orleans operated by the Hebrew Educational Society. His wife—this is the first time we learn he had married—was in charge of the French department and assisted in German. Established in 1866, when Reconstruction was just beginning in the South, the school quickly achieved a reputation as one of the finest in the city. When Dr. Baar arrived it had an enrollment of more than two hundred pupils. Many were gentile children from the "best families" in New Orleans.[16] Its new professor not only added prestige to the faculty but became an overnight favorite with its students and their parents as well. "He is unrivalled as a teacher of German and Hebrew," the *Messenger* told its readers, "and has won golden opinions from all sorts of men."

Despite his heavy academic schedule, the new professor found time to write, and within a few months he repeated in New Orleans the success as an essayist he had first demonstrated in Washington, D.C. Indeed, he blossomed as an expert in pedagogy, a field in which he was highly qualified. "The first and most important law in education," he wrote in an essay on Rousseau published in the *New Orleans Sunday Times* on June 9, 1871, "is to individualize, and that man who best understands the individual nature of his pupils is . . . the most efficient teacher and educator." That same month, in the paper's Sunday edition, he contributed an essay on Jean Paul Friedrich Richter, the German novelist. (It was reprinted in the *Messenger* a few weeks later.) In July there was another essay, titled "Pestalozzi," dealing with the theories of John Henry Pestalozzi, the Italian educational reformer whose schools (all of which failed) combined regular instruction with manual labor. "No abstract method will ever make an eminent teacher," Dr. Baar argued in the essay. "The real master must be able to pave his own road, that is, guide his scholars without a lantern. . . . He must be able to say: 'La methode c'est moi.' " The following month, changing his field of interest, he published a piece on Sir Walter Scott.[17] This enormous output seemed to prove that the German-Jewish immigrant professor had become exceedingly articulate in English.

Yet, while Dr. Baar's reputation was flourishing, the school itself was floundering. In 1873 its enrollment declined to 160 pupils. Poor management may have been the reason, for in 1874 it was embarrassed by mortgage indebtedness and went through a reorganization. Its new president introduced a number of changes to stabilize the school's weakened status; one was the promotion of Dr. Baar to principal.[18]

Early in 1876 there occurred another one of the frequent acts of fate that changed the direction of his life. Word reached him from Liverpool that the wealthy Quaker woman who admired his sermons had died and—disinheriting her relatives—had left him her entire estate of about £9,000, over $45,000 in American money. In her will, she made it clear that she had left him the money because of the spiritual benefits she had derived from listening to his sermons. Dr. Baar at once embarked for Liverpool. Upon arriving, however, he learned that the deceased woman's next of kin were planning to contest the will. Feeling he had no legal or moral right to the money, he renounced the inheritance in their favor and returned to America.[19]

His appointment as superintendent of the HOA was made shortly after he got back to New Orleans. He apparently was persuaded to take it by Emanuel Lehman, a trustee, who may have heard of him from business friends in Liverpool and New Orleans. Dr. Baar left for New York in the fall and officially took charge of the orphanage on November 1, 1876. Although he and Jesse Seligman were total strangers, the two got along well together and soon established a firm and durable relationship. Under their joint administration began what might be called the HOA's golden age—a period, lasting two decades, during which it would acquire a national reputation as one of the finest institutions of its kind in America.

With Dr. Baar as superintendent, the orphanage for the first time had what it had been always seeking—the right man in the right place. He was to remain in the post longer than all of his predecessors' terms put together. And his impact on the children was to prove exceedingly durable. Traces of his influence were to linger on until 1941, the year the HOA closed.

Behind the Baars 7

For an educator who had eloquently argued the case for individual-izing children, Dr. Baar's initial reforms seemed to contradict every-thing he had ever said or written. All were in the direction of more regimeniation, tighter discipline, and stricter conformity. In fact, he eventually managed to achieve the goal his predecessors had been working toward but only partially attained: the militarization of the HOA. No wonder then that, many years later, survivors of his regime would refer to it as being "behind the Baars."[1] This was no exag-geration. Never again would life for the residents be as remorselessly controlled and restrictive. What is surprising, though, is that alumni from the Baar years remembered them with a good deal of pride and affection, as if they had successfully passed through an ordeal that had tested the limits of their stamina, character, and morale.

Seeking a "better control and a stricter vigilance," he told the soci-ety in his first annual report, in 1877, he had "drafted the boys into 13 military companies. These companies, drilled twice a week by a competent teacher, and headed by a sergeant, or monitor, selected from their own ranks, have to place themselves every morning in a military line, and are examined by the officers of the house as re-gards their cleanliness and outward appearance." When they saw the boys lined up in military ranks, visiting society members were im-mensely impressed. So were other important visitors. "The institu-tion had greatly improved in the short time he has assumed control," the *Messenger* commented on December 29, 1876. A few months later, the *New York Times* echoed this view. In an article headed "Compassionate Israel," which described how the city's Jews cared for their poor, it mentioned the asylum first and praised it highly. The reporter was particularly impressed by the military bearing of the boys and the "rigid inspection" they received before marching off to school. Their appearance, he wrote, was "sufficient evidence that they get an abundance of good food, comfortable clothing and kind treatment"—a judgment he seems to have arrived at without consulting the boys themselves. The paper also had complimentary things to say about the children's educational attainments. Of the seventy children in grammar school sixty-five had been promoted; and of this group twenty had been "jumped a class." In addition, three older boys were attending City College, which was unusual because orphanages as a rule did not provide inmates with higher education.[2] According to the prevailing view, orphans were not entitled to any more schooling than was necessary for them to earn a living after they were discharged.

Dr. Baar's first innovation quickly became a permanent part of asylum life. The organization of the boys into military companies would lead, in a few years, to the establishment of the cadet corps, an elite group of older boys, dressed in Civil War Union Army uniforms and equipped with mock rifles. The sergeants who officered it would evolve into the monitorial system, a British idea Dr. Baar liked and introduced. Thus, the older boys who gave commands on the drill field were also authorized to give orders in the dormitories—and to expect the same instant obedience. And the morning review of the military companies would become the preschool morning inspection.

Soon the spotlight of public attention shifted from the HOA to Dr. Baar himself, the result of another innovation, his Saturday sermons to the children. Preaching was something his predecessors had never done at religious services: children were not considered suitable subjects for sermons. But Dr. Baar did not agree with conventional wisdom on the subject, probably because he was a born preacher for whom an audience in need of moral salvation was an absolute necessity. Since the residents provided the only available audience—and a captive one at that—he made the most of them. Tailoring his preaching to suit their intelligence and, more important, their shorter attention span, he developed five-minute homilies built around a single theme and geared to a level the children could grasp. Dr. Baar felt that the children listened to him with "marked attention," but he was hardly an unbiased observer. One Baar alumnus recalled that he often fell asleep during the sermons and is sure he wasn't the only one. However, he noted, they were good "when he listened."[3]

Visitors who heard his Saturday sermons gave them favorable word-of-mouth advertising in the Jewish community, publicity which helped attract even more visitors. One of them was a skilled pulpit orator himself and considered Dr. Baar's efforts worth publishing. He was the Reverend Isaacs and, on August 10, 1877, he began printing them in the *Messenger* under the heading "Sermons for the Young." In the first of these, Dr. Baar told his wards: "Everything depends on the strength of your will; by the means of this will you can accomplish the highest, noblest, the greatest things on earth." A few weeks later the published sermon focused on discipline, one of his favorite subjects. "Once accustom yourself to obedience, my children," he declared, "and everything will go right with you." Certainly everything seemed to be going right with Dr. Baar for two other papers, the *New York Herald* and the *American Hebrew*, also began printing his sermons.

On June 2, 1878, the HOA held its third annual Prize Day, an event so unusual for an orphanage that the *New York Times* sent a reporter to cover it. Two prizes of fifty dollars each were awarded to the most deserving boy and girl in a gala evening ceremony attended by a large number of visitors. Known as the Betty Bruhl Prizes, the money represented the interest from a trust fund of $2,500 bequeathed in Bruhl's name by her husband.[4] With Dr. Baar's encouragement, other trustees made similar donations for Prize Day, providing more awards for achieving children. The money was banked for the prizewinners and given to them when they were discharged. Although a small nest egg at best, it came in handy when they left the home to start a new life in the community. Year by year, the number of prizes awarded, the grounds for awarding them, and the amount of money distributed grew larger.

As the decade was ending, Dr. Baar was becoming more concerned about the lack of space for the growing number of new admissions. The orphanage had an open admissions policy and seldom rejected anybody unless they were sick or diseased. But with the rise of Jewish immigration from eastern Europe and Russia, the waiting list of needy children grew longer. To accommodate them, the girls were moved to an annex on East 86th Street.[5] At the same time the HOA rather abruptly stopped taking children from Brooklyn, then a separate city. Having no alternative, the Brooklyn Jewish community responded to the unexpected crisis by establishing its own orphanage for boys only in a rented house large enough to shelter sixteen boys. In August 1878, the new home received a state charter under the name of the Brooklyn Hebrew Orphan Asylum. But Brooklyn kept hoping that the New York home, to which it looked for leadership, would eventually change its mind and once again readmit Brooklyn children. As late as 1890, for example, it offered to turn over all of its assets, property, and its one hundred boys to New York, but this offer was again refused.[6]

With a Brooklyn home in operation, the wave of Jewish orphanage building in the city was under way. And like the new home, all the others were built because the first among them wouldn't or couldn't admit certain categories of children. In 1879, the third Jewish orphanage opened in a rented house on 57th Street and First Avenue. Operated entirely by women (assisted by an all-male advisory board), the Hebrew Sheltering Guardian Society planned to care for needy Jewish children, mostly nonorphans, either remanded by the courts or referred by the community. The society was reimbursed by the city for the remanded children but had to support the others out of their own funds.[7]

In the fall of 1880, Dr. Baar felt the time had come to start advertising himself. He had the HOA's print shop publish a volume of his sermons and sent copies to members of the society, leaders in the Jewish community, and to selected members of the German aristocracy. Although the volume was liberally praised in the city, the compliments Dr. Baar personally cherished most came in letters from the Crown Prince of Germany and the Duke of Gotha. Publicity about his Saturday sermons now reached the point where even gentiles were coming to hear him. The sermons fared well with a wide audience, as they had in Liverpool, because there was little specifically Jewish material in them. One gentile, impressed by the children's devotion and order at religious service, wrote Dr. Baar and asked if he might contribute to the asylum. Pleased by the request, Dr. Baar said yes.[8] He was also gratified by sales of his book, which went into a second edition in 1885.

Despite a great deal of discussion in the late 1870s over the need for a new and larger building, nothing was done about it until 1879, when the case for expansion became overwhelming. There were now 296 children under care—165 boys in the main building, 19 boys in the industrial school, 99 girls in the annex, and 13 children—11 boys and 2 girls—who were boarded out for lack of space. Half orphans outnumbered orphans 239 to 50. Seven children were neither orphans nor half orphans but came from destitute families.[9] In keeping them, the HOA was violating its state charter and yet it had been unable to turn them away. Their presence was a portent for the future.

Now, at last, the HOA made the decision it had been deferring for years: to build a new and larger home elsewhere. It planned to move to upper Manhattan on what would become Amsterdam Avenue between 136th and 138th Streets. An Irish farmer named Daniel Devlin owned it, and the society paid him $138,465 for it.[10] They chose the site because it was dry and healthy, not too far from the city and the homes of its members, and the price was reasonable. They may also have been impressed by another consideration: the site was on the crest of a hill that overlooked spectacular panoramic views in almost every direction—the Harlem River to the east, the Hudson River to the west, and the rest of the city laid out to the south.[11]

That winter the orphanage found itself confronted with the kind of emergency that strengthened the argument for expansion. An epidemic of scarlet fever broke out in the city and soon appeared in the asylum. Thirty children were stricken, placing the orphanage in an embarrassing situation. Eighteen were taken by Mount Sinai Hospital, which not only waived its contractual obligation never to take more than two children at a time but also set up a special isolation ward for them. Two victims were placed in German Hospital, but the remaining ten, all girls, could not be hospitalized anywhere, so great was the pressure for space in medical facilities. In desperate straits, the orphanage made room for them in the East 86th Street annex and isolated them as much as was humanly possible from the other eighty-nine girls living there. Eventually, all the children recovered except for two hospitalized boys who died. When the emergency was over, the society came to a self-evident conclusion: the new building would have to have its own hospital, including isolation wards.[12]

Ground for the new building was broken in the fall of 1881 and work on the foundation began the following year. While the digging went on, the orphanage bought more land to square off the site. The additional plots were part of a property known as the Donnelly estate and cost $43,000. Their purchase brought the total cost of the land alone to $181,465.[13]

The cornerstone was laid on May 16, 1883, when the building's walls reached the second story. Several hundred people attended the ceremony, mostly members of the society, their wives, and some dignitaries. When they arrived at the site after a long journey—horsecars went only as far as 125th Street and Third Avenue so many had to hire carriages for the final leg uphill—they found that a special platform had been set up for them in front of the half-completed building. Its brick and stone facade was draped by the green flag of the society, flanked by American, English, German, and French flags. Speeches were made by Mayor Franklin Edson, Chief Justice Charles P. Daly, and Carl Schurz. Congratulatory letters from President Chester A. Arthur, Governor Cleveland, and General Grant were read to the gathering, which politely applauded each one. Jesse Seligman laid the cornerstone himself, using a silver trowel. Inside the cornerstone he placed a metal box containing city newspapers, the latest reports of various city charities, American coins of 1783 and 1883, and a Jewish shekel.[14]

No one awaited the completion of the new building more eagerly than Dr. Baar. In his six years as superintendent he had become a passionate advocate of the orphanage as a superior institution for raising children. "I am bold enough to assert," he told the society in his annual report for 1883, "that we turn out from our Orphan Asylum as many worthy members of human society as there are sent forth in our world by our respective homes and families." To support this claim, Dr. Baar in the same report provided the names of three successful alumni: Henry Mauser and Bertha Brieger, who had been appointed head of the boys and girls departments, respectively, of the Cleveland Jewish Orphan Asylum, and Rosa Levy, who had been named vice-principal of a Jewish academy in Paris. These three were the leaders in what would soon become an established practice among Jewish orphanages in America—the hiring of qualified alumni from the HOA. It reflected the spread of Dr. Baar's reputation as a leader in the field of institutional care for children to every Jewish community in the nation and in Europe. Eventually, every Jewish orphanage in the United States would have one or more New York alumni heading its staff, and most of them were Baar-trained people.

The new building was ready in August 1884. First to move in were the girls, followed in a week by the boys. There were 370 children in all, living in an asylum built to shelter 600. In October the building was formally dedicated. Mayor Edson returned to make the dedication speech and two thousand visitors came to see the ceremony and inspect the new home. What they saw was quite possibly the most magnificent orphan asylum ever built.

Designed in Renaissance style, it consisted of a main building of four stories and two connecting wings and a small center wing of three stories—like a giant capital letter *E* with its spine resting on Amsterdam Avenue. A high central clock tower dominated the main entrance, whose doors were made of heavy oak. Inside, the only term sufficient to describe its facilities was palatial. Walking through the main floor from one end to the other, visitors found a synagogue, also used as an assembly hall, two large reception rooms for the use of relatives on visiting day, the trustees' room, the superintendent's office and other smaller offices, serving rooms, classrooms, and a library. Dormitories were located on the second and third stories in each wing. On the fourth floor of the main wing were two infirmary wards, one for each sex, which could be converted into isolation wards if necessary. Available also in case the dormitories became overcrowded was an auxiliary fifth dormitory.

Swimming baths for each sex had been built on the ground floor in the wings; each was nineteen by nineteen feet square and four feet deep. To ensure the safety of the children, six staircases had been designed, and all were connected with corridors in such a way that no part of the building could be cut off from at least two of them. In an emergency, the entire building could be evacuated in a few minutes.

A number of facilities were included that permitted the HOA to operate as an independent, self-sustaining community. All were in the basement—a laundry, a bakery, a kitchen, and storerooms. Every room was steam heated—something of a luxury in those days—and equipped with electric call bells. (The inmates were grateful for the heat but hated the bells.) Heat and electricity were furnished by a boiler and generator located in a small, separate building behind the center wing. Every room was lighted by gas, which was also stored in the asylum.[15] The entire home would be electrified around 1900, long before the rest of the city.

Such splendor had a high price, and it came to $660,000. With the cost of land included, the grand total came to just over $750,000. But the Jewish community, which bought the bonds that helped pay for it, considered the money well spent. After his first look at the new orphanage, the Reverend Isaacs referred to it as a "superb edifice." Returning for a second look in January, he declared it to be "the handsomest asylum in the country." Reaching for even grander superlatives after a third visit some weeks later, he described it as "a palatial home, occupying the finest villa location on the island" with "offices, reception rooms, and hallways . . . as elegant as in many fashionable hotels." At the same time, he offered a sobering comparison: while expenses at Lamartine Place in 1860 had been $5,000, the annual expenses now came to $60,000 and promised to rise still higher.

One facility in the old building that was conspicuously missing in the new one was the industrial school. Its omission was deliberate and reflected the failure of a principle. Originally, the school had been established chiefly for the purpose of teaching the older boys a trade; earning a profit was secondary. Within a few years, though, the urge to make a profit took hold and caused some changes in the school's operations. Hoping to attract more business by underselling established firms, the print shop added more equipment and hired more workers. One result was that the apprentices were soon crowded out. Another was the growth of heavy expenses and, soon, even heavier debts. The shoe shop had also become a losing enterprise, though its debts were smaller. Before the new building was ready, Jesse Seligman decided to let the industrial school die.

Yet the idea of providing children with a trade as the best way to make them self-supporting still seemed a good one. In January 1884, the Jewish community established the Hebrew Technical Institute, a school for training Jewish mechanics. It was planned as a free school where poor Jewish boys from immigrant families could be taught a trade. The orphanage not only sent children there but, for a time, contributed to its maintenance as well.[16] Similarly, in 1885 the Hebrew Benevolent Society of New Orleans announced that it proposed to erect a new orphanage where every male inmate would become a "miniature land owner." A strip of land would be assigned to every boy to till as long as he remained in the home. Acting as his broker, the asylum proposed to sell his produce and bank the proceeds for him. As a result, the child would become a farmer during his stay and leave the institution "a small capitalist." No record exists to indicate whether this project was ever carried out.[17]

When the State Board of Charities made its first annual inspection in 1885, its report officially and enthusiastically confirmed all the glowing praise the orphanage had received from previous visitors:

> No pains or expense have been spared to make it all that it should be, and although in some of the details . . . it does not quite meet with your examiner's approval, still taking it as a whole it is, beyond doubt, the most thoroughly equipped and well-built institution that has yet been visited. Everything has been done to make the ventilation of the dormitories good, and as the beds are now distributed, quite sufficient air space is given to each child, a thing rarely found in our public institutions. . . .
>
> Each dormitory has five separate water closets, a sink and washbasins. . . . In all the closets on the boys' side there are urinals as well. Each dormitory has its separate lavatory. The trough and spigot system prevails. Clean towels are supplied each child once a week, which are kept hanging over the foot of each child's bed.
>
> The dining room is on the first floor behind the chapel synagogue, and is a magnificent room, well aired, ventilated and lighted. . . . The meals are as follows: Breakfast 7 A.M.—Bread, butter and coffee. Dinner M.—Meat, vegetables, bread. Supper 6 P.M.—Bread and butter tea and stewed fruit of some kind.
>
> Iron bedsteads are supplied with straw mattresses, sheets, blankets, etc. A full change of sheets is made each week. The girls dormitory con-

tains 100 beds, the boys' 110. The total number of children at present is 456; 196 girls and 260 boys. They are all in excellent condition. A doctor visits the institution every day, and any illness that might occur is immediately attended to.

The inspector found only two minor faults and made recommendations to correct them. He suggested that gratings be placed in the lavatory troughs to prevent children from using water lying on the bottom that might be contaminated and thus spread contagion. His second request involved the toilet seats, which had one unusual feature: their operating mechanism held the seat upright until used by a child, after which they would, within a minute, pop up again automatically and trigger the flushing action. Presumably the automatic mechanism was included to ensure that the toilets would be flushed regularly. But the inspector felt that the timing was too long and wanted it reduced so that the seat snapped back the instant a child stood up after finishing. The asylum complied and the self-flushing toilets continued in operation until it closed.[18] They were so efficient that one wonders why they were not adopted for use in all public toilets everywhere.

One other item in the report deserves comment—the use of straw mattresses. Bed-wetting was a major problem in the dormitories. Every morning at least 10 percent of the children were found to have wet their bed during the night, producing soiled bedding and the pervasive odor of urine. Apart from punishing the bed wetters, which did little to solve the problem and indeed made it worse, no one knew what to do about it. Blankets and sheets could be washed but not the wet and smelly mattresses, so the mattresses were removed and replaced with another blanket. Periodically, the orphanage would return to the use of mattresses in response to criticism, then get rid of them and go back to blankets again. But replacing mattresses was expensive and the changes were hard on the children. If the inspector found nothing wrong in the dormitories when he visited, it probably meant that the HOA knew when he was coming and got everything clean and tidy before he arrived.

With the orphanage in its third and—as it would turn out—last building it would ever occupy, we get the first complete picture of what life was like for the residents. As might be expected, that life was simple, spartan, repetitious, predictable, nearly pleasureless and, hardest of all to bear, lived in almost total silence. Dr. Baar, for reasons he never explained publicly, forbid the children from talking to each other during almost all activities in their daily routine. For growing children, already deprived by placement in an orphanage, this was an intolerable restriction. They rose in silence at 5:45 every morning, washed and dressed in silence, ate their meals in silence, and went to bed without speaking more than a few minutes every day. Only during the few hours of play they were allowed every weekend did they get a chance to speak to each other. In between, they had to steal moments of speech at the risk of punishment.

Residents dressed in uniforms, despite some protest against the practice from the Jewish community. On school days the boys wore a single-breasted jacket with a single row of buttons, a white collarless shirt, short pants that reached to the knees, like Bermuda shorts, white stockings, and ankle-high heavy boots they jokingly called "canal boats." Every boy also had to carry a large red bandanna. The jacket and pants were made from a slate-colored cloth known as Kentucky jeans—said to be so strong and durable that it took six boys to wear out one suit. At Dr. Baar's instructions, the suits were made with only one pocket, in the jacket, and none in the pants. He didn't want the boys to go about with bulging pockets, which he considered sloppy. Much less is known about what the girls wore, but the same Baar alumnus who reported on the boys' clothing remembered that the girls wore middy blouses and skirts made of the same type of cloth and black stockings.

More formal and dressier clothing was worn for the Friday night service, the Sabbath, and on holidays. For these occasions, the boys wore a blue suit with a double-breasted jacket, short pants, white collar, and black stockings held up by garters; the girls probably wore white dresses and white stockings. Most likely the boys' blue suit was Dr. Baar's idea. In his 1884 report he spoke nostalgically of the "blue-coat boys" of England, out of whose ranks, he recalled, had come such men as Coleridge, Lamb, and Richardson, among others. A lifelong Anglophile, he often spoke as if he hoped to transform the HOA into an American-Jewish Eton or Harrow.

The only group that was permitted to dress differently was the kindergarten boys and girls, both of whom were required to wear an apron over their clothes to keep them from being soiled. Visitors found the kindergarten boys irresistible because they wore a Buster Brown collar and a flowing knotted tie with their blue suits. For some reason the girls in their white dresses did not attract the same attention.

Meals were seldom pleasant. Like everything else, they were locked into a changeless routine. When the meal bell rang—at seven for breakfast, noon for lunch, and six for supper—the children marched to the dining room in columns, entered, and lined up along-side their table. Covered with oilcloth, the long tables seated sixteen, eight to a side, with a monitor at the head. Wood benches served as seats. At the first bell, everybody sat down; the second bell signaled grace before meals, spoken in Hebrew; everybody began eating at the third bell; the meal took about fifteen minutes, ending with the fourth bell, the signal for grace after meals; and the fifth and final bell was departure time, when everybody stood up, faced, and marched out when their turn came. No talking was permitted during meals, and governors patroled the aisles between the tables observing the children as they ate.

Apart from their routine, meals were unpleasant because of one regulation, rigidly followed: the children had to eat everything they were served, their tastes, preferences, and allergies notwithstanding. If a child didn't eat everything, the entire dining room had to wait until his or her dish was clean. Any delay or refusal to finish led to punishment.

For some reason water at meals was rationed, one cupful to every two children; seconds were not permitted. Since water was never scarce, this policy seemed completely unjustified. To the children, it was another one of many apparently senseless rules laid down arbitrarily by adults which they were compelled to obey without question. Introduced by the Harts at Lamartine Place, the practice had never been changed. (One possible explanation for the water rationing is that it was a means to control bed-wetting.)

The meals themselves, if you accept the memories of Baar alumni, had improved only slightly since the *New Era* exposé in 1875. Breakfast consisted of a cereal—farina, oatmeal, hominy—bread and butter, and coffee or milk. According to one graduate, the cereal was usually cold, the butter rancid, and the coffee watery. Few could recall school-day lunch menus. One popular lunch was the frankfurters served on Wednesdays, when the Ladies Sewing Society met. In an article on the HOA published in the July 1890 issue of the *Illustrated American*, lunch was described as consisting of "soup, meat, vegetables, and some kind of sauce or dessert." This sounds like the Sunday lunch, for soup was never served on weekdays. Supper wasn't much better than lunch, according to some Baar alumni. One recalled it being two slices of buttered dark bread, a mug of tea with milk, and a mug of water, while another remembered such fruit and vegetables as prunes, barley, and lentils. (If mugs of water were being served, it meant that the stringent—and senseless—water rationing policy of the past had finally ended.) Again, if you want to believe the

Illustrated American, supper was a well-rounded meal—"bread and butter, with fruit or sweet potatoes, and occasionally stewed plums, eggs or cheese, with tea or milk." Everybody agrees, though, that the best meals were served on weekends. On Friday night, there was herring, which most of the children enjoyed. But its smell was so strong that it couldn't be completely washed out of the dishes that night. As a result, the Saturday morning cereal always tasted slightly fishy. Saturday lunch was meatballs, with bread pudding for dessert, and occasional treats like apples or ginger bread. Best meal of the week was the Sunday dinner, when the trustees and other visitors came to watch them eat—a spectacle the Reverend Lewin had condemned. The children were served soup, a roast meat, and a sweet for dessert. Aware of being watched, the children rarely presented any disciplinary problems at Sunday dinner, and the food was so much better than the weekday variety that no one had trouble eating it all.

Because no snacks were served between meals and there was no way to obtain them (except by sneaking out, which was against the rules and grounds for severe punishment), the children were always hungry at bedtime. And when they were hungry it was harder to sleep. Although there were occasional midnight raids on the storerooms to steal food, the only such incident that occupied a permanent place in the memory of Baar alumni was an event known as the Prune Raid.

One summer's night in 1899, a group of boys got the idea of raiding a storeroom and stealing some prunes and apricots. Unknown to them, another group in the same dormitory had a similar idea: raiding the dining room to get a few pitchers of cool water. It was a very hot night and although they could have obtained water in the washroom it was always tepid in the summer.

Both groups, one starting earlier than the other, left the dormitory stealthily and moved toward their separate objectives. Like patrols, each group crept forward with lookouts in front and rear to warn the others of the one person they most feared to meet—the night patrol. Both missions accomplished their goal and the groups seem to have met each other on their way back to the dormitory. But this happy ending was spoiled the next morning when one of the prune raiders got sick and vomited terribly. In the ensuing investigation, the whole story was wrung from the guilty parties. Unable to distinguish between the two groups, the governors lumped them together and they became known as the Prune Gang. One gang member recalled that the punishment they received was long and severe, lasting nearly three months.

In his article on the HOA in the *Illustrated American*, the writer noted with some surprise that the "amount of hired help required is remarkably small for so extensive an institution." Apart from the superintendent and four teachers (who also worked as governors in the dormitories), twenty-eight persons were employed. Their number was so small because the older girls worked as unpaid housekeepers. Before leaving for school every morning, they made three hundred beds—including those in the boys' dormitories—and swept and dusted as well. After meals, the girls cleared the tables, swept the dining room, washed the dishes, and set the tables.

Though this was exploitation, the girls managed to turn their daily drudgery into opportunity. While making the boys' beds, some slipped notes under certain pillows; in the dining room they slipped notes under certain plates. How the girls learned where the boys they wanted to reach slept and ate was a considerable feat, for the sexes were kept segregated and communication between them was strictly forbidden.

School-day mornings were always a bit hectic. While the girls were cleaning up after breakfast, the boys shined their shoes, checked their clothing, and, if necessary, attended sick call, held in a basement playroom. Two lines of boys were waiting for the doctor when he arrived—one for those who needed building up, the other for those who were constipated. The first line received cod liver oil, the second, castor oil. Any really sick cases were sent to the infirmary, which also treated cuts and bruises. In the 1890s the HOA's consulting physician was placed on a daily schedule in order to deal with the medical needs of a large and growing population.

Dr. Baar made only two appearances on weekdays, both in the early morning. How he spent the rest of his time is a mystery. The first was at the service held before breakfast and the second was at eight, for inspection of the boys. Mrs. Baar inspected the girls at the same time. Inspection was the morning's most important ritual and the entire staff would turn out for it. Held in a basement playroom on most days, it was sometimes moved to the playing field in good spring weather. The boys formed four long, precisely aligned ranks through a procedure known as "toeing the line"—placing the tips of their shoes against four long cords stretched out on the floor. There were about one hundred boys to a line, and the lines reached from one end of the playroom to the other. Precisely at eight—Dr. Baar's punctuality was legendary—he would appear in the playroom carrying a rattan switch. Already standing at attention, the ranks stiffened a bit upon his entrance. At a signal, the boys stretched their hands out, palms up, each holding a red bandanna. Passing down one rank and up another, Dr. Baar spoke only to those boys who failed inspection for one reason or another: dirty hands, uncombed hair, sloppy dress, unwashed ears, unshined shoes. Offenders were ordered to step up front. These he punished by whacking them hard across the palm with the rattan switch.

Dr. Baar seldom spoke during inspections, but when he did his remarks were usually admonitory. His favorite comment, invariably directed at repeat offenders, was "You are a *narsty* fellow." As he spoke, in a German-tinged British accent, he would point at the offender with his right hand, forefinger crooked over the middle finger, and shake it emphatically. When inspection ended, he left the playroom, not to be seen by anyone the rest of the day.

Everybody left for school when the inspection ended, about 8:30. Half remained to attend P.S. 192, a primary school set up, with city approval, for the youngest children, who were taught by the governors. The older children attended Grammar School No. 43 at 129th Street and Amsterdam Avenue. Supervised by the monitors, the boys marched out in column formation for the seven-block downhill walk to the school. On many days the column was verbally abused by neighborhood Irish gangs. From them came a torrent of insults—"sheenies," "dirty Jews," "Christ-killers," "kikes," usually accompanied by stones or snowballs, depending on the season. All this was done at a safe distance, for the rowdies were vastly outnumbered by the column. But the monitors, obeying orders, would not permit anyone to break ranks to pursue the tormentors. At times, though, when the abuse became especially vicious and prolonged, they would relent and allow a few of the bigger boys to leave the column and drive off the rowdies.

The situation got so bad in the 1880s that the orphanage had the home's officer, a retired city policeman named Mike Brady (whom the boys loved and affectionately nicknamed "Pop") accompany the children to school. Brady's presence alone wasn't enough to stop the verbal abuse, but he was spry enough to scare off the rowdies when they got too close to the column. He was less successful, though, in stopping the fights that broke out in the school yard. Fighting was a regular feature of school life because of a tacit understanding among the boys that any insults to their religion had to be resented and fought. Since the insults never stopped, neither did the fighting.

Each side would choose one big, strong boy to challenge the other. The two champions would fight with bare fists in a rough ring made by their respective supporters. Often the same boys would be chosen for weeks or months at a time. One Baar alumnus recalls a series of almost daily duels between an asylum boy named Nathan Frank and an Irish boy named Nugent. Frank won every time, he says. The HOA champion of another day was Benny Noah and his rival a "long-eared, lanky, clumsy Irishman" named Connolly. Again, it was Noah who always won. Indeed, if the memories of Baar graduates are to be honored, asylum boys won all the fights at No. 43. This hardly seems likely. Still, considering the rigorous life they led, the pent-up feelings they held against the asylum's discipline, the absence of opportunities to release them, and their general good health, there are good reasons for believing that they won most of them.

For Mike Brady, the school-yard fights always trapped him in a three-way conflict between loyalty to his employer, loyalty to his own people, and his love of fighting. Although he tried to stop the fights, Baar alumni report, there were times when he seemed not to be trying hard enough. On such days the dilemma was usually resolved for him by the principal or the custodian.

Despite the rowdies, the children enjoyed going to school because it got them out of the orphanage for a few hours a day. As a rule, no child was allowed to leave without permission, which was seldom granted. Only the grammar school children got out regularly and they made the most of it. During such brief intervals as changing classes, boys and girls found moments for glancing encounters, and brothers were able to meet sisters. Inevitably, there were also opportunities to meet and establish friendships with neighborhood children, most of whom were not related to the rowdies. In some instances, tenuous romances sprang up between home boys and neighborhood girls. For example, one girl named Queenie Ellis would pass by the boys side on 138th Street every weekday night, when the boys were studying in their classrooms on the main floor, and give a special whistle. Upon hearing it, the boy it was intended for would rush to the window and wave at her. But nothing came of this affair. When the boy was discharged and tried seeing Queenie on a regular basis, their friendship promptly collapsed.

With perhaps one exception, the teachers, also mostly Irish, were very fond of the "Hebrew Boys," as they liked to call them (though the girls went to No. 43 they were far fewer in number). It was hard not to like the Hebrew Boys for they were ideal students—always punctual, well-behaved, their lessons always done. Though a minority in the school—about 15 percent of the enrollment—they invariably won most of the prizes and honors for scholarship. And the teachers showed their appreciation in many ways. One Baar old-timer recalled that during a bad snowstorm in 1896, which prevented the home children in his class from returning for lunch, his teacher sent out for sandwiches and milk, which she paid for out of her own pocket. Another alumnus remembered how his teacher found a way to allow him to be with his aunt, who had unexpectedly turned up at school but was not permitted to see him. Violating school regulations, the teacher sent him out of class on a phony errand that made it possible for him to be with his aunt for a while. If the HOA children were paragons at No. 43, it wasn't entirely because of their superior intelligence and sterling character. They were compelled to study every night and they had to behave lest complaints about them reach Baar and lead to punishment.

The one place where life was hardest for the children was in the dormitories. Apart from the steam heat, there were no comforts available in them; they were vast, open rooms with no furniture except beds and no decorations anywhere. If there was one good thing to be said about them, it was that they were extraordinarily well lighted and ventilated, there being windows on at least two sides. A hundred or more children slept in a dormitory, in beds laid out in precise rows so that anyone could quickly check out their occupants by glancing down the aisles.

The beds were actually iron cots ingeniously designed to also serve as chairs and wardrobes. Each cot had hooks on the headpost from which clothes could be hung, and a retractable shelf under the cot that could be pulled out and used as a seat for dressing. Since the children were not permitted to have any personal possessions and the only clothes they owned were those they wore, there was no need to provide them with lockers or chests. Both boys and girls slept in nightgowns.

Privacy of any kind was impossible in the dormitories. All activities were open, public, and collective. In the morning, for example, everybody woke at 5:45, in the predawn darkness, and had an hour to wash, dress, and prepare for services and breakfast. Governors and monitors went about waking up anyone who continued sleeping after the rising bell sounded. Some children were shaken into wakefulness, others had their cots overturned. Lolling on the cot was a luxury that could not be tolerated. Washing was the first morning chore and it was done in huge lavatories at the end of every dormitory. In it were basins and towels and rows of toothbrushes in numbered cases along the walls. Dr. Baar was a strong believer in the use of toothbrushes, and the numbered cases was his idea.

Almost every activity carried out in the dormitories was done "by the numbers"—in response to numbered commands. For example, undressing at night proceeded as follows:

1. Jacket off
2. Sit down
3. Right shoe off
4. Left shoe off
5. Right stocking off
6. Left stocking off
7. Pants off
8. Take clothes away
9. Go to bed
10. Get in bed

When everybody was in bed, various attempts were made by the monitors to compel sleep, also by the numbers. First, a monitor would count to three hundred, slowly. Next, official sleep-testers visited every bed and blew in the eyes of its presumably sleeping occupant. Those who blinked were routed out of bed and punished. Even trickier were the monitors who went about gently asking, "Is everyone asleep?" Anyone foolish enough to reply was beaten.

Standing punishments were frequently employed by the monitors for various infractions, and some were ingenious. The simplest of these was to order the boys—no one is quite sure how the girls were punished, or if they needed to be—to stand in a line, one behind the other. In one variation, they had to stand with their arms upraised, either empty or holding a pillow. But the real genius was the monitor who thought up the "crack" variation. This one required the boys to stand in a line, in tight formation, each practically leaning on the one in front of him. If anyone moved even slightly, or did anything else forbidden, like whispering, the monitor would rap the head of the last boy in line and yell "Crack!" Upon being struck, the last boy was required to knock his head hard against the head of the boy in front of him; he, in turn, repeated the process in a continuing chain reaction, until every boy had had his head rapped. As each boy was struck, he was expected to yell "Crack!" If a boy had a friend standing in front of him and was unwilling to knock him hard, the monitor would intervene and punish the reluctant one with a hard rap. For the monitors, the beauty of this variation was that the boys punished themselves, thus saving them a lot of effort, not to say bruised knuckles.

Dr. Baar once told the society, "It is indeed seldom or never that we resort to corporal punishment. . . . Self-control and mild forbearance on the part of the teachers are some of the reasons why our children amicably associate with each other; why the big ones do not strike the little ones, but form one strong united band of social companionship." One wonders now what place he had in mind, for there was little "social companionship" in the dormitories, where the "big ones" had carte blanche to strike the "little ones." Although it is hard to believe that Dr. Baar was ignorant of what was happening in the dormitories, most old-timers claimed that he was not aware of the brutality because it was kept from him. Whenever he appeared, some Baar alumni recall, "supervisors and monitors were on their most innocent behavior." Moreover, the "kids were afraid to report rough treatment." It was also not easy for a child to see Dr. Baar; he was about as approachable as a monarch on a distant throne.

Ingenious as the monitors were at inventing punishments, they were often surpassed at the art by the governors. According to the recollections of a number of Baar alumni, one "applied a sewing machine strap which left ugly welts on the skin"; another liked to come behind a victim suddenly and "knock his head with his knuckles"; a third specialized only in kicking shins; a fourth loved to take two boys and "knock their heads together"; and a fifth enjoyed kicking boys with his "pointed shoes." When it came to punishments, every governor was free to do as he pleased. In Dr. Baar's administration, all the governors were former home boys who knew of no other means of maintaining order except through physical punishment and harsh restrictions. Slapping or punching a boy was almost second nature to them, as reflexive as blinking or breathing. And seldom did the punishment fit the crime. As a result, most boys who were beaten severely for the most trivial infractions felt deeply humiliated and developed long-standing grudges against their persecutors. Even in the 1950s, when some alumni were interviewed, they still remembered certain incidents with undiminished clarity and hatred.

There were never any organized protests against the beatings from the boys themselves. Ironically, the only vocal objections came from an outsider. In the late 1880s, a gentile farmer living on the 138th Street side would cry out in protest when he saw or heard a boy being beaten or mistreated by a monitor in the classrooms at night. So frequently did he protest that monitors in the classrooms opposite his farm were careful not to punish anyone if they saw the old farmer looking across the street. Unfortunately, he seems never to have brought his complaints to Dr. Baar.

One of the few pleasures the residents enjoyed was seeing their parents on visiting day, held on a Sunday afternoon once every three months. Over a thousand people would visit the orphanage each time and stay for two hours, the most Dr. Baar would allow. Under previous administrations, parents were permitted to visit once a month. But Dr. Baar, fearful that parents might bring contagious diseases, curtailed their visiting privileges. Not everybody looked forward to visiting day; full orphans without relatives were depressed by it. Out of sympathy for their feelings, the Reverend Isaacs once urged the HOA to abolish this "quarterly exhibition" and allow more frequent visiting. His suggestion was ignored.

If parents brought food, money, or candy, Dr. Baar would not permit the children to keep them. He thought the food was potentially hazardous to their health; he felt they weren't ready to use money yet, so he kept it for them until they were discharged; and he considered the consumption of candy a corrupting indulgence. In addition, parents had to be exceedingly communicative on visiting day, for Dr. Baar would not allow children to write letters to them afterward. Furthermore, any letters sent to the children were censored. Apparently he hoped to maintain the children in a perpetual moral quarantine, totally isolated from unwholesome outside influences until they could return home transformed. To Dr. Baar and the trustees, the parents themselves represented the least wholesome of all outside influences.

The supreme privilege was to be granted permission to visit one's parents one day a year, during the summer. It was not granted lightly. A child had to have a near-perfect behavior record all year long to earn the right to the annual one-day visit. In every dormitory the governor in charge assigned one boy or girl the duty of carrying a notebook to record all infractions and the demerits meted out for them. Those whose demerits passed a given total were denied the privilege of the summer visit, among other things. Too many demerits could keep them from certain play periods, deny them the next weekend dessert, or exclude them from the next special treat. By the time summer came, there weren't many boys (the girls were considerably more obedient) who received approval to see their parents.

Baar often complained to the society that the children needed more recreation. "I do not know what I admire more in them," he remarked in one report, "the elasticity of their minds or their bodily physique in passing through such a process." He was referring to their over-organized daily routine, involving school from nine to three, German and Hebrew classes from four to six, homework at night, and vocational training of sorts (mostly for the girls) on weekends. Obviously there was very little time for play. Only in the summer were the children allowed a few hours of leisure every day. But to enjoy it they had to rely on their own ingenuity. No one had toys and athletic equipment was unavailable. If a boy wanted to play baseball, he literally had to make his own ball. It was done by wrapping the ravelings of an old cotton stocking around a piece of cork, covering it with strips from old sheets or similar rags, and sewing them together with old shoelaces. Any kind of decent stick served for a bat.

Dr. Baar, who knew more about cricket than baseball, allowed the boys to form their own team, which played teams from the neighborhood and from two other orphanages, the Hebrew Sheltering Guardian Society and the Brooklyn Hebrew Orphan Asylum. Games with visiting teams were always great occasions for the entire home; even Baar often came to watch them. Visitors usually complained about the playing field; it was hard, gravelly, grassless, and uneven.

Apart from baseball, there were games like One-O-Cat, played with two sticks, and Prisoner's Base, a running game with a lot of rough physical contact. An annual picnic was held on the grounds during the summer, and there was also the annual excursion up the Hudson to such places as Indian Point. Every morning the cadet corps drilled for a few hours; the rest of the year it drilled only on Sunday mornings. Although it was vacation time, the children still could not escape some schooling. Religious classes were scheduled for some mornings and every afternoon for two hours. How the children endured the hot classrooms during the long summer afternoons is something difficult to imagine today.

If their life offered few pleasures and promised even less expectations, it nevertheless did provide some compensation (at least in the 1880s). The neighborhood was still rural and a delight to live in. In its first few years, the orphanage was an alien presence, a semi-Gothic brick and brownstone intruder perched on the crest of a hill amid a wide open landscape. Amsterdam Avenue down to 132nd Street was filled with vacant fields ending in a rocky cliff. Known as Donnelly's Woods, this area was uninhabited except for an empty house, which the children liked to believe was haunted. North, the nearest building was a fire station about ten blocks away. Behind and to the west was an unobstructed view of the Hudson River. The only road between the orphanage and the river was Broadway, then known as the Boulevard—a rather elegant name for an unpaved street. At the time, though, all the streets in the vicinity were unpaved and, in bad weather, all but impassable. Still, Broadway and the river were sights that kindled the fantasies of hundreds of HOA children. For example, one Baar old-timer recalled that Broadway then served as a "speedway" with "fine turnouts for horse-drawn carriages." Whenever he passed the second and third floor hall windows facing west, he would look out expectantly, hoping to see something exciting. One sight that always thrilled him was the Albany coach, pulled by tandem horses and guided by a red-coated footman with a hunting horn. It passed by on the Boulevard once a day. Even more fascinating to him was the teeming river traffic—tugs, lighters, sloops, steamboats, Hudson Line paddle wheelers. To him the view west was always "a grand sight" and one of his few happy memories.

Another Baar alumnus never forgot the Saturday afternoon in 1887 when the first cable car, a double-decker, climbed up Amsterdam Avenue, crested the hill at 135th Street and crossed in front of the orphanage. It drew a crescendo of cheers and applause from the hundreds of children who had gathered there for that moment.

There were times, though, when the neighborhood's isolation proved to be a liability. Such was the case during the Great Blizzard of 1888. Beginning on March 12, it presented the orphanage with the first test of its ability to survive as a self-sufficient community. Dr. Baar was worried by two possibilities: a food shortage and a medical emergency. Neither occurred. On the first day of the blizzard, the asylum found its hero: "Pop" Rosenberg, the baker, fought his way through snow, wind, and waist-high snow to reach the building. Since no fresh food of any kind was to be available for nearly a week, the fresh bread he baked daily was welcomed as if it were manna. By the third day, snowdrifts covered the main entrance and reached the second story. The orphanage was isolated from the city, unable even to use a telephone, for all the lines were down. But it survived without any sign of strain. No one got sick and the only problem was boredom. Dr. Baar dealt with it by ordering classes to be held every day of the blizzard. To alumni, it is remembered as a period of three uneventful and tedious days. When it was over, the snow lay on the ground for days afterward and provided the children with an unexpected source of pleasure. It also prevented the cadet corps from drilling the next Sunday morning, but no one seemed to mind.[19]

The End of an Era   8

In the fall of 1888 many cities all over America were planning for what was expected to be the biggest patriotic event since the Civil War—the George Washington Centennial in April 1889. Since Washington had been inaugurated in New York that city was organizing the most spectacular celebration of any in the nation. Three days of festivities were decreed as the minimum acceptable period of homage due the first president.

On April 29, President Benjamin Harrison, the guest of honor, would arrive, be welcomed regally by civic dignitaries and prominent citizens, and lead the centennial ball that evening. The following day he would reenact the first inaugural at its original Wall Street site and review the greatest military parade ever staged in New York as it moved up Broadway to Washington Square Park. Ordinary New Yorkers would assume the primary ceremonial role on the third day, May 1, and march in a parade of their own called the Pageant of Peace. Organizations representing the most prominent ethnic, business, labor, political, and fraternal groups would be invited to participate. Most of their members were foreign-born and the parade would give them a chance to express their loyalty and appreciation to America. One of the smallest groups, comprising about five thousand college and grammar school children, was known as the Educational Division.

As an inducement to all units to perform at their very best—the city's civic pride was involved—the centennial committee announced a marching contest. The prizes were a gold and silver medal for the two best adult groups and a blue banner for the best unit in the Educational Division.[1]

Although the HOA was not a school it was nevertheless invited to participate in the centennial. Its cadet corps had appeared in a number of parades in 1888 and had performed well enough to attract some praise. No one expected them to win, for they were orphanage boys. Indeed, the HOA was the only orphanage participating in the parade and, as it would later turn out, the only Jewish unit as well. Still, the home's resources all but guaranteed that they would make a better showing than most of their rivals.

To begin with, the orphanage's military training instructor, a former Police Department drill sergeant named Lt. Schwauke, was one of the best in the city. In physical appearance, Lt. Schwauke was a monolith of a man—tall, massively built, with a huge walrus moustache that concealed most of his mouth. Out that hidden mouth, however, thundered a parade-ground voice that made many boys cringe when they heard it. One thing about him that was always mentioned in hushed tones was the large fleshy knob over the index finger of his right hand. This disfigurement was the result, so it was said (no one dared ask him outright), of a Civil War wound. Lt. Schwauke was ruthless in the pursuit of perfection, and the cadets, about 150 hand-picked boys, responded smartly. They had little choice, for mistakes aroused his wrath, which was devastating.

Another resource, and an invaluable one, was the orphanage's own military brass band, probably the only boys' band in the city at the time. It had been reorganized in July 1888 after having been disbanded (though no one knows why) since 1885. Its instructor, George Wiegand, was also first-rate. Wiegand, like most musicians in the city at the time, was German and spoke English with a heavy accent. He was also bandmaster for the Seventh Regiment, a member of the New York Philharmonic, and a popular composer and arranger.

In his own way Wiegand was every bit as formidable as his colleague, Lt. Schwauke. And the most formidable thing about him was his incredibly developed ear for music. On practice days the band was warmed up for him before he arrived by a talented eighteen-year-old college student named Martin Cohen, who was also colonel of the cadets. Band alumni claim that Wiegand could detect wrong notes played during the warm-up while riding the Amsterdam Avenue cable car several blocks away. Upon entering the rehearsal room, they recall, he would at once pick out the errant musician and scold him.[2] Because of this unnerving gift, the boys took care to play correctly during rehearsal, lest Wiegand pounce upon them when he arrived. A martinet like Lt. Schwauke, he had extremely high standards and he quickly brought the band up to the level of quality he demanded.

A third advantage the HOA had over its rivals was its own parade ground, the rocky, uneven playing field. It was available any time Lt.

Schwauke wanted to use it. During the school term, though, the boys had time for drill only on Sundays.

Whether the uniforms the boys had been wearing—Union Army blue and probably Civil War surplus—were an asset to the corps is a moot matter. Still, anything with color was better than their dull grey Kentucky jeans, and the boys enjoyed wearing them. The shiny brass buttons and the genuine military hardware made them all feel like real soldiers. Officers were given army swords and epaulets, while the boys in the ranks received real rifles with their firing pins removed. Assembled in formation, the corps with its four companies, led by a colonel, made an impressive appearance on the field. Each company had its own captain, lieutenant, sergeants, and corporals, and commands would go down the ranks in authentic military cadence.

Through the fall and winter of 1888, the cadets and the band (plus a tiny drum corps of eight) were drilled relentlessly by their respective instructors. Of the two groups, the band had to work the hardest and the longest. Its members not only had to learn their instruments and rehearse together as a unit but also had to be taught to march and play with the cadets. This made training doubly tedious for them, for it meant going from Wiegand on weekday nights to Lt. Schwauke on Sundays, when all three units rehearsed together.

With the coming of spring, the rehearsals assumed an intense quality and the orphanage itself began to reflect a state of nervous expectation. On the night of April 30, few boys could sleep and the excitement in the dormitories made it harder to keep order. For once no rising bell was needed to wake them in the morning. By 4:30 "we were all up," recalled Louis Freund, a cornetist in the band, many years later. In the predawn darkness the boys were "shining our shoes, getting our uniforms ready, polishing our instruments, practicing." They were wearing a new uniform for the parade—Continental grey with knee breeches. About an hour later, all three units, totaling nearly two hundred, accompanied by Dr. Baar and some governors, headed downtown. It was a sunny, cold, windy day, not perfect parade weather yet crisp and exhilarating.

Downtown the city that greeted them presented a thrilling sight, one they would remember for the rest of their lives. Buildings everywhere were decked out in patriotic bunting and flags flew from thousands of windows. About a million spectators filled the streets, many of whom had arrived hours earlier to get choice spots along the parade route. President Benjamin Harrison, surrounded by a huge entourage of dignitaries and politicians, sat in the reviewing stands in Madison Square.

One man who was very pleased with himself that morning was the chief marshal of the parade, Gen. Daniel Butterfield. Fifty thousand marchers had been recruited, thus fulfilling the centennial committee's goal of making it the biggest parade in the city's history. To judge the marching contest, the general had placed fifty men along the parade route, which began at 57th Street and Fifth Avenue, went south to 15th Street, east to Broadway, around Union Square, and ended at Canal Street.[3]

After a long impatient wait in a side street near Fifth Avenue, the HOA's contingent finally received the signal to march. Preceded by a boy carrying a blue pennant with the initials "HOA" in white letters, the group stepped out onto Fifth Avenue and into the parade. From the moment they began marching, they drew enormous applause, for their bearing was erect, their movements precise, their ranks perfectly aligned.

At one point in the parade an incident occurred that would achieve instant immortality as one of the asylum's most durable anecdotes. An Irish policeman who noticed the pennant-bearer apparently misread the initials because the wind had whipped the pennant backward. Approaching the boy with a broad, proud smile, he asked, "Ancient Order of Hibernians?" Shaking his head, the boy motioned to the contingent coming up fast behind him. He then saw a huge banner carried by two boys which read "Hebrew Orphan Asylum Cadet Corps." The policeman laughed heartily, as if a joke had been played on him.[4] Apart from this case of mistaken ethnicity, nothing unusual happened during the long parade. In fact, the cadets were greeted everywhere with approving cheers and loud applause. By the time they reached Canal Street, they were feeling a heady sense of triumph that made them forget all the endless hours spent at drills and rehearsals.

Although the contest winners weren't announced immediately, newspaper stories the next day provided a strong clue as to how well the boys had performed. The *Times* commented: "Of all the boys in the educational division, the representatives of the Hebrew Orphan and Benevolent Society received the greatest amount of applause. With their band of little fellows, led by a drum major whose age was not more than twelve, their appearance everywhere was the cause of much cheering. Their marching was described by the ladies as 'perfectly lovely.' "

The *Herald*'s reporter apparently found the boys irresistible:

A CUTE DRUM MAJOR
After the Brooklyn boys came the ladykillers of the division, 150 boys of the Hebrew Orphan Asylum, headed by the cutest little uniformed

band, led by the cutest little drum major, all in blue and gold, that mortal ever laid eyes on. The band, comprising thirty pieces, all boys of the asylum, and all less than fourteen years old. The music was wonderfully good. The drum major, Joseph Jellenik, is just thirteen years old. But the way he whirled his staff was a caution. All of the 150 boys outside of the band carried Belgian rifles. The orphans with their band created a genuine sensation and were greeted with a waving of handkerchiefs and applause all along the line.

Although the *Tribune* also praised the boys' performance, its comment was the briefest: "The little cadets marched finely and their bandmaster, who is said to be the smallest in the United States, twisted and swung his stick like a veteran, and was much applauded." The *Sun's* story was the only one to describe the boys' special uniform:

> Seventy-five of the Weir Battalion, School 10, Brooklyn, in neat blue uniforms, with white leggings and belts, Major F.H. Nichols commanding, started applause, which was drowned by cheers and laughter a moment later at the sight of a fat little youngster waving his drum major's baton sedately in front of the boys band of the Hebrew Benevolent and Orphan Asylum. One hundred and fifty little fellows, in gray suits, with knee breeches, marched behind him, and were followed by the Columbia Institute Cadets in dark blue uniforms.

The judges obviously agreed with the crowds along the parade route. All fifty of them declared that the HOA's cadets had won the coveted blue banner. About six months later, on Thanksgiving Day, the banner was delivered. Two military heroes came up to make the presentation: General Butterfield, the parade marshal, and General William T. Sherman, the only major Civil War hero on either side still alive. Sherman, an old friend of Jesse Seligman's, had moved to New York a few years earlier. About a thousand visitors, chiefly society members and their families, attended the ceremony, held in a courtyard. A small platform had been erected there, to be used as a dais by Seligman and the two guests of honor.

The program began with an exhibition drill by the cadets and a concert by the band. (One piece deliberately omitted was "Marching through Georgia." Sherman hated it so Seligman advised Dr. Baar not to include it in the band's performance.) When the entertainment was over, Seligman introduced General Butterfield first. After some short congratulatory remarks he presented the banner, which was about six feet wide and five feet long and showed the Gilbert Stuart portrait of Washington in gold and silver thread on a field of blue. On the left side of the banner was the inscription "Awarded to the

Hebrew Benevolent and Orphan Asylum Society of the City of New York, for fine bearing in the Civic and Industrial Parade."

It was accepted for the boys by one of the cadets, who thanked him in a brief speech. It was obvious that everybody was waiting to hear Sherman, as if his presence there was the real award rather than the banner. Nearly seventy then, he was making one of his rare public appearances, as a favor to Seligman. He may also have had a personal reason for being there: he had been an orphan himself, which made it easier to identify with his young audience. His speech was not much longer than Butterfield's but a good deal more mixed in content, mood, and feeling:

> When I came out this afternoon I hardly knew what part I was to take in this ceremony. The president of this beautiful college and I have been personal friends for over thirty years. We met far away on the coast of the Pacific, in San Francisco, in times when we needed men, and he was one of them. It was at his request that I came here, and to witness this ceremony has been a sincere pleasure to me.
>
> To you, boys, I shall say, always bear in memory that flag which you have received and earned. I am sure the judges who apportioned it to you were impartial. Go on in the same course. Be ever firm, persevering, industrious, and give your hearts and souls to whatever you undertake, and it requires no prophet to tell what your future will be.
>
> You look upon this flag as a trophy earned by your patience and industry; but look in the center of your files. There is the old flag that we love so much, the stars and stripes. Gather around it always, boys, and look to it as the emblem of the country you have to serve for the next thirty or forty years, and see that it remains as pure and strong as it is now.
>
> You are orphans, I know, but you are well cared for, and the more you have to struggle the more of men you will be and the better elements you will have in you. Stand up for your rights, boys, because before the law and before the Constitution and yonder flag, you are just as good as any other boys in the country.
>
> Let us pray that the day may come when we shall be perfect brothers of all nations, when we shall all love each other as brothers should. God bless you my children. I hope that you will have happiness in this life. War did not bring happiness.
>
> We old men saved you boys in the past. You now take up the history of the country where we left off, and there is One above, righteous and just, who will hold you responsible for the labor of your lives, that you may do your duty and leave to others to finish the great work until the consummation of all time. You start out with health and all the hopes and glories of the future before you. But realize one-hundredth part of youth's ideal, and you will have done well.[5]

According to the *Times* the next day, Sherman's speech made the boys feel "two inches taller." A fifer in the drum corps, one of the smallest boys in the home, made the reply:

> We have heard and read of you, General, and your honored name is a household word among us. They say I am too little to play a conspicuous part in the ranks of our orphan soldiers, but to show you how deeply I appreciate the military art, I am proud to tell you that I belong to our famous corps of fifers, and that I do my duty in the best style possible. Dear General, may you live long, and believe that I and all the boys of this asylum assembled around you feel deeply the honor you do us in being present at this occasion.

Dinner followed the ceremony, and it was a banquet—six hundred pounds of turkey and "enough cake and candy and ice cream to freight a ship."[6] The huge banner was framed and hung in the dining room. (It remained there until the home closed in 1941. No one knows what happened to it afterward.)

In a sense, Sherman's speech to the cadets could be considered his valedictory to the nation as well, for he died fourteen months later, in February 1891. At his funeral, the cadet corps, band, and drum corps performed for him for the last time. The route taken was exactly the one used for the centennial, and the asylum's contingent was the last unit in that long and mournful procession.[7]

For everybody connected with the HOA the winning of the centennial banner, though a minor triumph, was converted into a landmark event. Jesse Seligman and the trustees were enormously pleased and proud, while Dr. Baar basked in the glow of extravagant praise. His boys' performance was seen (by him and many others) as both a vindication of the institutional system and, of course, his own administration as a shining example of what that system could accomplish at its best. Long established as the fountainhead of wisdom on matters concerning the care of the children, he was now enthroned in his authority, immune to criticism from any source.

When news of the HOA's centennial victory appeared in the Jewish press all over America, it evoked enormous astonishment everywhere. This was because the very existence of a Jewish cadet corps and military band was extraordinary. At the time they comprised the only Jewish paramilitary units of their kind in America, if not the world. To the Jewish community in New York, they had the effect, among other things, of providing living proof against the charge that Jews were not patriotic. And it was particularly important for their morale to know that the only Jewish unit of its kind was also the best.

Overnight the cadet corps and the band became the pride of the HOA, which began using them for what today would be called public relations. They proved to be especially effective in fund-raising. In fact, the first call for this service came early in 1890, when the United Hebrew Charities of Boston invited the band to a fund-raising event held in a theater. Dr. Baar happily agreed to let them go. For the boys in the band, the excitement they felt the night before they left for Boston was almost exactly like the night before the centennial. In its first out-of-town appearance, the band was a sensation, entrancing an audience that would dearly have loved to hear them play all night long. Afterward the Boston Jewish community expressed its pleasure by sending the HOA a handsome testimonial.[8]

Boston's request for the band alone, without the cadets, set a pattern for the future. Of the two units, it was the band that always attracted the most engagements. Although the boys in the band never received any direct payment for their services, they didn't mind the work involved. Indeed, they loved engagements and looked forward to every performance. An engagement required them to leave the HOA for up to half a day to visit a strange place and entertain people who usually treated them well. Frequently there were unexpected fringe benefits, such as refreshments or donations of small coins from delighted spectators. At other times the benefits were less tangible, though still worth savoring. For example, when Admiral Dewey made a triumphal visit to New York harbor after his victory at Manila Bay during the Spanish-American War, the HOA band was one of many similar units waiting on a fleet of special barges to welcome him. As the admiral's flagship passed in review, their drum major, twelve-year-old Benny Greenwald, twirled his baton while standing on the barge rail, his legs held firmly in place by Martin Cohen. In the parade held later to honor the admiral and celebrate America's victory over Spain, a hundred HOA children—boys in blue serge suits, girls in white dresses—marched down Riverside Drive together with children from city schools. They were preceded by the HOA band and the cadet corps costumed in Rough Rider uniforms. Leading them all was little Benny Greenwald in a West Point uniform twirling a silver-topped baton as he strutted down the drive.[9]

Nor would any band member ever forget their appearance at the dedication of Montefiore Hospital, in the Bronx, where Theodore Roosevelt, then governor, was the guest speaker. Before leaving, Roosevelt shook hands with every boy in the band.[10] Hospital and synagogue dedications provided the band with many of their engagements. It is safe to say, in fact, that no cornerstone of any building erected by Jewish organizations in the city (or the suburbs) was suitably laid unless the HOA band was present to provide the music.[11]

Without realizing it, the HOA had become an informal training school for band musicians. Every year the band lost some members through discharge, and many of them found jobs with various professional bands. In fact, it was the prospect of earning a living at music that attracted many boys to the band and led them to accept practice and rehearsals with considerably less complaint than did the cadets. Their training under Wiegand, though not extensive, was apparently sufficient for the level of music performed by most bands in the city at the time. Few bands then were permanent organizations with a regular conductor and scheduled engagements. As a rule, they were groups hastily assembled for a single occasion and then disbanded. By the mid-1890s, however, there were so many band alumni floating about that the idea naturally occurred to some of them to form their own band. But none actually did so until October 1894, when twenty-one alumni formed the Jesse Seligman Military Band. It was named as a posthumous tribute to the late president of the HOA, who had died some months earlier.[12]

Jesse Seligman's death was a blow to the city's Jewish community, which saw him as a martyr to anti-Semitism. The previous year Jesse's son Theodore, a recent Harvard graduate, had applied for membership in the Union League Club, in New York. He wasn't anticipating any trouble because his uncles Joseph and William had helped found the club after the Civil War and his father had been a vice-president. In addition, he had such distinguished sponsors as Elihu Root and Joseph Choate, among many others. Yet, incredibly, Theodore's application was rejected. The reason, as the membership committee tactlessly explained, was not "personal" but "purely racial." What it meant was that the club's formerly open membership policy had been slowly changing against the admission of Jews— a symptom of the anti-Semitism then slowly and quietly surfacing in American social life. Infuriated by the rejection, Jesse at once resigned. His resignation was not accepted. But it didn't matter; so great was his bitterness that he never returned to the club. Soon afterward his health began failing, and he decided to take a trip to California with his family. In reality, though, he was fleeing the city to escape the intense humiliation he felt. To his friends he said that he never again wanted to live in New York. He never did, for he died in California. His body was borne back to the city in a special train and more than 2,000 people, including 150 HOA children, attended his funeral at Temple Emanu-El.[13]

One person who felt Seligman's death quite keenly was Dr. Baar. Having worked together for eighteen years, they had grown very close during their long collaboration. Between them, they had built the HOA from a small, obscure orphanage into an institution with a national reputation. Seligman's sudden passing foreshadowed the aging superintendent's own fading mortality.

His successor was Emanuel Lehman, a founding partner of the Lehman Brothers brokerage firm. Although Dr. Baar got along well with Lehman, it soon became evident that his authority with the trustees was slipping. One sign of his waning influence was reflected in the outcome of the first issue that came up between them, the need for expansion. Once again the HOA was overcrowded, with seven hundred children living in a home built for six hundred. Discussion about what form the expansion should take had started in 1893, but now, in early 1895, a choice had to be made. There were two views on the subject: the trustees wanted to add two wings to provide for five hundred more children; Dr. Baar argued instead for a separate building for the girls.

In his disagreement with the trustees, Dr. Baar appeared to be fighting bigness and its depersonalizing effects on the inmates. "With seven hundred children in the house," he told the trustees, "we have already in the better sense of the word a so-called 'machine-education'; if you take several hundred children more . . . you will reduce the asylum, pardon my expression, to a mere boarding establishment." To the trustees, this argument may have sounded like a self-deluding numbers game. Why was seven hundred still an acceptable figure and twelve hundred the point at which the orphanage became "a mere boarding establishment"? Dr. Baar never seems to have provided a satisfactory explanation.

Nor was his preference for a separate girls' building supported by anything more substantial than a Victorian view of the relations between the sexes. Apparently he favored none whatever. What frustrated him was that boys and girls were somehow still managing to communicate with each other despite his strict regulations. "We have often found correspondence between the sexes," he advised the trustees, as if this were a cardinal sin. He was referring to the notes the girls were slipping under pillows when they made the boys' beds in the morning. His solution, though, seemed far-fetched, almost like putting the girls in a nunnery. To their credit, the trustees rejected the idea and ordered the construction of the two wings.[14]

Eighteen ninety-six was a year of important anniversaries. In April, Baar celebrated his seventieth birthday. At a testimonial dinner held that month, Lehman presented him with a solid silver inscribed loving cup. "Overcome by emotion, he made a very touching response."[15] A week later there was an unveiling of a memorial to Jesse Seligman, a bust by Sir Moses Ezekiel. It was placed in the lobby, thus making it the first thing visitors saw when they entered.[16] The two new wings were dedicated in November, on Thanksgiving Day. This event, which Baar had tried to prevent, also happened to coincide with his twentieth anniversary as superintendent.[17]

The following year it was Lehman's turn to be honored. But the occasion would be long remembered more for what he gave to HOA than for what he received. On February 15, his seventieth birthday, he presented the HOA with a $100,000 Industrial Fund, the interest to be used to help alumni to learn trades, professions, or establish themselves in business through low-interest loans. For many children fortunate enough to receive grants from the fund, it was the first step toward a successful career after their discharge. In providing the fund, Lehman was making the point that training boys to become mechanics was not the sole acceptable route to self-support, as it had seemed in the seventies and eighties.[18] Jacob Schiff had recognized this earlier when he set up the scholarship fund of 1891 with an annual income of $300. The money was earmarked for talented boys who wanted to pursue an artistic or scientific career. Although girls were originally ineligible for scholarships, this policy was later changed. Both the Lehman Fund and the Schiff Fund represented the sort of investments in their future that natural parents might make for their own children.

In the summer of 1898 the HOA was suddenly confronted with the greatest crisis in its history. As the spring school term was ending that year, a large number of children became violently ill. All the victims complained of the same symptoms: sharp stomach pains, high fever, diarrhea, discharge of mucus and blood, and an ulcerated and inflamed large intestine. Dr. Jacobi diagnosed it as epidemic dysentery. With each passing day more children joined the sick list. By the end of the first week in July, nearly a hundred children were laid up. When the infirmary in the central building became full, one boys' dormitory was emptied and turned into a hospital ward for the most serious cases. Decades later a member of this group still retained one vivid image of his stay in this improvised emergency ward: the long line of boys waiting outside the toilets, their bodies writhing in pain and their faces reflecting this agony, as they waited their turn to move their bowels.[19]

Early in the third week of the epidemic five children died, including several who were about to graduate from Grammar School No. 43. One victim, Celia Lipschitz, had been a playmate of Dr. Baar's only daughter, May. A pretty girl with curly blond hair, May was adored by all the girls. At the morning service after Celia's death, Baar presented a side of himself the children had rarely seen. Appearing in the synagogue with a long, gloomy face, he started the service in a tentative, halting manner. Then he lost control, broke down, and wept.[20]

That week the number of seriously ill children rose to nearly 20 percent—157 out of a population of 865. Nor was there any sign that the epidemic was slackening. Some progress was made nevertheless because Dr. Jacobi had by then determined its cause: impure water. Still, he didn't know the source of the contamination, and he couldn't even begin to trace it until the home was evacuated. The trustees agreed, though not without some qualms about the immense task involved. Conducting a mass evacuation of children was difficult enough, but doing it in the middle of a raging epidemic called for an effort bordering on the heroic. The sick children and those with no relatives were transported to two sanitarium buildings the HOA rented in Far Rockaway. Of the well ones, some were sent to other institutions while others were sent to live with relatives. The entire operation took about a week or so—perhaps the most spectacular administrative feat accomplished during Baar's regime. Subsequently three more deaths occurred: two children and an adult, the chief steward. This brought the toll to eight, a figure that proved to be final.[21]

For many children it was the strangest—in some instances, the happiest—summer of their stay in the home. The luckiest ones were those who were moved to Far Rockaway. With no governors or monitors to harass them and few rules to follow, the well ones, and the sick ones as they recovered, lived like vacationers on an extended holiday. Few among the group sent to live with relatives had as pleasant a summer. Many went back to crowded East Side tenements and their Yiddish-speaking parents, whose Orthodox religious practices and undisciplined style of living seemed foreign to them. As one Baar alumnus put it long afterward, it was like being sent back to "another world."[22]

With the HOA empty, Dr. Jacobi and his staff were able to trace the source of the contaminated water to neighborhood facilities. After consulting the city's health and sanitary authorities, they agreed to follow the latter's recommendations. First, the asylum was disinfected, its plumbing completely overhauled, and new fixtures installed. Second, two large filters to purify the water were installed at the point where it entered the building's plumbing system. The cost of these renovations came to $20,000.[23] The third step agreed upon would take more time—the construction of a new, five-story building that would include a quarantine center for new admissions and two isolation wards on the top two stories, plus a tower staircase to provide access to them. (The Reception House, as the new building was named, would not be ready until 1902.)[24] In October, when the renovations were completed, the children returned.

Hurried along, perhaps, by the strenuous exertions required of him during the epidemic, Dr. Baar made a decision that he probably had been mulling over since his seventieth birthday. In December he announced that he would retire early in 1899. This was no surprise to Lehman and the trustees. Dr. Baar was now seventy-two, an old man who walked with a marked stoop. To alumni who remember him in his last years as superintendent, he had the appearance of "a sage, a learned scholar." His retirement attracted a good deal of attention, including a long story in the *Times*. He and his wife took an apartment near the HOA, to be near the children they loved.[25] The HOA had been their life for twenty-two years and they could not give it up easily. Dr. Baar visited frequently and gave occasional guest sermons at the Saturday services. Alumni came to him for advice about their life and career. What delighted him most was hearing about his successful children. And there were at least half a dozen who did very well indeed, including two who achieved international fame. To Dr. Baar, these few plus a great many more whose careers were substantial if not outstanding, were proof that the orphanage system worked and should be supported.

The most famous of all Baar alumni was Edwin Franko Goldman, the bandmaster and march composer. Goldman was admitted to the HOA in 1887, about a year after his father died, at the age of nine. Apart from the fact that he was a half orphan, he had nothing in common with the other children whose life he was to share for the next six years. He was a second-generation American and a Southerner, having been born in Louisville, Kentucky. Both his parents, David Goldman and Selma Franko, were also Southerners from New Orleans. And unlike the families of most new admissions, his parents were cultured, in comfortable circumstances, and extraordinarily talented, chiefly in music.

Goldman's father, who had been sent to Germany for his education, was one of the most brilliant men in America. At one time or another he had been a lawyer, college professor, linguist, judge, orator, lecturer (in ten languages), rabbi, and newspaper editor. In addition, he was an amateur musician endowed with virtuoso talent on the piano and violin.

His mother was equally gifted. She was a member of the Frankos, the most famous musical family in America in the post–Civil War period. In the 1860s the Frankos—five child prodigies at home on both piano and violin—joined with Adelina Patti, the Spanish soprano, to form an act that toured America and Europe. At a concert they gave in Washington, D.C., in 1869, their performance left one listener, a boy named John Phillip Sousa, in a state of rapture. "It was the first time I heard real music," he was to write in his autobiography, "and it inspired me to do better." Selma met and married David Goldman in New Orleans. One recent resident of the city that both became acquainted with early in their marriage was Dr. Baar, then principal of a Jewish school. Although burdened with children—ten were born but five died—the Goldmans moved a great deal, depending on which of David's multiple careers he was pursuing at the moment. In Terre Haute, Indiana, where David was working as a newspaper editor, he became seriously ill and died, in 1886, at the age of thirty-eight. His death was a permanent blow to his wife; Selma mourned him the rest of her life and never remarried. Left with five children to support, she moved to New York, where most of her brothers and sisters were either performing, teaching, conducting, or writing music, and started teaching piano and violin. But it took a long time to build up a clientele and Selma sometimes didn't have money to feed the children. Fortunately, Dr. Baar learned that she was in the city and he prevailed upon her to leave the two oldest boys, Edwin and Walter, with him. She agreed, though reluctantly, and with the understanding that she would take them out as soon as her income permitted.

On Edwin's first day there, Dr. Baar called him into his office and "spoke gently" to him. To Edwin, he "looked not unlike Peter Cooper, with the same sort of whiskers under his chin. He told me about my parents and how talented they were. He hoped that I had similar talent." Dr. Baar's personal interest in Edwin immediately set him apart from the other children. As he wrote in his unpublished autobiography, *Facing the Music,* he was given "special privileges and treated as a member of Dr. Baar's family." Goldman never forgot this. In his memory, Dr. Baar would always remain a great disciplinarian with "a heart of gold."

Although his mother, uncles, aunts, and cousins had been performing in concerts by the time they were five, Goldman began his musical career at an age when the Frankos had ended theirs as child stars—when he was ten. His extraordinarily late start was not his fault. His mother had been too busy bearing and raising children to find time to teach him. Still, she did tell him about the family's musical tradition, and he dreamed of becoming part of it. When the HOA band was reorganized in the fall of 1888 in preparation for the Washington centennial, Edwin was one of the boys who volunteered to join it. For no particular reason he was assigned to play the alto horn. But the horn bored him; he didn't like the idea of playing only afterbeats. Soon, he was dropped from the band for having "absolutely no talent." Dr. Baar was astonished when he heard this judgment; he persuaded Wiegand to try Edwin on another instrument. Wiegand offered him a cornet. From the moment he blew his first notes, the boy was transformed. He progressed so rapidly in the first few weeks that Wiegand invited him to come to his home twice a week for additional lessons in harmony. "At last I was started on a musical career and I was happy," Edwin recalled.

For the rest of his stay, Goldman was to devote all of his free time after school to music. At eleven he became the band's only soloist, promoted to this eminence by Wiegand. Dr. Baar, who followed his progress like a doting father, often went down to the band room to hear him practice. But there is evidence, however, that his mother didn't approve of his preference for the cornet. In a family so utterly committed to the violin and piano, brass instruments presumably were regarded with something akin to horror. At any rate, when he was twelve, Mrs. Goldman obtained Dr. Baar's approval to visit the home twice a week to give him piano lessons. It was too late; Edwin was committed to the cornet.

When his mother was securely established as a teacher, she decided it was time to take her two sons home. Walter consented at once but Edwin—incredibly—refused to go. He told his mother that he was very happy in the asylum and wanted to stay. What effect these words had on her is difficult to imagine; she had struggled for years to become self-supporting and reunite her family. Unable to change Edwin's mind, she let him remain, certain no harm would come to him while Dr. Baar was superintendent. Goldman may well have been the only child in the history of the HOA to prefer the asylum to his own home.

One thing Edwin never lacked while there was recognition. At twelve he was awarded a gold medal with the inscription "Best Boy in Band." At thirteen he was appointed the replacement for Martin Cohen, who had graduated from college. Like Cohen, his main duty was to warm up the band before Wiegand arrived. Although he never said so, it seems likely that his lifelong dream of organizing a first-rate band capable of performing the finest symphonic music may have first come to him then, as he rehearsed thirty small boys in the band room of the HOA.

Whatever it did for his ego, the dual role of solo cornetist and band leader left him in a conflict for the next few years, and he wasn't always certain which of the two he really preferred. And he would soon be facing an even more serious conflict. When he was fourteen, a trustee offered to send him abroad for study, but he wasn't interested. Instead, he took an examination for admission to the National Conservatory of Music, on East 17th Street. Passing easily, he won a scholarship that entitled him to study there the following year. But when it arrived, he was hesitant about attending. It was 1893 and he was fifteen. That June he graduated from Grammar School No. 43 and was unanimously voted the most popular boy in the class; he was also awarded a prize for scholarship. Next, he took the entrance examinations for City College, passed with high grades, and was admitted. Now on the verge of being discharged from the HOA, he was confronted with a hard choice for a poor boy to make: college and the security of a well-paying profession or a far more chancier career as a musician. Without much agonizing he chose music.[26]

Goldman then embarked on what was to become one of the most spectacular careers in the history of music in America. At the National Conservatory he studied composition with Antonin Dvorak. Within a year, Jules Levy, the world's greatest cornetist, accepted him as a free student. In 1895, when he was seventeen, he was engaged by the Metropolitan Opera Orchestra—the youngest musician ever to perform with that organization. (Although the appointment was merited, nepotism played a key role. The Metropolitan's conductor was Nahan Franko, Edwin's uncle. To keep the relationship a secret, the boy was listed on the roster as Edwin F. Goldman.) He stayed with the Met for ten years. Although he enjoyed performing, he also knew that he wanted to be a conductor. And being with the Met gave him an exceptional opportunity to study all the great conductors—Toscanini, Mahler, and Damrosch, among others—from his seat in the pit. At the same time, he acquired a good deal of personal experience by organizing and conducting a number of small ensembles, none of them permanent.

Six years after he left the Met, in 1911, Goldman put together a select group of the finest brass players he could find to form the New York Military Band. For a number of years the band gave occasional concerts, all well-received, but no regularly scheduled performances.

In 1917, though, Goldman got the idea of presenting free summer concerts and, after overcoming all sorts of obstacles, gave his first performance on the green at Columbia University. His motivation for starting the outdoor concerts was partly economic. He wanted to provide employment for musicians during the summer, when concert halls were closed.

The biggest obstacle of all, it seems, was getting people to accept the idea of summer concerts in the first place. Apparently no one had thought of it until Goldman came along—an astonishing thing when one considers the vast number of summer concerts available now in the city. But New Yorkers were delighted by the idea and thousands of them went to Columbia to hear him. The event became a triumph for Goldman and his "Symphony Orchestra in Brass," as one delighted critic described his superb band. Since then, the Goldman Band, transferred to Central Park, became a popular, enduring fixture of summer life in the city. Its success enabled him to devote more time to his other major interest, composing marches.

In 1932, the year his lifelong friend John Phillip Sousa died, he received the most satisfying honor of his entire career. At a Central Park concert that summer, Sousa's widow presented him with her late husband's favorite baton. In her speech, she said she was sure that Sousa would have wanted him to have it. The gesture was more than symbolic. Since Sousa's death he had in fact become the dean of American bandmasters. His reputation as a composer had soared equally high: his march "On the Mall" is considered by some to be second in popularity to "The Stars and Stripes Forever." The acceptance of Sousa's baton was, in a sense, the climax of his life. The former thirteen-year-old leader of the best boys' band in the city had become the best bandleader in America.[27]

Throughout his career Goldman never forgot what the HOA had done for him. All his life, for example, he remained a close friend of Dr. Baar's daughter, May. He treasured the honors for music he had won as a boy and kept them apart from his other medals and awards. And it was a group of HOA boys who gave him one of the most memorable birthday parties he ever received. On January 1, 1928, his fiftieth birthday, eight members of the HOA band paid a surprise early morning visit to his Riverside Drive apartment. After being let in very quietly—the "surprise" had been planned—they broke into "On the Mall" followed by "Happy Birthday." Goldman came out of his bedroom a few minutes later, smiling broadly.[28] He died in New York in 1956, at seventy-eight. At his death the city not only lost its favorite bandsman but an extraordinarily popular citizen. With his bushy white hair, engaging smile, and cheerful manner, Goldman was said to have been known by sight to more New Yorkers than any other public figure.

Julius Tannen, the second most famous alumnus of the Baar period, was a vaudeville star who is generally considered the father of modern stand-up comedy. He was also the first great Jewish comic in America. Born Julius Tannenbaum in Chicago and orphaned at three when both parents died, he was sent to New York to live with an aunt. A mischievous boy, Julius got on her nerves with his endless pranks. By the time he was six, her patience was exhausted and she placed him in the HOA, in 1887. Although the HOA's severe discipline abruptly squelched his prankish behavior, his lively personality wasn't entirely suppressed. After a while, it surfaced in a new form, as humor. Tannen became known for his ability to write and present skits, sketches, and monologues at dramatic shows and Prize Day ceremonies every June.

Like Goldman, his contemporary, he was discharged in 1895. But unlike Goldman, he had no outstanding talent that pointed the way to a career and he was not seeking higher education. Nor was his first job, as a furniture salesman, a promising one. He made a success of it, though, because he interjected a witty line of comedy patter into his sales spiel. Customers loved it and were charmed into buying furniture. In addition, it led to many requests for his services outside the store as an entertainer. With Tannen, so it seems, began the tradition of the Jewish salesman who graduates to show business by softening his hard sell with humor.

When he was twenty, he decided to turn professional. At the time, in 1901, he was working as a secretary to J. Ogden Armour, the Chicago meat packer. (He had learned shorthand in the HOA.) In a show he gave for employees before he quit, he presented an impersonation of George M. Cohan, who happened to be performing then in the city. Tannen took his bow with a mock curtain line he had thought up with Cohan's family act in mind: "My father thanks you, my mother thanks you, my sister thanks you, and I thank you." By coincidence, Cohan was in the audience and heard it. Not long afterward, when the Cohan family had finished a rousing performance and had taken many bows for it, George sensed that a curtain line was needed to get them off stage with a flourish. Then, remembering Tannen's words, he came forward and spoke them. The applause was thunderous. From then on, they became part of the Cohans' act. Tannen never publicly revealed that he was the author of the most famous curtain line in vaudeville. Cohan, it should be noted, never thanked Tannen for handing him that nifty curtain line.

In his first engagements, Tannen—who shortened his name when he went into vaudeville—made an instant, refreshing impression on audiences because his comic style and appearance were so different from that of other performers. While they drew laughs with slapstick physical humor, his act was purely and elegantly cerebral. All he did was to walk out on stage and talk. And talk. And talk. At first, he presented only monologues, but they were witty, topical, and original. Audiences laughed at what he said, not at what he did. While other comedians wore outrageous costumes to provoke laughs as soon as they appeared on stage, Tannen dressed in an ordinary business suit. He had a thin face, long neck, and, in his early years, always wore a pair of rimless pince-nez perched on the end of his nose. It gave him the look of a stock broker who had wandered on stage by accident. His delivery was stentorian and nonstop. Years later, when a drama critic labeled him a chatterbox, he agreed and thereafter billed himself as "Julius Tannen—Chatterbox."

Within a few years Tannen became a headliner and played all the best vaudeville houses in America, including the Palace in New York. In 1908 he was invited to perform at the London Palladium, an honor accorded only to the best American entertainers. As he went from one triumph to another, he worked at improving and enlarging his repertoire of comic techniques. He became celebrated for his exquisite timing. One of his innovations was the delayed punch line, preceded by a pregnant pause. Example: "A woman has the right to be as homely as she wants to be"—pause—"but this one has abused the privilege." He developed the ad lib to a fine art and regularly cut down hecklers with crushing insults. He became expert at mimicry and was one of the first entertainers to present impressions of famous people. Fittingly enough, one of his most famous impressions was that of George M. Cohan. It was his revenge on Cohan for having stolen his curtain line. He pioneered in the use of one-liners. And he is said to have thought up the idea of a "master of ceremonies" to introduce a series of unrelated acts. Whether true or not, he was acknowledged by all his contemporaries as the best emcee in show business. From 1925 to 1929 he was the emcee for the biggest revue on Broadway, Earl Carroll's Vanities.

Although very popular, Tannen never attracted the kind of idolizing followers that were drawn to such performers as Will Rogers. This was because he was more of a comedian's comedian, the professional that younger performers studied carefully and tried most to imitate. Still, he is credited with getting Will Rogers "off his horse" by writing his first monologue for him. Rogers quickly became more of a celebrity than Tannen ever was, for his comments were softened by a folksy delivery and a gentle smile.

Between the rise of the motion picture, which killed vaudeville, and the depression, which wiped out his fortune, Tannen was reduced to bankruptcy in the early 1930s. So he did what many other performers were doing at the time—he went to Hollywood. No longer a star, he played character parts in a great many movies, the best known being *The Miracle of Morgan's Creek*. In 1962, the Masquers Club of Hollywood gave him a testimonial dinner at which Jack Benny, Bob Hope, and George Jessel, among many others, acknowledged their debt to him. He was honored for being a superb monologuist, a first-rate impressionist, a great ad-libber, and a master of timing. Three years later, in 1965, he died at the age of eighty-four.[29] But long before then he had helped elevate American stage humor from low, vulgar, slapstick comedy to an artful entertainment suitable for any group of listeners.

Louis Freund, another highly successful Baar boy, achieved his fame quietly but securely in what was then a new industry, the electrical contracting field. A New Yorker by birth, he was seven when his parents both died in the same week in March 1884. Relatives in Philadelphia cared for him briefly but couldn't keep him. They sent him back to New York, where he was placed in the HOA. Freund became a favorite of Dr. Baar's when he joined the band as a cornetist.

At the age of fourteen, he was planning to attend City College after his discharge; Dr. Baar talked him out of it. He told Freund that it would be a very hard life for him to work all day, attend college at night, and then do his studying after midnight. It would be harder still because he had no family or relatives to return to who could give him any kind of support. Although all this was absolutely true and sound fatherly advice, it was not an impossible course of action, given Freund's ambition, intelligence, and determination. But Dr. Baar's own plans for him, though, make one wonder about his real motivation. He wanted Freund to stay in the HOA another year so that he could teach cornet in the band. He knew that Edwin Franko Goldman would be discharged at the same time and losing his two best cornetists in the same year may have been too much for him. At any rate, Freund stayed on. As a substitute for college, Dr. Baar got him into the Hebrew Technical Institute, where he studied electrical engineering. An excellent student, he won three prizes upon graduation—twenty-five dollars, a set of electrical manuals, and a set of drawing instruments. They were more than enough to launch his career.

The electrical industry was young in the closing years of the century and Freund had no trouble finding work. But he had trouble of another sort unrelated to his job. Some boys in the factory were anti-Semitic and two of them challenged him to a fight. His first fight was with a boy a head taller than himself. "I beat him so badly that he never returned to work," Freund recalled in the 1950s. He also won the second fight. After that, no one bothered him. "I think the training we got in the HOA made us all tougher," he observed. While getting started in the business, Freund earned extra money as a member of alumni bands. For a while, in fact, he organized and led his own band, named after himself.

Eventually, he formed his own electrical contracting company, Louis Freund, Inc., which became very successful. He was elected president of the New York Electrical Contractors Association and remained in that post until 1957, when he became its historian. He was also a charter member of the Electric Board of Trade and a member of the Board of Governors of the National Electrical Contractors Association.[30] In 1958, at the age of eighty, he died. One wonders what his life would have been like if he had rejected Dr. Baar's advice and gone to college instead of to trade school.

Two other Baar boys deserve brief mention. Martin Cohen, who led the HOA cadets at the Washington Centennial, went to the College of Physicians and Surgeons at Columbia University. After graduation he became one of the best known and most successful ophthalmologists in the city. For thirty-eight years he was a consultant surgeon in his specialty at the Manhattan Eye and Ear Hospital. In the 1920s he was a consulting ophthalmologist at the HOA. From 1903 to 1952 he published about eighty scientific papers and invented a number of medical instruments as well.[31] Lionel J. Simmonds, a younger contemporary of Cohen's also went to college, became a governor, and then assistant superintendent. In 1920 he became superintendent—the first alumnus to run the asylum in which he had arrived as a resident.

Dr. Baar died in 1904 at the age of seventy-nine. His funeral was held in the HOA's synagogue, attended by hundreds of alumni who had grown up under his regime.[32] No monuments were erected to his memory but none were needed. The orphanage he had left in 1899 changed in a number of ways after his death, yet much of its inner essence would remain pure Baar until it closed decades later. At the time of his death, when many of his boys were doing well, Dr. Baar liked to believe that his training was solely responsible. This was only partly true, of course. Most of them were helped along by trustees and members of the society who actually took a personal interest in the children. Without their support many of the successes might never have been.

From Philanthropy to Social Work 9

In visiting and ascertaining the conditions of the applicants, they heeded not the threatening sky above, nor the frozen earth below, to turn in the narrow alleys and gloomy streets sacred to the poor. In our visits we clambered up to moldering fetid garrets, and groped our way through all the dreary haunts where poverty and misery, driven by extorting landlords and dire necessity are compelled to herd with vice, through the tainted moral atmosphere, where innocence dies, and youth is corrupted, a fountain poisoned at its source.[1]

This excerpt from the report of the Committee on Charity is remarkable, for it portrays committee members as intrepid missionaries on a rescue safari into darkest poverty. Like European colonizers, the members concerned themselves primarily with self-glorification rather than the wishes of the people. The 1870 report similarly referred to the "joyous comrades of the asylum" and the "golden stream of benevolence." In 1871 Jesse Seligman relished "the pleasing conviction of having done all in our power to ameliorate the condition of suffering humanity." Also in 1871, G. M. Leventritt, chair of the committee of governors, included the following attempt at verse in his report:

> There's a language that's mute,
> There's a silence that speaks,
> There are words that can only be read
>   on the cheeks,
> And there's our orphans, and from their
>   eyes you can deduce health, happiness,
>   and prosperity.

Leventritt's words illustrate the society's approach to the children: the members "deduced" their state rather than asking them directly.

Despite this authoritarianism, the orphans at the HOA had a better life than most orphans. Because of the benevolence of the members the HOA was the best endowed orphanage in America. That secure financial support kept the HOA free from the obsession with efficiency common in almost all orphanages in nineteenth-century America. Efficiency was simply providing the bare necessities at the least possible cost. Since the money to operate orphanages was always hard to obtain, and the number of children placed in them kept growing, their budgets were always being strained to the limit.

The HOA didn't overlook efficiency but it did refuse to enshrine it as an ideal. Instead, it measured its success by how well it could develop the moral, physical, religious, and cultural lives of the children entrusted to its care. This goal was established before the Civil War by many orphanages, but was forgotten as the orphanage became the dominant form of child care for dependent children. The HOA, however, continued to honor this goal right up until the day it closed. It always spent more for services and facilities than other homes, and its per capita cost was always higher as well, usually by 15 percent or more. The astonishing thing about the HOA is that when it was more overcrowded than at any time in its history—in the early 1900s—it was providing more medical, social, recreational, and cultural services than it had in the early 1870s, when its population was much smaller.

In 1874 the HOA began receiving public funds for the first time. That year the state legislature amended its charter and authorized the city to reimburse the HOA the sum of $110 per child per year plus an additional $13.50 if it provided some education. As might be expected, the new law had an enormous impact on the HOA's financial position. Thus, in 1874, when its budget was $32,000, the city paid it $23,000.[2] Such support couldn't have come at a more propitious moment. The HOA was growing faster than many other homes in the city and needed the extra money. At the same time, money was becoming harder to get because there was a greater demand on charitable funds, a reflection of the new migrations from Russia. By the early 1880s, the number of poor Russian Jews in the city had increased to the point where they were being regarded as a calamity, not just a burden. Providing relief for them was straining the resources of the Jewish community.

As if anticipating this problem, the HOA since the Civil War had been acquiring a new generation of members. Among them were a number of German Jews who had made their fortunes outside the city but had subsequently gravitated there because it had become the business and financial capital of America. It was also the city with the nation's biggest Jewish community. As a result, the city acquired practically every Jewish millionaire known—more than forty, according to one newspaper account. Most of them joined the society because it was the most prestigious Jewish charity in the city.

The acknowledged leader among the millionaires was Jacob H. Schiff, one of the giants of Wall Street. Schiff had once been an immigrant himself, though hardly a poor one; his family were bankers in Germany. He had arrived in New York City after the Civil War at the age of eighteen with $500. But the money was far less important than his genius for high finance. No Horatio Alger hero, Schiff practically started at the summit and stayed there. In 1873 he became a junior partner in Kuhn, Loeb, a German Jewish firm. Two years later, after marrying Solomon Loeb's daughter Therese, he was promoted to a full partnership. By the time he was thirty he was a millionaire.

Schiff joined the society in the 1870s and contributed heavily to it. For example, he founded the Scholarship Fund of 1891 in June of that year, a grant of $300. The money was the annual interest from railroad bonds, and Schiff specified that the scholarship be awarded to a boy who desired a noncommercial career, preferably in the arts or sciences.[3] The HOA remained one of his pet charities throughout his life, and he visited occasionally. One alumnus who saw him there in the early 1900s recalled that he never forgot the "awesome figure of Jacob Schiff being conducted through the HOA." Wearing a silk hat and spats—more or less his daily uniform—"he had with him an entourage of other directors or assistants. Not once did he stop to chat with a child or to ask the children if they were satisfied with their food or if they had any complaints."[4] What the awed boy didn't realize was that Schiff, accustomed to dealing with the biggest people on Wall Street and the leading officials in government, would have felt uncomfortable talking to a child.

Otto H. Kahn, a junior partner in Kuhn, Loeb, was treasurer of the HOA from 1901 to 1902. He got interested in the Metropolitan Opera and supported it virtually alone for many years.[5] Isidor and Oscar Straus belonged to the family that owned Macy's and Abraham and Straus. Isidor and his wife were on the Titanic and died because each refused to enter a lifeboat without the other. Oscar, a trustee from 1885 to 1920, was appointed minister to Turkey in 1894 and was named Secretary of Commerce in 1906 by Theodore Roosevelt.[6] Other millionaires included the Bloomingdales, the Sterns, Philip and Emanuel Lehman, Henry Rice, Theodore Rosenwald, Marx Ottinger, Benjamin Russak, Jack A. Dreyfoos, Julius Ochs Adler, William Guggenheim, Jacob F. Bamberger, Julius Goldman, Edward Lauterbach, Jacob Goldsmith, Victor H. Rothschild, and Jonas Sonneborn.

Members seldom visited the HOA unless there was a special occasion to make the trip worthwhile. Trustees, as officers, were the only exception; the bylaws required them to hold a weekly meeting on Sunday. Reserved solely for their use, the trustees' room was large, ornately decorated, and furnished only with long tables and heavy chairs. Around 10:30 every Sunday morning the trustees would begin arriving, each in his own chauffeured limousine. Most were dressed in frock coats and striped trousers. Waiting to greet them was the front-door monitor, a special assignment established by Baar. It was the front-door monitor's responsibility, among others, to escort every trustee to the meeting. By 11:00 the entire driveway down to the field would be filled with limousines.

The central figure at these meetings was the superintendent. He would present a number of reports dealing with expenditures, changes in personnel, population, and anything else he considered important. If any of his reports raised questions, he was expected to answer them. At times, he was given instructions to follow. No matter how well he stood with the trustees, every superintendent—including Dr. Baar—must have entered the trustees' room every Sunday morning feeling a little like a man on the spot.

Meetings usually lasted an hour. Upon leaving, one former front-door monitor from the Lowenstein years recalled, the trustees "invariably took home with them a fresh loaf of rye bread just baked by our baker Morris Rosenberg, who was a genius."[7] When this practice began, and why, no one knows. Surely there was something incongruous, to say the least, about solemn men in formal dress leaving an orphanage with a loaf of bread tucked under the arm. Still, who could refuse the work of a genius?

Most trustees went home at once, although a few stayed to watch the cadet corps drill on the field. Seldom did those who stayed spend any time with the children. The idea that philanthropy should include personal attention to the recipients of charity, particularly when they were children, wasn't fully accepted as yet. Isaacs of the *Messenger* had been urging it on his readers for years but hardly anyone seemed to be listening. Most contributors felt that their duty was done when they gave their money. Others believed that the children were receiving all the attention they needed simply by being in the orphanage. But the lack of personal attention, which critics were pointing out as the chief weakness of the orphanage system, was something no asylum could remedy. Even Baar realized this. In his 1882 report he expressed the hope that outside children—meaning the children of members—would look upon the HOA as a "school of sympathy." He wanted them to make friends with the children and visit them regularly. No evidence exits to show that any of them did. But there were some men who took a more generous view of their responsibility toward the children and gave as much of themselves as they did of their money. These few may have given several generations of orphans the only human warmth they would experience during their years in the HOA.

One man who filled this role longer than any other was a gentle hero named Seligman Solomon. There was probably no one like him connected with any other orphanage in America. For more than two decades after the HOA opened, in 1860, he was a daily visitor there and devoted more time and effort on behalf of the children than any other person concerned with their welfare. What motivated him to do it is not known, but one reason may have been the extreme poverty into which he himself was born, in a little town in Germany, in 1822. Though his early life is a mystery, he is said to have attended public school and learned arithmetic and calligraphy. For a few years he held a position as court clerk. In the early 1840s he emigrated to the United States and settled in New York. After a slow start in the dry goods business, Solomon switched to real estate and made a huge fortune almost overnight.

One of his closest friends at the time was Myer Stern, a member of the society. Stern persuaded him to join it. Indeed, Solomon did much more; he retired from business and devoted the rest of his life to charity, though he was only thirty-eight years old at the time. Every day he turned up at HOA and did anything he could for the children. He brought them food and sweets and would often take his meals with them—a practice the administration probably didn't like but was reluctant to stop. Solomon played with the children, joked with them, and consoled them when their spirits were low. Nor did he forget them when they were discharged; he found the boys work if they had none and made sure they were properly paid. He even visited boys in their home to see if they needed guidance with their personal problems. These activities suggest that Solomon was going beyond philanthropy into social work, and that he can be credited with beginning the movement toward individualized care at HOA.

Although he spent most of his time in the HOA, he did not turn down others outside it who were also in need. He sent groceries to hungry families and fuel to fireless homes. He helped Christian families as freely as he helped Jewish ones. As a philanthropist, his methods were completely unorthodox: he never investigated any requests for assistance to see if they were genuine but simply gave what was needed. It never bothered him that some requests might be fraudulent—a lack of worldliness that puzzled his colleagues in the society. None, however, could afford to criticize him. During his lifetime he recruited about one thousand new members into the society, a record that was never equaled. Curiously, Solomon's name never appears in the annual reports despite his work there. Perhaps the administration considered him a threat because the warmth he showed the children was a reproach to the HOA and its dehumanizing routines.

Eventually Solomon's fortune ran out and he was reduced to the poverty into which he had been born. In the late summer of 1884, he fell sick and died the following February. His dying wish was to be buried with his beloved orphans in their plot at Salem Fields, in Queens. His death was mourned by hundreds of alumni and residents, who knew him as "Papa Solomon." Seeking to honor his memory, they decided to erect a suitable monument over his grave. A monument committee was organized and collected contributions from over a thousand residents, alumni, and friends. On May 9, 1886, in the presence of five hundred people, mostly alumni, and the asylum's choir of forty voices, the monument—a twenty-two-foot-high granite obelisk—was dedicated by Dr. Baar. Jesse Seligman delivered the oration and Myer Stern, Solomon's friend for over forty years, offered the eulogy. The epitaph on the monument read: "A Father to the Orphan and Humanity's Noblest Volunteer," and on the reverse side was the text from Job 29:12: "Because I delivered the poor that cried, and the fatherless, and him that had none to help him."

As the monument was unveiled, many in the audience wept. Some stood around it for a long time after the ceremony was over. Anyone who visits the Orphans Plot in Salem Fields today will find the monument still there in the middle of a row of thirteen headstones marking the graves of inmates. "Papa" Solomon's monument towers above the stones; he is still looking after his children.

For many alumni it alone seemed insufficient to honor Solomon's memory. In March 1887 a group of them got together to form an alumni organization they named the Seligman Solomon Society.[8] Thanks to Dr. Baar, the new organization held its first meetings in the HOA. The goals it established for itself reflected the members' hopes of carrying on the work of their hero. These included aid to members, assisting newly discharged graduates, and the establishment of a Seligman Solomon Prize Fund, the interest to be used for cash prizes to one boy and one girl every year at Prize Day.

Within a few years the new society acquired close to a thousand members. Its most important annual event was an anniversary dinner held in a big downtown restaurant. In the early 1900s the entertainment at these dinners was occasionally provided by such celebrated members as Edwin Franko Goldman and Julius Tannen. Faithful to its goals, the organization helped many graduates find jobs after they were discharged.

Seligman Solomon's career was duplicated to a lesser extent by another officer and contemporary, Morris Tuska. In some respects their lives were markedly similar. Tuska, born in Hungary, had come to America as a boy of thirteen in 1844. He too was highly successful in business at an early age. In 1871, when he was forty, he also decided to retire and devote the rest of his life to charity. And like Solomon he did not relish being "a mere distributor of money," nor did he believe in what was then called "scientific charity"—that is, investigating first and giving later. For the next thirty years Tuska was to spend his time at three charities—three days a week at the HOA and one day each at the United Hebrew Charities and the Hebrew Technical Institute. He was an officer in all three. When he died in 1903, Dr. Baar wrote a highly eulogistic biographical sketch of him for the Seligman Solomon Society's journal that year. This suggests that the assistance Tuska provided was more indirect than personal, and that he wasn't as close to the children as Solomon had been.[9]

Edward Lauterbach, a younger man who probably knew Tuska but not Solomon, first became concerned about the children in 1883, when he was elected a trustee. He was one of the most successful corporate lawyers in the city, and an expert on railways. A lifelong Republican, Lauterbach wrote the gold plank for his party's platform at its convention in 1896—the plank William Jennings Bryan attacked in his famous "Cross of Gold" speech at the Democratic convention the same year. He served the HOA on two levels: his firm handled all its legal work without charge and he himself took a personal interest in helping alumni find careers. They expressed their appreciation by making him an honorary member of the Seligman Solomon Society. In 1921, when he had been a trustee for over forty years, about two thousand men, women, and children attended a special testimonial in his honor at the HOA. At his request, the HOA was also where his funeral was held when he died two years later. The HOA's memorial to Lauterbach was singularly appropriate for a man who had helped children become professionals: the library was named for him.[10] His portrait, depicting a kindly man with a modified Santa Claus beard and moustache, greeted all children as they entered the library.

The last of the personal philanthropists was Louis Strauss, a stock broker associated with a Wall Street firm. Strauss became a trustee and chairman of the scholarship committee in the twenties. That position gave him the power to approve scholarships for deserving children, mostly boys since few girls applied for them. Those seeking a scholarship had first to obtain the superintendent's recommendation but final approval came from Strauss. Although everybody knew about the scholarships, precise information about them was unavailable. Neither the qualifications for applicants nor the number of scholarships available in any given year were ever announced. Still, it was understood that very high grades or exceptional musical or artistic talent were considered the absolute minimum. But the ultimate test came in the interview with Strauss. Applicants had to convince him that they had the personal resources—determination, ambition, character, and stamina—to succeed in a hard, competitive world.

According to alumni who successfully survived the interview, Strauss, who sat behind an enormous desk that made him appear intimidating, was actually friendly, supportive, and encouraging. Indeed, one applicant in the thirties, Mollie Herman Fisch, found him sympathetic and "really concerned about me." She hoped to earn a degree in physical education, and Strauss approved a scholarship for her at the Savage School for Physical Education, a private school. After graduating she earned two more degrees and became a high school teacher in physical education.

What Mollie didn't know at the time of the scholarship interview, however, was that she had made a lifelong friend. Strauss kept track of her afterward and continued to follow her career and her life for the next thirty-three years, until he died in 1968. Nor was she the only HOA graduate he befriended. Whenever she talked to Strauss she learned of other scholarship winners he was treating in the same way. To all of them he was *Uncle* Louis, a surrogate relative who invited them to have dinner with him or his family. Every year his sister would invite Mollie to share Thanksgiving Day dinner. "I was made to feel like a member of the family rather than a guest. He listened to us as an uncle listens to nieces and nephews. His acceptance of me as a person, and his willingness to share my every little accomplishment helped me immeasurably."[11]

What Uncle Louis and the others had done was to move philanthropy from a purely money-based, indirect relationship with the children into something close to social work as we know it today. Behind it was the growing feeling that the need to individualize the children, to give them personal attention, was essential if they were to leave HOA as reasonably normal human beings. That concern would become dominant as the Baar era ended and the twentieth century began.

The Young Reformers   10

Dr. Baar's decision to retire in 1899 was a case of perfect symbolic timing. As the twentieth century loomed he clearly was not the man to lead the HOA into it. Yet his departure was probably viewed with some regret by the trustees. For twenty-three years he had run the HOA with clockwork efficiency and seldom had given them anything to worry about. Now they were faced with the always onerous task of finding a suitable replacement—a search that would take considerably longer than anyone anticipated since Dr. Baar's next two successors stayed only a few years each.

David Adler took charge in June 1899. Neither a rabbi nor a scholar, his only qualification for the job seems to have been that he had taught German in high school. A former resident of Brooklyn, he had a wife and two teenage children, Albert and Martha. Since *Adler* is German for *eagle* and his wife became the matron, his administration would soon become known as "Under the Double Eagle."

Life under the Double Eagle was a lot more pleasant than it had been behind the Baars. Adler seems to have been aware of the abuses of the orphanage system and did his best to correct them by introducing a great many changes. One of his first targets—the subject of growing criticism by child welfare workers—was the drab Kentucky jeans uniform worn by the boys. But the clothes he chose to replace them were only a shade better: though not precisely uniforms, they could easily have been mistaken for them. Few alumni remember much about them except for the pockets. Each suit had two pockets in the trousers, none in the jacket. Under Dr. Baar, there had been only one pocket, in the jacket, and none in the trousers. If this was an improvement, the boys didn't know what to make of it; few of them owned enough possessions to fill even one pocket. Blue hankies were issued to replace the red bandannas they had been using. Shoes, though, remained "canal boats." It is not known whether the girls' clothing was changed. It most likely was not because fewer objections were heard against it.

Meals, too, were different. To everybody's relief, prunes were banished from the menu. Instead, there were "sweet potatoes for nine months and herring for three." The new diet was welcomed at first, but its appeal diminished when its novelty wore off.

Sick call, too, was not the same—at least in one respect. Castor oil no longer had to be taken alone. Under a new, presumably more humane, procedure, those for whom it was prescribed were first given two spoonfuls of coffee, apparently to deceive their stomach. Next came the two spoonfuls of castor oil, followed immediately by two more spoonfuls of coffee. It didn't help: the castor oil still tasted awful.

Female suffrage received its first recognition under the Double Eagle. Adler abolished the practice of having the girls make beds and clean the boys' dormitories. The boys were ordered to do these chores themselves. Naturally many objected, regarding it as an affront to their masculinity. Clandestine flirtations suffered as well: there were no longer any love notes under the pillows to read at night. But epistolary romance wasn't entirely dead. Since the girls continued to clean up the dining room after meals, there would still be notes under the dinner plates.

Dr. Baar's ironclad rule on absolute silence for all activities was almost totally eliminated. Except for meals, talking was permitted everywhere else. Of all Adler's reforms, none was greeted with as much joy as this simple one of being able to talk like ordinary children. All at once the HOA erupted into noisy life, and the image of marching young robots was shattered forever. As for marching itself, it too was abolished except, of course, for cadet corps drill. The new superintendent also decreed the end of most whistles and bell signals on the playing field.

For the first time, the children were allowed to send and receive mail, but that right was slightly circumscribed. Incoming mail was not opened, as had been the case previously, although outgoing letters had to be submitted for review. However, report Double Eagle alumni, none of the letters were ever edited or changed in any way. If this was censorship, none complained. What the children wanted most was mail from their parents because it was important to their morale, and Adler allowed them to receive it.

Especially thankful for the new regime were the college boys, for it provided them with an unexpected windfall—an allowance of twenty-five cents a month. Thus they became the first residents ever to receive spending money—a privilege that made them the envy of the entire orphanage. But if Adler was idealistic enough to expect that the allowance would encourage thrift, he was to be totally disappointed. At the end of their first year he called the college boys into his office and asked them how much money they had saved. An embarrassed silence ensued and all hung their heads in shame. One by one, each confessed that he was in debt.

The most important reform proclaimed by Adler was the abolition of corporal punishment. But this claim is hard to take seriously because he didn't abolish the monitorial system at the same time. As long as there were monitors the beatings in the dormitories would never stop. What does seem likely, though, is that the discipline imposed by the governors relaxed considerably. This was because Adler hired the first two governors since the early Baar days who were not alumni. Not having grown up in the HOA, they were not schooled in its discipline and thus inclined to be more gentle and lenient. Their gentleness helped lower the general level of brutality in the dormitories, at least while they were physically present. The flaw in Dr. Baar's system of promoting the college students to governors was that it accomplished no change in perspective. Despite their new status and authority, they still thought of themselves as residents. But instead of feeling more responsible toward the younger boys, a new governor was likely to exact retribution for the beatings he had endured years earlier. Since no girls were receiving college scholarships at the time the problem did not exist on the girls' side, where all the governesses were outsiders. In hiring outsiders as governors, Adler was taking the first step toward breaking the self-perpetuating cycle of monitorial brutality.

Inevitably, Adler was compared to Dr. Baar and, understandably, always came off better. In addition to his changes he tried to get closer to the children than his predecessor ever had. Adler's approach seemed an attempt to ingratiate himself with the children. "He made his appearance among [them] more often and came in contact with them more frequently, even at unexpected times." To one alumnus, Adler's "twinkling eyes under his busy brows usually carried a smile and lacked the austerity of Dr. Baar." He loved to appear on the playing field, "where the little ones flocked to him"—a show of affection Dr. Baar could never inspire. The children also developed a fondness for Adler's family. His son, Albert, who was about fifteen, joined the boys in their cadet drills and games and managed their entertainments for them. His daughter, Martha, "was more intimate with the girls than May Baar had been." Some children were even invited to have their meals with the Adlers in their large apartment overlooking Amsterdam Avenue. To the lucky few it was the honor of honors, and they remembered it the rest of their lives.[1]

In his first annual report, in 1900, Adler wrote: "Rigid means of discipline are almost unnecessary, as our children really appreciate kind treatment." Yet he seemed to contradict this liberal view a bit later: "On the way to and from school, in the lecture room, in the school rooms, and in the dining room, absolute order is constantly maintained." Adler was assuring the trustees that despite his reforms, the HOA wasn't dissolving into anarchy.

In that same report Adler touched on an issue that reflected concern about the children's highly insulated and restricted life. "I do favor frequent excursions, especially in small groups, to give our children opportunity to learn of the outside world," he wrote. "Too long a stay in such institutions produces a kind of awkwardness and impractibility."

Since the only time to get the children out came in the summer, he arranged more activities during the school vacation. In the first summer of his regime he allowed thirty older boys and girls to visit their families every Sunday. He also arranged day outings to various "watering places" for groups of thirty to forty girls and boys. But swimming was a problem because there weren't enough bathing suits to go around. The governors resolved it by letting the girls wear them in the morning and the boys use them in the afternoon. Bathing suits then were sexless—calf-length, dark-colored, one-piece outfits—so it didn't really matter who wore them.

One area Adler didn't reform—though reform would have helped make it more tolerable—was the admission procedure. On their first day in the Reception House, newcomers, girls as well as boys, were examined in the nude, vaccinated, bathed, issued new clothing, and given a baldy haircut. All of it was done with numbing dispatch. The effect on new admissions was, to say the least, utterly traumatic. Newcomers then spent six weeks in quarantine in the Reception House, after which they were either placed in the main building or sent to foster homes. Those who went to the main building had to cope with another first-day experience—being placed in a dormitory among one hundred children. For most admissions, the first day would always remain their worst day in the HOA. Indeed, first-day horrors were embedded so firmly in memory that they were never forgotten. As a six-year-old boy, recalled one alumnus, he was placed in a dormitory on 138th Street, facing the Montefiore Home for chronically ill Jewish patients across the street, on Amsterdam Avenue. As it happened, his father was a resident there. He cried so pitifully that an old man from the home heard him and crossed the street to talk to him. He pleaded with the man to call his father. The resident returned, and a minute later his father appeared on the street. Momentarily forgetting the rules, he ran out of the asylum and went to his father, who gave him a bottle of soda pop. "That quieted me," he recalled, and eased his first-day anguish.[2]

Physical reactions to admission were common. One remembered vomiting, another defecating in his trousers, a third breaking out in a bad stutter, and a fourth losing his appetite completely for two days. For others there were just feelings and impressions summed up in such phrases as "overpowering strangeness," "complete bewilderment," "being closed in," "vastness," "institutional smells and voices," and "frightened." In most cases, understandably, the underlying emotion was fear. A few, like the boy with soda pop, seemed to have almost total recall of that day's events. One remembered the tub bath, which embarrassed him, and a brand new outfit of clothes, the infamous Kentucky jeans, which he hated on sight. Later he was placed between two boys and marched to his first meal, lunch. As he waited to enter the dining hall, a boy near him made a funny face to cheer him up. He laughed heartily. "Suddenly I felt a most terrific slap on the side of my face." A monitor who had happened along at that moment had struck him.[3] One girl, admitted in the 1930s, also had a bitter memory of that first day. "I will never forget when I went through that gate. My father took me to the Home and did not tell me of his intentions. He brought me to [an] office. I sensed something was wrong and grabbed my father's leg. He kicked me away and ran out. I cried for a long time."[4]

Only a rare few remember anything pleasant happening to them on the first day. One boy, admitted in 1892, had such a relatively untroubled experience: "Miss Hadel, the matron, bathed [me] and changed my clothes. She was kind and friendly. I was placed in the 6th primary; Miss Hirsch, the teacher, was also kind. The strangeness soon affected me and I started to cry. Miss Hirsch called in David Lefkowitz, a rabbinical student who was acting as governor while on vacation from the Hebrew Union College. He took me into the teacher's room, played with me, soothed and calmed me and them returned me to my class."[5]

Unlikely as it seems, there was one recorded case in which the first-day horrors were reversed, with the HOA being traumatized by a newcomer. On November 18, 1902, there arrived a boy named Harry

Garguzen, age not known. Even less is known about the circumstances that led to his admission. The record of his stay in the HOA
is summed up in a one-sentence entry in the massive black admissions register: "This boy was brought here by Educational Alliance
on recommendation of Dr. Frankel of UHC [United Hebrew Chari-
ties] but was returned after having been found to be unmanageable."
How long the boy lived in the HOA before "being returned" is not
shown in the ledger. Neither are there any details about the behavior that led to his prompt discharge. Still, one wonders how any boy,
no matter how incorrigible, could have withstood and defeated the
steel-fisted authority of the institution. What the HOA didn't know
at the time, though, was that it had held no ordinary mortal in its
grasp; it had been dealing with "royalty."

Nothing more was heard about Harry Garguzen until 1919, when
he turned up in Paris as "Prince Michael Romanoff," the son of Czar
Alexander III and brother of Nicholas II. It was the beginning of a
long and highly publicized career as an imposter, swindler, con artist,
confidant to celebrities, bon vivant, and highly successful restauran-
teur. He returned to the United States in 1922 with a British accent
and the title of "Count Gladstone" and ran afoul of the immigration authorities. They locked him up in Ellis Island, from which he
promptly escaped. He soon resurfaced in New York society as Prince
Michael and charmed the wealthy widows who loved to hear his
tales of Old Russia. The police didn't find him charming, though, because he passed numerous bad checks signed, with imperial brevity,
"romanoff." As a result, he was in and out of jail, deported once to
France, and endlessly involved in deportation proceedings. At these
hearings, one witness who was invariably called to testify was the
superintendent of the HOA, Lionel J. Simmonds. Although they seem
to have accomplished little, the hearings did serve to reveal the true
facts about his life. He was born Harry F. Gerson in Vilna, Lithuania.
At the age of six he was taken to America in 1900 by his parents,
who settled on the Lower East Side in New York. He left home,
took to the streets, peddled newspapers, was arrested as a vagrant,
and wound up in the HOA. Between the ages of eight and eighteen,
he was shuttled between various Jewish orphanages, each of which
declared him incorrigible and got rid of him. For a brief period he
worked as a buttonhole maker—practically the only honest labor he
ever performed. During these bleak years he seems to have fanta-
sized himself in the role of a noble person, out of which emerged the
dapper, worldly, and royal "Prince Michael Romanoff."

In the late thirties he quit New York for Hollywood, attracted a great many celebrity friends and, with their sponsorship, opened a restaurant in Beverly Hills. It became an exclusive hangout for such friends as Darryl Zanuck, Joseph Schenck, Robert Benchley, and John Hay Whitney, to name just a few. In 1958, these friends and many others influenced Congress to pass a special bill that made him a naturalized citizen. He retired from the restaurant business in 1962 and lived in elegant retirement for nine years, until he died in 1971. In his last year, according to friends, he was collecting material for his memoirs.[6]

Under Adler physical training became compulsory for the children. It was held twice a week (once for each sex) in the basement gym in each wing. As a rule, any compulsory activity was hated but few felt that way about physical training. That was because the instructor was an irrepressibly cheerful man named James DeForest. Of all the staff hired to train the children, DeForest was easily the most popular and the most colorful. He "was like fresh air let into the Home," a grateful alumnus remembered decades afterward with a feeling akin to hero worship. Jimmy—he didn't mind the children calling him by his first name—was Irish, in his twenties, and always seemed to be smiling. Amid all the grim adult faces they saw every day, his smiling face stood out in radiant contrast to theirs.

Born into a circus family, Jimmy worked as a trapeze artist until an accident ended his career. He then decided to try boxing. The ring had been a lifelong interest of his, and during his circus travels he had personally met and befriended every heavyweight champion from John L. Sullivan onward. After moving to New York, he took the part-time job at the HOA to keep him going between bouts.

Jimmy left the HOA around 1907, when he opened his own training gym for fighters at 59th Street and Madison Avenue. Opening it was a dream he had had for years, since he had long known that he would never make it as a prizefighter. Realizing this, he had turned his talents to other aspects of the ring, such as promoting, matchmaking, training, advising, and managing, and had done well in all of them. These activities and the gym now required all his time, and he had to give up his job at the HOA. Leaving the children he had grown to love was not easy for him, and it was, of course, much harder for them to accept his going. At his last two sessions a lot of tears were openly shed when he made his farewells.

Overnight, though, his gym became a hangout for HOA alumni. Jimmy even invited some of them out to his home in Allenhurst, New Jersey. Within months a number of them got together to pay him the highest honor it was within their power to bestow: they organized a

military band named for him. The DeForest Military Band met once
a week to rehearse and was in business for at least two years.

DeForest later became the most famous manager and trainer of
his time. He trained Jack Dempsey for his championship fight with
Jess Williard. Then, changing sides, he trained Luis Firpo for his bout
with Dempsey; Firpo knocked the champion out of the ring in the
first round. DeForest died in 1932, and some of the most bereaved
mourners at his funeral were HOA alumni. "He was one grand guy,"
an alumnus recalled, in a statement that could serve as his epitaph.[7]

Progressive as it was in most respects, Adler's regime had its problems, some of which were inherited from Baar's regime. One doubts
that Dr. Baar, even if he was aware of it, would have discussed sexual
abuse with the trustees or the staff, so the subject never received official attention. However, his son, Victor, is accused of sexual abuse
by an alumnus. The incident allegedly took place in the tailor shop.
According to the alumnus, who was eleven at the time, he had gone
to the shop on an errand and found it empty, except for Victor. Then
a twenty-year-old college student, Victor told him with a friendly
smile that he had a quarter for him in a trouser pocket. Without questioning why Victor would want to give him a quarter, he accepted the
invitation. But there was no quarter in the trouser pocket, just a large
hole through which his hand thrust embarrassingly deep. Victor's
smile grew lewd. Frightened, the boy withdrew his hand quickly and
ran out of the tailor shop. He stayed away from Victor after that and
never revealed the incident to anyone until much later.[8]

This kind of abuse seems to have been widespread in the boys'
dormitories, though few alumni would discuss it. One mentioned a
"really vicious character who forced his attentions upon the smaller
youngsters."[9] And another remembered that when he had to stand in
front of a certain boy he would always be molested. Only by reporting
that boy to the governor was he able to have the practice stopped.[10]

After Dr. Baar retired, molestation among the boys either increased or grew more obvious because Adler was unable to ignore it.
Unfortunately his method of dealing with it was secret and punitive.
"There was an investigation of the boys," according to an alumnus,
"which assumed the relations of an inquisition so that some boys
under severe chastisement mentioned the names of innocent com-
panions so as to escape as much of the punishment as was possible or
endurable. I was one of the victims and I cried bitterly at such injus-
tice for several days and nights."[11] This punitive approach probably
worsened the situation instead of lessening it. Although it seems
likely that some molestation was present on the girls' side, it is

Dr. Hermann J. Baar. (*Seligman Solomon Society Souvenir Journal,* 1924)

Seligman Solomon. (Seligman Solomon Society Program, Dec. 29, 1889)

Aerial view taken in the 1930s. (H.O.A. Association, Inc. Collection)

Lionel J. Simmonds in the 1950s.
(Photo by Ben Attas)

The cadet corps. ("This Is Your Life," souvenir program, May 28, 1958)

A standing lesson held by monitors of boys' dormitory M-4 one night in 1937. (Photo by Roy Morris)

Calisthenics on the roof of the Warner Gymnasium in the late 1920s. (Courtesy of Mildred Stember)

The championship basketball team of the 1939–40 season. (H.O.A. Association, Inc. Collection)

Friendly Home girls listening to the radio in the late 1920s. (Courtesy of Mildred Stember)

A Godmothers Association club in the 1920s. (Courtesy of Mildred Stember)

Chicken farming at Edenwald in the 1920s. (Courtesy of Mildred Stember)

Farming at Edenwald in the late 1920s. (Courtesy of Mildred Stember)

Swimming pool at Edenwald in the late 1920s. (Courtesy of Mildred Stember)

Girls canoeing at Camp Wehaha in the late 1920s. (Courtesy of Mildred Stember)

Campers in the late 1920s.
(Courtesy of Mildred Stember)

Cornet player practicing in the 1920s. (Courtesy of Mildred Stember)

Daily News publicity photograph from 1927.

The Harmonica Band in the 1920s. (H.O.A. Association, Inc. Collection)

Drum corps members horsing around in the 1930s. (H.O.A. Association, Inc. Collection)

COMING TO NEW HAVEN

HEBREW ORPHAN ASYLUM BAND

of New York

Who recently won first prize in Graphic Musical Festival and also winner of several cups, will play at a

CONCERT

given for the Benefit of the

Jewish Home for Children

on Sunday Night OCT. 12 at 8:30 P. M.

at the HYPERION THEATRE

Novelty Numbers from Local Professional Talent and other features.

Seating Capacity Limited and we advise our members to make reservations as soon as possible. Send your remittance in to the Home and reserved ticket will be forwarded to you. Committee will also solicit.

DON'T MISS THIS TREAT

COLUMBIA PRINTING CO., 174 COMMERCE ST., NEW HAVEN, CONN.

Publicity flier from the late 1920s. (H.O.A. Association, Inc. Collection)

Posing at the entrance of the HOA in the 1930s. (H.O.A. Association, Inc. Collection)

Hamming for the camera in the 1930s. (H.O.A. Association, Inc. Collection)

not known whether any investigations were ever held there. Female alumni would not discuss the problem.

At the annual meeting in April 1901, Emanuel Lehman declined to run for reelection, and Louis Stern succeeded him as president. Co-founder and co-owner of Stern Brothers Department Store, he was one of the best-known merchants in America and a leading citizen of the city. In 1897 he had been appointed by President McKinley to represent the United States at the Paris Exposition. While there, he had performed his duties so well that the French named him a knight of the Legion of Honor. Unknown to him, his fellow Republicans back home gave him another honor: nomination as borough president of Manhattan in the election that year.

Like many colleagues in the society, Stern was a self-made man. In 1867, he and his brother Isaac, both immigrants from Germany, had opened their first dry goods store on West 22nd Street and Sixth Avenue. The store was successful from the start and the brothers began expanding it after their first year in business. By 1878 they had moved the store to a building of their own on west 23rd Street. Both became millionaires. Stern build a mansion on Fifth Avenue and bought another home in Tarrytown-on-Hudson. He joined many clubs and museums and contributed to many charities, not all of them Jewish.[12]

A few days after the 1901 annual meeting, the HOA was the subject of extravagant praise from the *New York Times*. In an editorial on May 3 headed "Health Conditions among Children," it reported that there had been no deaths in the HOA in eighteen months, an achievement it called "a remarkable showing." Moreover, "the hospital ward is empty." In the past winter, it observed, a scarlet fever epidemic that had killed many children in the city had produced only two cases in the HOA. But both recovered and the disease was contained.

Attempting to explain this record, the *Times* seemed to be taking sides in the growing controversy over the merits of institutional care versus foster care. "The remarkable health of the children in this institution," it declared, "is due to no other causes than a plain and wholesome diet, pure water, regular habits, well-regulated exercise, good sleeping accommodations, and plenty of amusements without excitement." Then, taking this argument a step further than most pro-institutional advocates would go, it asserted that the situation of children "living in the most favorable conditions at home is less conducive to health and longevity than that of an inmate of an institution whose records show that health and happiness is perfectly consistent with an oversight and discipline which, important in the average family, are indispensable to the well-being of children." At a time when the supporters of foster care were saying that "the worst foster home is better than the best institution," the *Times* was arguing, in effect, that a really good institution was superior even to normal family life. One wonders what the children in the HOA would have thought about that extravagant position.

The annual meeting in 1902 was overshadowed by an event so unusual that it received a good deal of publicity in the press. That afternoon two former residents, Harry Kornfelder and Laura Simon, were married in the HOA by a third former resident, Rabbi Samuel Langer. Rabbi Langer himself had been married there by Dr. Baar some years earlier. Bride, groom, and rabbi received an "ovation" from the children after the ceremony.[13] The juxtaposition of two seemingly unrelated events on the same day—the annual meeting and a wedding—was probably more than coincidence. The trustees who witnessed the wedding were provided with proof of the benefits of their largess. Here were three graduates taking part in the community's most sacred ritual, a ceremony that seemed to epitomize the work of the HOA at its finest. What better argument could there be for the merits of institutional care?

In 1903 Adler resigned and returned to Brooklyn, where he resumed his teaching career.[14] His popularity followed him home, for many alumni went to visit him there and others maintained lifelong friendships with his children.[15] Rudolph I. Coffee, his replacement, attracted some publicity because he was so young—only twenty-six. He is said to have been the youngest superintendent ever to be placed in charge of a charitable institution in the United States. A bachelor from Oakland, California, Coffee was a rabbinical student at the Jewish Theological Seminary in New York. He worked even harder than Adler to ingratiate himself with the children.

Coffee's publicly proclaimed goal was to "deinstitutionalize" the HOA as much as possible. Using Adler's reforms as a point of departure, he extended them and added some of his own. For example, he abolished the practice of having the children identified by a number and ordered that they be addressed by their first name. First-day admission horrors were eased a bit by abolition of the baldy haircut. (But it didn't last; it would be reinstituted by the medical staff when he left.) The boys' clothing was changed again, this time to a style and cloth which made it impossible to tell that they came from an orphanage. In addition, two pockets were added to their jacket to match the two in the trousers that Adler had given them. The need for them was still questionable since "money was just as contraband and candy was invisible." A better brand of shoes replaced the old canal boats. Hankies, red under Dr. Baar and blue under Adler, became—inexplicably—red, white, and blue under Coffee. They were used sparingly, if at all; it made the boys feel unpatriotic to soil them. As one alumnus put it, "We were afraid to blow our noses for fear of offending the government." Apparently few if any changes were made in the girls' clothing.

Coffee removed the last restriction to speech; now the children could talk everywhere, including meals. The meals were changed again—less herring and sweet potatoes and more lentils. This led to some grumbling and the old question: Is this an improvement?

Another innovation was the appearance in 1904 of the first literary publication produced by and for the children themselves, *The Chronicle of the H.O.A.* It was published by the Literary Society of the H.O.A., a new club that probably got started under Adler's administration. Its editor was Harry Schneiderman, an honor student at Grammar School No. 43, who left the HOA the same year to attend City College on an HOA scholarship. Three editions of the *Chronicle* were published but no copies exist today.[16]

Coffee became a hero to the boys when he had the HOA buy them their first, real, factory-made baseballs. Gone at last were the days when they had had to improvise their own from scrap materials. In fact, he did more for athletics than any of his predecessors even though—perhaps because—he was totally and irredeemably unathletic. Though desperately eager to be considered a sport, the new superintendent couldn't play at anything. Still, he was good-natured about his shortcomings. He once agreed to have himself photographed on the playing field holding a bat with a ball tied to it with a string. After a year or so, he learned enough to be able to bat balls out to the boys.[17]

In his first annual report, in 1904, Coffee proudly announced the "absolute abolition of corporal punishment." This was curious, since Adler had proclaimed the same thing a few years earlier. Coffee's statement must be considered as administrative rhetoric intended to please the trustees, for he, like Adler before him, did not abolish the monitorial system. The end of corporal punishment would be frequently declared but its demise never actually took place.

Only in religious training did the new superintendent seem more stern and less ingratiating. He imposed stricter discipline in religious school and doubled the length of prayers in the synagogue. Children caught stealing had to recite the book, chapter, and verse of the Bible dealing with the eighth commandment. It was the price they had to pay for having a rabbinical student in charge.

In Coffee's first year a milestone was reached: the HOA's census rose to 1,003, topping the one thousand mark for the first time in its history. "The facilities of our home are now taxed to the uttermost capacity," he told the trustees. But his recommendation to ease the problem wasn't too imaginative: enlargement. For various reasons, though, the trustees were unwilling to go along with it. Twice in forty years the asylum had uprooted itself and moved into bigger quarters elsewhere, and they were not eager to repeat the process a third time.

Coffee was ordained a rabbi in 1904, thus earning the right to be called "Doctor." This event foreshadowed his eventual departure from the asylum, for his ambition was to lead a congregation. But finding one would take time.

In most respects, Dr. Coffee's administration was a carbon copy of Adler's. It, too, was troubled by sexual abuse, which was "rife," in the word of one alumnus. And Dr. Coffee reacted to it exactly as Adler had. He "had each and every boy before him in a secret inquisition, in which each kid was asked if he had such relations," the alumnus observed. "Such an official inquiry could only have been touched off by the widespread character of the situation."[18] The outcome of the inquisition or if girls were also involved is not known.

There is no evidence to suggest that Dr. Coffee's secret inquisition affected his popularity. Indeed, many boys hero-worshipped him and he appears to have been the most fatherly superintendent the HOA ever had. "We were always welcome to visit him in his office or living quarters and pour out our feelings to him," one still grateful graduate remembered, adding: "He was a real father to us all." At his last few morning services, Dr. Coffee invited anyone to whom he had made unredeemed promises to visit him. And, the same alumnus insists, he honored them all. "Natural parents could not have done more for us. We sorely missed Dr. Coffee when he left."[19]

In the next fifteen years, Dr. Coffee served in congregations in Pittsburgh, Chicago, Toledo, and Oakland, his hometown. Then his career took another turn: he became a Jewish chaplain for the California prison system. At various times he provided counseling for prisoners at Alcatraz, San Quentin, and Folsom, among others. In addition, he held important posts in national Jewish charitable organizations and was elected president of the Jewish Committee for Personal Service, a welfare organization for prisoners. He died in San Francisco in May 1955.[20]

Had Dr. Coffee remained at the HOA, he would have had to deal with the crisis of overcrowding that now threatened it. But the problem was not the HOA's alone; it was only a tiny part of the national crisis in child welfare at the time. Since the early 1880s there had been ever-increasing migrations to America from eastern Europe and Russia. In the process of settling into their new home, many immigrant families were broken or destroyed by disease, unemployment, abandonment, or death. The parents of families that suffered these disasters often lacked the resources to cope with them. Private charities provided some help, if one knew where to find them and was willing to plead for it. Public funds for such purposes, except to institutions, were nonexistent. The upshot was that hundreds of thousands of children all over America were orphaned, abandoned, homeless, and left to fend for themselves. In an attempt to care for them, the nation's third wave of orphanage building got underway. From 1890 to 1905, over four hundred orphanages were built to shelter the new crop of dependent children. Even these were not enough.

Some eastern cities, for example, were dumping unwanted children on other inland cities. The *New York Times* reported on December 13, 1902, that carloads of children had been shipped out by city institutions to Milwaukee, Wisconsin, because there was no room for them. The change, in this case, was not an improvement. Many wound up living with Wisconsin Indians, who were themselves living on the edge of starvation. Others were found living and begging in the streets of Milwaukee.

Ironically, the new orphanages came under attack as soon as they were built. Institutional care was no longer regarded in professional child welfare circles as the best way to raise dependent children. In 1899 the National Association of Charities had declared that foster home care was the method of choice—an event that made a deep impression on child-care workers. More and more one heard the rallying cry of foster home care supporters that "the worst foster home is better than the best institution." The cry grew louder even though there was little objective evidence to document it and even though it was clear that many foster homes did not live up to the superior reputation being thrust upon them.

The vast reform efforts of Adler and Dr. Coffee must be considered against the background of this deepening controversy. They seemed eager to prove that it was possible to humanize an institution. How well they succeeded is a moot question, but the conflict between the two systems of care was one that would become the major preoccupation of the next superintendent, Solomon Lowenstein.

Individualizing the Children   11

At first glance, Solomon Lowenstein seemed to resemble most of his predecessors, for he was a Reform rabbi, twenty-eight years old, and a fine speaker. Yet, in one major respect at least, he differed from all of them: he was the first superintendent with experience in what was then beginning to be called social work. For two years, while studying for the rabbinate at the Hebrew Union College, in Cincinnati, he had been head worker in a Jewish settlement house. After his ordination he was appointed director of the United Hebrew Charities in that city, a post he held for three years. In 1904 he was named to the position of assistant manager of the United Hebrew Charities in New York City.[1] With five years of experience in welfare work, Lowenstein was unquestionably the most qualified man ever to become superintendent of the HOA. His arrival was possible only because the practice of social work—some were boldly calling it a profession—had itself arrived, in the decade before World War I.

In his relations with the children, Lowenstein was invariably "kind and gentle," alumni report, yet he was never as ingratiating as Adler and Dr. Coffee. Some remember him as distant and formal, for he never addressed children by their first name. On the other hand, he never used the title of doctor; it might have widened the distance between himself and the children. He stayed close to the children by taking interest in their food. At noon Saturday, when the best meal of the week was served, he was often there to share it with them. The meal was meat loaf and beans, side by side in a long pan. Lowenstein would stand in the middle of the huge dining room and eat a portion of each from a plate he held in his hands. He ate "voraciously," one alumnus noted, even faster than the children. Now and then, without notice, he would turn up at other meals, apparently to sample the food for himself.[2] Despite this interest he made no attempt to "father" the children, like Adler and Dr. Coffee, or to become attached to any of them, as Dr. Baar had. Still, he was well liked and is now fondly remembered by alumni who knew him.

Lowenstein's goal, it was clear from the start, was to carry on the work of individualizing the children begun by his two predecessors. *Individualize the child!* The phrase had become a rallying cry for child welfare workers and, like them, Lowenstein was firmly committed to it. Yet the irony of his regime was that the HOA had grown (and was continuing to grow) far beyond the capacity of any administrator to do much about it. As we have seen, the census had gone above 1,000 in Dr. Coffee's administration; now it was climbing rapidly toward 1,100.

How was it possible to individualize such an army of children? Aware of the paradox, Lowenstein remarked on it in the 1906 annual report: "It is manifestly impossible that only one person shall be acquainted with the lives and personalities of over 1,000 children. It is absolutely necessary, for purposes of proper order and discipline, that the children be dealt with in large masses." Some children were receiving individual attention, he pointed out, though under Darwinian circumstances. "The children of greatest ability, most forward, and the children of least ability, most backward, the best behaved and the ablest, the worst behaved and the least capable are those who receive the most special consideration." Invariably forgotten were the mass of children in between. What he hinted at too was that there wasn't enough staff available to give the children even a modicum of attention. At the time, there were four governors for the boys and three governesses for the girls, or about one adult for over one hundred children. Of this group only one or two had either the time or the inclination to spend any more time with the children than their supervisory duties required. The male governors were all college students preparing for another career while the female governors were hoping to get married and leave.

Ironically, Lowenstein gave his own children as little attention as the asylum's staff provided the inmates. According to his son Nathan, who was born in the asylum and spent the first twelve years of his life there—more than most inmates, incidentally—Lowenstein was often too busy to spend much time with his family. He was also very strict with them. Nathan and his two youngest sisters, both also born in the HOA, grew up under the same severe discipline that governed the other children. As a result, Nathan recalled, he was not happy there.

Although he would have preferred to think about ways to individualize the children, Lowenstein couldn't afford the luxury of dwelling on it. That was because he had inherited the HOA's share of the worst crisis ever faced by the city's Jewish community. Its source lay in the spectacular mass migrations of Jewish immigrants from Russia and eastern Europe. In the first decade of the twentieth century Jewish immigrants were arriving at the rate of one hundred thousand or more a year. By 1915 there would be a million and a half Jews in New York City, giving it the largest Jewish population in the world. Almost all were poor and required some form of assistance—often furnished by relatives already here, frequently by Jewish charities of all kinds—to survive their first few months in America. Jewish leaders and charitable agencies had persistently tried to divert part of this flow inland, but their efforts usually failed. Most immigrants settled on the Lower East Side, turning it into the most overcrowded community in the nation. There they lived in circumstances only slightly better—occasionally worse—than those they had left in their native land. Many went to work in the garment trade, working in sweatshops where they earned subsistence wages or less, while others lived from hand to mouth at marginal occupations.[3]

The upshot, inevitably, was a staggering increase in Jewish dependency, especially among children. The number of abandoned, homeless, neglected, and even delinquent Jewish children rose to unheard-of levels, but there was no room for them in existing Jewish facilities. Nor were funds available to build more. Already, in 1904, about 750 Jewish children were known to be living in Catholic, Protestant, and public institutions—something that had not happened since the HOA opened decades earlier.[4] In his 1906 report Lowenstein noted that seventy-two Jewish children had been transferred to the HOA the previous year from non-Jewish institutions. Moreover, no one had any idea of the number of other Jewish children living in the streets.

Seeking a solution to the crisis, the HOA in 1903 became the first Jewish home in the city to reintroduce boarding out, or paying a family to keep a child, on a large scale. Until it moved uptown to Amsterdam Avenue, the HOA had always boarded out some children, but only as a temporary, emergency measure, used chiefly for placing underage, sickly, or unmanageable children or to prevent overcrowding. The numbers involved had always been small and no one had ever regarded it as a substitute for institutional care. Now, however, the HOA turned to it as a last resort, as did other Jewish homes.[5] Overnight, what had begun as a last resort became an accepted, routine alternative to institutional care.

Indeed, boarding out helped make foster care respectable. It appeared to be a more responsible system than the one used for decades by the Children's Aid Society, which—in the beginning, at least—literally gave children away to any families that would take them without caring too much about what happened to them afterward. Although the society, responding to strong public complaints, had later engaged agents in midwestern cities to follow up on the children placed, the system still continued to draw a good deal of criticism. Boarding out was preferred because the families involved were accountable to the institution that provided the children. Thus, foster parents were quasi-employees whose homes had to meet standards approved by the agency.

A year after the HOA began its boarding-out program, it joined with other Jewish homes in the city and the United Hebrew Charities to form a central agency to deal with the problem in an organized fashion. The new agency, called the Bureau of Boarding and Placing-Out Jewish Dependent Children, represented the first attempt by Jewish asylums to work cooperatively. To assist it, the city's Department of Charities took the unusual step of hiring a special examiner for dependent children to help the bureau locate satisfactory Jewish homes for either boarding out or adoption. It also agreed to subsidize boarding-out children at the same rate paid for institutionalized children—$110 per year per child.[6] Paradoxically, the city seemed willing to do all it could to help children provided that help was given *outside* their own home. Most private agencies and child welfare workers favored allowances to keep children at home, which would have been cheaper and probably better for the family. In 1905 the HOA established a special widows' fund for this purpose.[7] Deserted mothers were included later.

In its first four years the new bureau placed out over one thousand children, of which one-third were HOA children.[8] The pressures that led the HOA to resume boarding out also started the trustees thinking once again, reluctantly as always, about moving to a new and larger site. Though cool to the idea a few years earlier, they now seemed resigned to its urgency. One development that had led them to consider it was that the neighborhood had lost its rural character. Homes and apartment buildings were springing up all around, spurred by the construction of the IRT subway uptown, in 1904. Like most asylums, the HOA had always felt that it could do its work better in a rural setting, away from the presumably corrupting influences of city life. Yet there would be nothing but talk about moving for many years to come.

Under Lowenstein, there were few dramatic reforms, though life continued to improve for the children. He achieved one minor triumph for individualization by removing the long dining room benches that sat eight children to a side and replaced them with chairs. His major achievements, though, were in the area of recreation, which he systematized. In his first winter he arranged, together with the board of education, a series of ten illustrated lectures, given on alternate Friday nights. The lectures provided a mixture of the exotic, patriotic, and inspirational: Life in the Philippines; Travel in the Orient; Ben Franklin; City of Washington, D.C.; Real Success in Life; and Life of the Esquimeaux.[9] This was Culture, and the children sat through it dutifully, attentive if not engrossed. In 1906, though, Lowenstein introduced Real Entertainment, the sort that held the children transfixed. That was when motion pictures were shown for the first time, the screenings paid for by a trustee. They were presented on the field, at about 7:30 P.M., in good weather, with all the children invited. A huge white sheet hung from windows of the central wing provided a screen. The projector was set up around midfield. And the first movie ever shown was, one alumnus recalls, "The Great Train Robbery."[10] Within a few years, the movies were moved to the girls' courtyard so that they could be watched from the dormitory windows or the fire escape. The boys loved to sit on the fire escape and let their legs dangle. One alumnus remembered being fearful about joining them on the fire escape because he feared a catastrophe if it collapsed, so he watched from a window.[11]

More clubs were organized, run by the children themselves. The cadet corps continued drilling on Sundays, and to a larger audience now, for the HOA allowed neighbors to come in and watch. As usual, famous visitors came to review them. One year the guest of honor was Charles Evans Hughes, then governor of New York. A special reviewing stand was erected for him on the Broadway side of the field.[12] Still the best in its class, the cadet corps for two years straight had won the first-place banner in competition with other units. In April 1906 it gave a special exhibition at the Seventh Regiment Armory, where it was reviewed by Major General Frederick D. Grant, son of the Civil War hero.[13] The military band, still the best boys' band in the city, was now led by Philip Egner. Training the band seems to have qualified him for more important work—an appointment as bandmaster at West Point.[14] When he left, there was talk that he would have trouble bringing West Point's band up to the level of the HOA band. To the children, the HOA band was easily as good as Sousa's, perhaps better.

One minor though significant innovation introduced by Lowen-stein was to place a female counselor in charge of M-6, the youngest boys' dormitory. His rationale for this change was that the five- to seven-year-olds in M-6 needed a maternal figure to support and nur-ture them through their first trying years. Although the first woman hired for this assignment, Mildred Stember, was single, nineteen years old, and starting her first job, she proved to be the perfect choice. There were 120 boys to be looked after, monitors to super-vise, and a rigid, taxing schedule to follow. Every day, from the rising bell to lights out, she had to shepherd the boys through the HOA's clockwork routines and somehow find time and energy to give each a modicum of attention, affection, and solace. Yet she managed it so well that her boys soon began calling her "Ma" Stember. Lowenstein was so pleased with the experiment's outcome that he mentioned it in his 1910 annual report. And there would be a female counselor in M-6 almost until the day the HOA closed.

Other things didn't change much either—corporal punishment, for example. Lowenstein, too, proclaimed its abolition. Yet, like Adler and Dr. Coffee, he kept the monitorial system that guaranteed its survival. In any case, he knew little of what was going on in the dormitories because he was away so often, attending meetings and conferences. After his first five years or so the children saw as little of him as they had, decades earlier, of Dr. Baar. In his absence, the home was run by the assistant superintendent, Lionel J. Simmonds, an alumnus himself and a former Baar boy. Simmonds had been pro-moted to the job in 1907.[15]

Clearly the HOA was not so much moving ahead as it was mark-ing time. It was accumulating honors and pausing to admire them. In the process it had begun to lose some initiative. For the truth was that none of the changes it had introduced could compare with the revolutionary steps being taken that same decade at a smaller insti-tution located nearby, the Hebrew Sheltering Guardian Society, at 150th Street and Broadway.

From the time it opened, in 1879, the HSGS had been a carbon copy of the HOA, whose authoritarian structure it had adopted, in-cluding its monitorial system. Its sudden leap to leadership came about through the efforts of three unusual men—Adolph Lewisohn, Samuel D. Levy, and Dr. Ludwig Bernstein. First on the scene was Levy, who was elected to lead the board of directors in the 1890s. He hoped to individualize the children but he didn't know where and how to begin. Next came Lewisohn, a philanthropist who had made his fortune in mining. In 1901 he was elected president of the society that supported the home. A maverick and a loner who had been a close friend of Seligman Solomon, Lewisohn shared.Levy's hopes and was prepared to support any progressive plans he had. Two years later arrived the man the other two had been seeking, the director who would carry out the changes they wanted, Dr. Bernstein. He was then twenty-seven and had taught German in high school.

Unhappy with what he found in the home, Dr. Bernstein set about changing things. He began by organizing clubs, a few the first year, many more the next, until by the end of five years there were forty-three social and cultural clubs in operation, each governed by its own members. He encouraged parents to visit the home more frequently and even let them hold meetings of their own. Nor did he object to them speaking Yiddish. In fact, when he learned some parents couldn't communicate with their children because they didn't speak English, he provided interpreters for them.

Finally, in 1908, Dr. Bernstein took a monumental step that neither the children nor the staff expected (though it had the approval of Lewisohn and Levy): he abolished the monitorial system. In its place he established two self-governing units, a Boys Brotherhood Republic and a Girls Brotherhood Republic. (The idea wasn't new; he borrowed it from a small home in Ithaca.) Each republic was to elect its own officers and make its own rules.

For a home with about eight hundred or so children, the overnight transfer of authority from staff and monitors to the republics must have seemed to outside observers like an act of administrative lunacy. But the republics worked—and they did a good deal more than govern the children. They also operated a savings bank, managed a fast-growing library, and sold candy, stationery, and toys from a co-op store, using the profits to provide spending money for the poorest children. The republics overreached themselves, however, when they demanded that the home change its menu to something more sumptuous. Dr. Bernstein hastily intervened and squelched the plan. Even a children's democracy had to know its limits.

With the monitorial system abolished, the HSGS looked forward to its next giant step—moving to a new site and setting up a cottage-plan home. Under the cottage system, children lived in small groups in their own fully equipped homes, each supervised by a cottage mother. Like the republic idea, the cottage plan was not new. Sheltering Arms, a Protestant home at 129th Street, not far from the HOA, had set up one of the earliest in 1870. It was not a real cottage system, however, for each of the four "cottages" was actually an unusually large self-contained apartment inside a wing of the home. Sheltering

Arms, incidentally, had borrowed the idea from a German cottage home in Hamburg, and there were others like it scattered all over Europe. In fact, it was while on a trip to England that Levy visited a British example, Barkenside. Highly impressed, Levy went home a convert and soon persuaded Lewisohn and Dr. Bernstein that the cottage system was a superior method of child care. To Levy, it seemed to combine the best elements of institutional care and foster home care. Within weeks, the HSGS had a building committee campaigning for funds. Lots of money was needed because a cottage system not only required more property but also cost more than the traditional asylum. After looking at 150 sites in and around New York City, the committee settled on a 175-acre plot near the village of Pleasantville, in Westchester, thirty miles from the city. The choice may have been influenced by the fact that Lewisohn lived just a short distance away.[16]

So far as is known, the vast changes at the HSGS produced no visible waves at the HOA. No attempt was made to emulate them by abolishing the monitorial system. If Lowenstein himself disliked it, he never seems to have said so publicly. Apparently the trustees still had faith in it. On the other hand, the cottage idea appears to have evoked mixed feelings on the part of Lowenstein and the trustees. While paying homage to the cottage system, both were at the same time loyal to their own system. They sincerely believed that it was an exception of its kind, not to be compared with those that had given institutions a bad name.

Whatever their feelings about the HOA, the truth was that institutional care was a doomed system. Its death knell was signaled to all America in Washington, D.C., in 1909 at the First White House Conference on the Care of Dependent Children. It was called by President Theodore Roosevelt, who invited over two hundred leaders in philanthropy, social welfare, and child care to attend, including such figures as Andrew Carnegie, Jacob Schiff, Jane Addams, Jacob Riis, Lillian Wald, Booker T. Washington, Homer Folks, and Charles Loring Brace. Invitations were also sent to a number of leading institutions, including the HOA, represented by Louis Stern and Solomon Lowenstein, and the HSGS, represented by Adolph Lewisohn and Dr. Ludwig Bernstein.

President Roosevelt himself chose the keynote—explicitly anti-institutional—for the conference: "Home life is the highest and finest product of civilization. Children should not be deprived of it except for urgent and compelling reasons." In discussing his nine-item agenda, the delegates attacked institutions, supported foster homes, and praised the cottage plan. After a day and a half of such talk, Lowenstein was becoming more and more aroused. Finally, late on the morning of the second day, he asked for the floor. While agreeing that "congregate institutions should be divided into cottage groups," he also wanted to "protest against the idea that has been given circulation here this morning and that seems to be taken for granted . . . namely, that life in a congregate institution is necessarily of a gloomy, cheerless character. I happen to live in one in which there are about 1000 children who are not gloomy or cheerless. . . . I spend a good deal of time with the children, and do not find them unhappy or dull. We try to bring as much joy and happiness into the life of the children as possible. . . . The children can derive much happiness from such life and can be prepared to do excellent work after their discharge."[17] His remarks were greeted coldly, without applause. The conference had been called to write an epitaph for the orphanage and Lowenstein had had the temerity to suggest that the nearly departed had not been a total villain.

On the second day the delegates agreed to fourteen conclusions, the essence of which was that dependent children should first be kept in their own homes whenever possible, with foster homes as a second choice, and institutions as a last resort, provided they were cottage homes.

To the HOA, at least, the message of the conference was unequivocal: it would have to convert to the cottage plan. A year later, in 1910, the trustees at their annual meeting appointed a committee to consider removal to a new site; and the committee, in turn, asked Lowenstein to explore and report on the relative merits of city property versus country property before they began their search. As it happened, 1910 also marked the fiftieth anniversary of the opening of the HOA. The occasion was celebrated in April, in the Hippodrome, with an evening's program of patriotic festivities. Five thousand spectators came to see it, filling every seat in the house. When the curtains parted at 8:30, the audience gasped in wonder and broke into applause: lined up on stage were all 1,200 HOA children, the boys in military-style khaki-colored suits and broad-brimmed gray field hats and the girls in white or yellow dresses and white satin hair ribbons. As they started to sing "America," the audience cheered wildly for a few moments. The rest of the program was in the same flag-waving vein, with drills and band music (including a cornet solo by Edwin Franko Goldman sandwiched between speeches). In the finale, a spectacular number called "Rally 'Round the Flag," the cadet corps marched on stage with real Springfield rifles loaded with blanks.

With flags waving, the band blasting a Sousa march, ranks of cadets wheeling toward the audience and firing volleys of blanks, and smoke filling the orchestra pit, the rousing scene brought down the house.[18] Thrilled by it, the audience went home feeling that the HOA was a grand institution.

The fiftieth anniversary was the subject of a story in the *American Hebrew* on April 8 that featured an interview with Henry Bauer. The former "Little Mischief" of Lamartine Place was now nearly sixty years old and working as a night guard in the HOA. Discharged in 1864, a year after the move to East 77th Street, he had endured many misadventures in the decades that followed. Henry was now happily back in the only real home he had ever known—the only HOA graduate to have lived in all three HOA buildings.

Ironically, in the midst of all the praise being heaped on the HOA, its sponsors were seriously considering its extinction, at least in its current form. In his report to the building committee later that year, Lowenstein recommended that the HOA move out of the city. "The best of child-caring institutions today are found in the country," he noted, and singled out the HSGS as "the best yet devised for any children's institution." This was an enormous concession to make, but Lowenstein had a reason for doing so. Aware of the trustees' pride in always having been "in the forefront of all child-caring institutions of any denomination whatever," he suggested that this place could be lost if they didn't act promptly. "In recent years we have been outstripped by several non-Jewish institutions whose needs demanded an early removal. The HSGS has likewise been compelled to move and has followed the progressive tendency of the times. It is within our power to decide now whether this primacy among Jewish child-caring institutions shall belong to it or shall continue to remain with the HOA."

Lowenstein was throwing down the gauntlet, but many trustees disagreed with the idea that institutions were obsolete and that foster homes were superior. Indeed, one curious aspect of this controversy was that many Jewish communities favored institutions. And for a good reason: most Jewish institutions were considerably superior to their gentile counterparts. As the last religious group to build homes, they had benefitted by having so many bad examples to study and avoid. In addition, Jewish institutions were invariably built with the support of an entire community behind them, rather than by individuals or parishes, as in the case of gentile institutions. As a result, there was usually more money available for facilities and services.

One incident that suggests the prevailing Jewish attitude toward institutions took place in February 1910. Early that month Dr. Samuel Wolfenstein, superintendent of the Cleveland Jewish Orphan Asylum, arrived in New York City to carry out a questionable mission. Having read a few months earlier that Lowenstein was "eminently satisfied" with the HOA's boarding-out system, Dr. Wolfenstein, a known opponent of foster homes, asked Lowenstein if he could personally investigate the HOA's homes. Lowenstein obligingly sent him a list of 116 homes with 201 children living in them and invited him to visit any of them any time—unannounced. Now, list in hand, Dr. Wolfenstein hired a taxi and visited fourteen homes that morning, all on the Upper East Side. Afterward, he reported that his "findings were depressing in the extreme." There was not a single home, he concluded, in which he would have placed a "dependent or orphaned child in preference to its being placed in any of our orphan homes."

Around noon, however, a visit to the HOA gave him a wholly different impression. There he saw "over 1000 children, very comfortably seated at their wholesome meal, all neat and clean. . . . How attentively they were looked after, how the attendants watched for their wants and their comfort, and how well they looked. What a difference between this sight and the sights I saw in the boarding homes."

But Dr. Wolfenstein's investigation wasn't over. In the afternoon he visited the homes of widowed or deserted mothers who were receiving allowances from the HOA almost equal to those paid to foster mothers. Their homes were on the Lower East Side, in the heart of the ghetto. In them he saw "such trying scenes I have not witnessed since the year 1866 when . . . I visited the Russian cities of Kovno and Vilno." In short, the children living with their mothers were even worse off than those in boarding homes. What did Dr. Wolfenstein recommend? More Jewish asylums, of course: at least ten in the city and its suburbs, with a total capacity of five thousand children, or about twice those already in homes.[19]

Dr. Wolfenstein's report received a good deal of publicity in the press, which embarrassed the HOA. To answer his charges, Lowenstein ordered an investigation of his own. Carried out by two men connected with charity work in the city, their report apparently contradicted Dr. Wolfenstein's. Lowenstein discussed their report and the HOA's system for recruiting boarding homes some months later, at a meeting of the National Conference of Jewish Charities.

If its procedures were carried out as described, the HOA's system was probably the most rigorous and thorough in the nation. All applications were investigated by a special agent working full-time. An applicant had to prove that the family had an income of its own apart from the money it would receive as payment for the care of children. Five written references from unrelated persons were required. Children were placed only with Jewish families but only those with no small children who would take attention away from the boarded children. The vast majority of those who applied were rejected—523 out of 603 in one year, the HOA reported. Homes approved by the HOA had to undergo a second investigation by the city's Board of Health. However, no home accepted by the HOA was ever rejected by the city. After the children were placed, the foster parents were required to insure their attendance in a public school and register them with the nearest religious school. The HOA gave the children clothing, supervised their health, and paid for incidental expenses. After the home was in operation, it received additional supervision from a third authority—the State Board of Charities. In 1909, as it had every year previously, the state had placed the HOA in Class I, its highest rating.[20]

No system is foolproof, of course, and it is possible that not all of the regulations had been followed in the homes visited by Wolfenstein. He may have also, by coincidence, managed to pick the worst homes for his tour. It is also possible that, given his hostility to foster homes, he was unwilling to admit the existence of even one good home.

On July 1, 1912, the HOA suffered the loss or primacy that Lowenstein had warned about. It was the day the HSGS's new home, renamed the Pleasantville Cottage School, was opened. That morning at their old home at 150th Street and Broadway, 480 boys and girls lined up in groups numbered according to their assigned cottage. Each child had a cottage number pinned to a garment and carried a small American flag. At a signal the entire formation, led by the home's band, started marching down Broadway, which had been cleared of traffic for the occasion. The formation stopped briefly at 137th Street, just behind the HOA. Looking uphill toward the institution they would be seeing for the last time, they saw hundreds of HOA children "many feet deep, watching, and some weeping." Having taken part in joint activities for years, there were many among both groups who knew each other. A few, in fact, were related. As the column stood in silence, the HOA band played them a last and touching farewell, and marched down to join them. Then, cheered on by the HOA children, the column—hundreds of little flags waving in many small hands— accompanied by two bands—moved down Broadway. It turned east on 125th Street and headed for the New York Central station on Park Avenue for the train ride to Pleasantville.

Cottage mothers were waiting for them when they arrived, but the children were too excited to give them any attention. For the first few hours they reacted to their new surroundings with hysterical delight. They ran in and out of cottages, jumped on beds, flushed the toilets, opened furnace doors, tried the windows, climbed inside high iceboxes, and chased each other across the home's enormous campus. As one HSGS alumnus would put it many years afterward, "we were explorers in a new world."

To that new world now came professional visitors from America and Europe, and all marveled at it. "The best equipped institution for children in the world," declared the director of the Child Helping Department of the Russell Sage Foundation. Echoing this view, the director of Harvard University's Social Ethics Museum wanted a display of pictures and charts describing the home for a permanent exhibit. Soon there would be imitators: within five years three new institutions would be constructed along the exact same lines. But the crowning moment of all came that first summer when President William Howard Taft visited Pleasantville after dropping in on Adolph Lewisohn, an old friend. He left wearing the gold button seal of the Boys and Girls Brotherhood Republics. What chagrin this caused at the HOA, for it had never been visited by a president.

Yet even the HOA was willing to admit, without condescension, that the Pleasantville Cottage School was unquestionably the best of its kind on the world. No one who saw it in the first flush of glory could say anything else. Its dozen or so cottages were organized like college fraternities or sororities. Each cottage was home to about twenty-five boys or girls who ate, slept, and studied there. Within each cottage, all ages were mixed, so that some siblings could live with each other—thus eliminating one big complaint about the HOA system, which grouped all children by age and school grade. Cottage residents did their own housekeeping and helped their cottage mother prepare the meals. A system of cottage councils was introduced to reinforce the republics.

Besides the cottage plan and the self-government, the new home boasted a third remarkable feature, which accounted for the fact that it had been named the Pleasantville Cottage *School*. It initiated one of the most innovative educational programs ever attempted in America. Three different kinds of education—academic, religious, and vocational—were combined into one interrelated curriculum. Of the three, the first two offered fairly conventional courses, except that all children were required to take German, Latin, Hebrew, and Jewish history. At the same time, they were also required to take vocational training, which began in the first year of school.

In the number and variety of trades taught, the vocational curriculum was extraordinary for its time. Boys were offered a choice of woodwork, machine shop, electric shop, mechanical and freehand drawing, sheet metal, metal springs, and printing. Girls had fewer courses to choose from: domestic science, freehand drawing, stenography, and typewriting. Both sexes were later offered radiotelegraphy and radiotelephony.

Unbelievably, there was one final astonishing twist to the entire program: it was arranged to enable the children to complete twelve years of work in nine. This was accomplished by stretching the school day from five hours to seven and a half hours and reducing the summer vacation to a few weeks. Every child was expected to finish high school before discharge. All in all, it was an intensive, unorthodox program, demanding a great deal of the children. Yet they appeared to thrive on it, for all their teachers were first-rate and the idea of finishing school three years earlier had enormous appeal.

In 1915 the home's curriculum was officially approved by the deputy commissioner of the New York State Board of Education— the first time that the state had officially recognized a secondary school program that did not require twelve years of attendance and the first time that an orphanage school had received an equal rating with the regular public schools. A year later its technical program was praised by the director of industrial arts at Teachers College, Columbia University. He found that children of twelve to sixteen were doing work that compared with that done elsewhere by sixteen- to eighteen-year-olds.[21]

With the Pleasantville Cottage School established as a showcase for the care of dependent children, it was obvious that the HOA could no longer claim primacy among child-caring institutions. Still, it continued to act like a leader. And in some respects it always remained far ahead of its rivals. For example, in 1911, the year before the HSGS moved to Pleasantville, it established its own psychological services, the first offered by any orphanage. Eventually, this led to the operation of educational and vocational guidance clinics and, inevitably, to the introduction of psychiatric services.[22]

Furthermore, few institutions did as much as the HOA in providing summer recreation and using it as a means for individualizing the children. Its chief vehicle for this service was the Junior League, organized in 1905 by young adults. Their goal was to promote the welfare of the children by stimulating interest in them among the youth of the community. At first its activities were conventional: contributing money, providing outside recreation, and visiting orphans or those without relatives on Sunday visiting days. Near the end of 1908, however, the HOA called on the league to consider an idea it had in mind for a summer project. At the time, anemic, fragile, or underweight children (mostly newcomers) were being sent for the summer to the Sanitarium for Hebrew Children in the Rockaways. Having grown dissatisfied with this arrangement, the HOA had conceived of what it thought was a better plan—using a farm for the same purpose. There being no money in the budget for it, the league agreed to sponsor the project for one summer on a trial basis. In 1909 the HOA rented a farm in Westchester. The farm consisted of a large house, formerly a boarding home, with sixteen acres, including a truck garden, barns, outhouses, and some livestock. Apart from staple foods and clothing, the entire cost of renting, equipping, and maintaining the summer home was paid for by the league.

That first summer the farm was open from June until the middle of September. During that period 434 children visited it, staying from one day to two months, depending on their condition. All loved it. For those who stayed two months it was the happiest summer of their lives. "We felt like normal children living with parents," one alumnus recalled. They helped with the farming, milked cows, rode horses, went on berrying parties—all without governors, monitors, or bells. Because of the variety and abundance of food served, they also gained weight. When September came, no one wanted to return to the HOA; a few had to be literally dragged off the premises.[23]

Needless to say, the summer home was an immense success, and the league rented it for the next four years. By 1912 it occurred to Lowenstein and some officers of the society that it could be an even greater success if it were kept open all year. A year-round facility would help relieve some of the overcrowding and also give the children placed there the kind of individual attention they couldn't possibly receive at the HOA. But Lowenstein knew that the Woodlands home was too small for this purpose and that the Junior League could not afford to pay for the larger facility he had in mind. The only possibility that remained—not an easy one—was to sell the idea to the trustees. But how? Money was tight now and selling them on anything new would be difficult. Lowenstein and his supporters seem to have managed it by telling the trustees that a large Westchester farm, besides being good for the children, would also make it possible to produce "a considerable portion of the food" needed by the HOA.

This wasn't true, of course; the farm could have produced enough vegetables for just a handful of children. But Lowenstein knew that the trustees felt that even charitable enterprises could be made to pay their own way in some instances. Naturally, when told that the farm could help with the expenses, the trustees were impressed and went along with the plan.

In 1913, the HOA leased a farm of seventy-five acres in Valhalla, Westchester, and had its house remodeled. After it opened sixty-three boys spent almost a year there. With the assistance of the board of education, a teacher was hired and assigned to the farm as a live-in tutor.[24] In the summer a number of older boys were sent there to help with the farming, though the harvest that September wouldn't have filled a few wheelbarrows.

The Valhalla farm's first year coincided with another event that showed how quickly it had caught the imagination of those who had been there and aroused the envy of those who hadn't. *Our Little World*, the second literary magazine written, edited, and published by the children appeared in September 1913. The twenty-four-page edition, whose cover carried a photograph of the HOA, contained articles, poems, lyrics written for familiar melodies, cartoons, drawings, jokes, gossip, and twenty advertisements. Six editors, three girls and three boys, produced the magazine, whose title came from one of the poems.

Two of the songs and one cartoon were about Valhalla, all reflecting an obsessive interest in the food served there. For example, one song titled "In Valhalla" has these lines:

> Eggs for breakfast, pie for dinner, wine at supper time,
> Lots of fancy cooking and really it is fine;
> In Valhalla, Valhalla.

The second song, sung to "Dixie," also celebrated the meals:

> *CHORUS*
> Then I wish I was in Valhalla
> Getting fat, getting fat;
> In Valhalla land I'll take my stand,
> And eat, and eat in Valhalla,
> O eats, O eats,
> Away in dear Valhalla.
>
> We get French fried toast and fish fried in butter,
> Makes you plump and a little fatter;
> Then hurry up and just get thin,

And Dr. S. will shove you in,
Getting fat, getting fat, getting fat, getting fatter.

The glorious prospect of getting fat is graphically illustrated by a cartoon titled "Before and after Valhalla." The before drawing shows a thin, glum boy in knickers while the after drawing depicts the same boy as a smiling heavyweight almost five times his former width. The gluttonous longings expressed in the songs and the cartoon reflect a hunger that goes beyond the desire for more and tastier food than the diet served in the HOA. To the children who were there, Valhalla was a resort rather than a farm. Although there was work to be done, it was underplayed; what mattered was the fresh air, the loose discipline, the relaxed tone, the easy camaraderie, the unpressured life, the chance for children to be themselves.

If a subgenre is ever established for orphanage literature, *Our Little World* should receive a permanent place in it. One can obtain a fairly accurate and reliable view of HOA life from its pages. There is a piece on "Alumni Day," an annual event during the Lowenstein years. Hundreds of alumni would return to the asylum on a summer Sunday, play baseball (married men versus single men), enjoy a meal, and see a movie. An article on "The Library," written by the librarian, reveals, among other things, that "five thousand eight hundred books were taken out by the boys and girls from October 20, 1912 to July 31, 1913." This averages out to about five books per child for a nine-month period. Three short items deal with outings: one to the circus, one to the American Museum of Natural History, and the last to a newspaper, *The Evening Post*. All took place during the summer and were part of the HOA's effort to continue the pursuit of culture for its children all year round. Humor and wit fill many pages, in such pieces titled "Personals," "Sociables," "Some Don'ts," "Here and There," "Social News," "H.O.A. Isms," and "Jokes."

One terribly sad short story, with echoes of Dickens, Horatio Alger, Jr., O. Henry, and Italian opera, provides a poignant contrast to the humor. Titled "The Little Violinist," its tragic hero is a poor little boy who plays the violin for pennies in the streets, is befriended by a rich little girl (who gives him a quarter), has his violin snatched by a bully and thrown under a wagon, manages to save it but is run over by a truck, is taken to a hospital near death, calls for his grandfather, and plays a last song for him on the violin. When the doctor comes, both are dead. The story exposes all the fantasies, fears, and pessimism of a child growing up in an orphanage.

Only one edition of *Our Little World* was ever published. Still, it

offered a seminal example. Six years later the children would organize to publish another literary magazine that would enjoy a run of
nearly fifteen years and win honors for editorial excellence.

The HOA gave up Valhalla in 1918, though, when it decided more
renovations were needed, which were too expensive to undertake.
Next year the HOA rented two camps in Bear Mountain Park and
sent sixteen anemic boys and girls there the first summer. Lester
Loeb, the first director, named them Camp Wakitan, for the boys, and
Camp Wehaha, for the girls. Although the camps, like the summer
homes, were originally intended for sickly children, their value for
all the children was soon recognized. Both camps gradually expanded
(with Camp Wehaha moving to another lake) until by the mid-1920s
every boy and girl was spending a few weeks to a month at camp
every summer.[25] As a result, HOA children were enjoying a luxury
available only to middle-class children.

Another service the HOA pioneered was after-care—helping a
graduate make the adjustment to independent living after discharge.
The transition was becoming more of a problem because children
were staying at the HOA longer, and the longer they stayed the
more difficult was their adjustment. Upon discharge, graduates were
leaving a highly structured way of life and entering the outside world,
which was strange and threatening now because they had to make
many choices immediately and rely on their own resources. Graduates returning to families or relatives had some help in this process
but orphans and others who preferred not to return home were suddenly on their own. For all of them, discharge was invariably a fright-
ening experience, more terrifying than almost any first-day horrors
they had experienced on admission to the HOA. For a few months
at least, often longer, graduates suffered what could be called severe
discharge depression, a syndrome marked by terrible loneliness, deep
insecurity, and intense anxiety about the future.

Although aware of this problem for decades, the HOA had never
taken any direct responsibility for it. In his own time Seligman
Solomon had attempted to bridge the gap alone by personally following up on many discharged children. Indeed, the major reason for the
formation of the Seligman Solomon Society had been to help alumni
through the adjustment period. Lowenstein had always felt that a
more organized approach was needed but it wasn't until 1916 that he
was able to establish some after-care facilities. That year he persuaded
the Junior League to sponsor the Corner House, at 21 Charles Street,
in lower Manhattan, for male graduates who had no home to return
to or relatives to live with. It was intended as a half-way house for
working boys, where they could live under semiprotective circum-

stances until they felt ready to attempt full independence. Twenty boys moved in at once and many more were soon seeking admission. To meet the demand, the adjoining building was leased in 1920, doubling its capacity. Even this proved insufficient and led to a waiting list—a list, incidentally, that included alumni of the Pleasantville Cottage School and the Brooklyn HOA, neither of which had any after-care facilities.

Not long after the Corner House opened, female alumni were provided with an equivalent facility. In 1916, the Friendly Circle, a group sponsored by the Ladies Sewing Society, established the Friendly Home for Girls as an experiment. Twelve older girls chosen by Lowenstein went to live with a house mother in a large apartment in the top floor of a building. There, while attending school, they did all the work of maintaining the apartment. At the end of the four-month trial period the girls were placed with families under terms that allowed them to work their way through high school and college. The experiment was termed a success, thus making the Friendly Home another HOA annex. In the next few years the new facility moved twice and, in 1921, set up a permanent home on West 140th Street, near Riverside Drive, only a few blocks from the HOA.[26]

The war years were a very difficult period for the children. By 1915 every bed was filled, and the same was true the next year. But 1916 set an all-time record for the number of children under care—1,755. Of this total, 1,329 were in the asylum and 426 in boarding out, the highest number ever reached in each category. When a polio epidemic broke out in the city that year, Lowenstein and the trustees began worrying. Fortunately, not a case of it appeared among the children. Still, the overcrowding led the State Board of Charities to give the HOA's building a Class 2 rating for the first time in its history. For the trustees, that rating may have been the last straw. At any rate, it was in 1916 that Lowenstein announced that the HOA would move to the suburbs and reestablish itself on the cottage plan.[27] Later, the trustees changed their mind about leaving the city. After a two-year search, they bought a one-hundred acre site in the Bronx, at 225th Street and Boston Post Road, for $350,000.[28]

Lowenstein was away when the purchase was made. He had taken a leave of absence after America entered the war in order to accept an appointment as deputy commissioner (with the rank of major) with the American Red Cross Commission to Palestine. He represented the Joint Distribution Committee, which had just been organized to help Jewish war refugees.[29] Lowenstein's war service marked the end of his career with the HOA, for he never returned.

Lionel J. Simmonds, his assistant, became acting superintendent and guided the HOA through the war years, in which it took a highly patriotic role. A Red Cross auxiliary was organized by the girls, who, in two years, sewed and knitted over 1,700 items for the soldiers, chiefly socks and sweaters. The cadets and the band were placed at the disposal of the various committees of national defense and performed at a great many bond rallies.

Alumni, however, made the greatest contribution to the war effort. About three hundred served in the armed forces, many as volunteers. Given their cadet training in the HOA, most of them had no trouble rising in the ranks. By the time the war ended, one was a captain, four were lieutenants, twenty were sergeants, and dozens were corporals. In addition, seven alumni became regimental bandleaders.[30] All told, it was a record that would have honored any military school. One alumnus received the Distinguished Service Medal and ten had died.

The body of one soldier, Louis D. Blumenthal, was brought back to the United States in June 1921. A special funeral service was then held for him at the HOA, attended by over a thousand visitors, most of them alumni. With the cadet corps in attendance and an HOA bugler playing taps, his body was buried in the orphans' plot at Beth-El Cemetery.[31]

When the armistice was celebrated in New York City, the cadets and the band took part in the victory parade, a role they had earned by their participation in the home front war effort. Both units had helped sell millions of dollars worth of Liberty Bonds and War Stamps. The HOA made them available to city hall and patriotic groups all through the war.

Not long after the war ended Dr. Abraham Jacobi died in July 1919. He had been the chief of the HOA's medical staff from the day the HOA opened, in 1860. Of the 13,500 children who had passed through the home since then, only 62 had died, about 1 per year.[32] It was the most extraordinary record ever compiled by any children's institution in the world. Dr. Jacobi himself had established a record of sorts by his fifty-nine-year association with the home. Despite his heavy private consulting schedule, he never relinquished his responsibility for the children of the HOA. A year before he died, for example, he got the asylum to install a full-time dental clinic with its own X-ray department and an eye clinic which provided semi-annual eye examinations for the children. Dr. Jacobi has not been forgotten by the city he served so well. His memorial is the Abraham Jacobi Hospital in the Bronx.

Lowenstein returned from war around the end of 1919 and joined the Federation for the Support of Jewish Philanthropies as the executive director the following year. Federation was a new organization, established in 1917. It represented yet another periodic attempt by the city's Jewish community to set up a central authority over its own wildly proliferating charitable and welfare agencies. In 1915, when someone took the time to count them, there were 3,637 separate agencies in existence. These included 858 congregations, 69 schools, 101 recreational and cultural agencies, 2,168 mutual aid societies, 164 philanthropic correctional agencies, and 277 other organizations with miscellaneous functions. Many of them duplicated each other's services and practically all of them competed with one another for funds. Federation was created to bring some order and structure to this chaos. It planned to eliminate or discourage overlapping charities, centralize fund-raising, allocate money, evaluate the community's total service needs, and attempt to establish standards.

Talk of federation started in 1910, when Brooklyn's Jewish community was the first in the city to federate itself. But it had taken another eight years before Manhattan and the Bronx, led by twenty-four agencies (including the HOA), formed their own federation. The reason it had taken so long was that each member agency was required to give up its individual contributors to Federation. An agency that lost its contributors also lost most of its autonomy, so few were prepared to accept this condition. Eventually, community pressure made federation inevitable, though, and in a few years the original Brooklyn Federation and its Manhattan-Bronx counterpart merged to form a single, city-wide agency.[33]

Lowenstein's appointment in 1920 as executive director of Federation made him an important figure in state and national welfare circles. In 1922 he was elected president of the National Conference of Jewish Social Work. The next year he was named president of the New York State Conference of Social Welfare. From 1932 to 1933 he presided over the New York Conference of Social Welfare and did the same for the National Conference of Social Welfare in 1937 and 1938. Mayor La Guardia of New York City consulted him on welfare matters, as did state and federal authorities. He died at the age of 64 in January 1942, overcome by a heart attack while walking in the streets.[34]

The coming of Federation, whatever it did for other Jewish agencies, had a critical impact on the Pleasantville Cottage School. Raising money became harder during the war, and the Federation's board was unable to provide the school with all the money it wanted. To reduce expenses, the school accepted more children and made a number of economies. Some board members felt that the school's lavish educational program was a luxury and should be dropped. The situation worsened in 1918, when a polio epidemic forced the school to cancel all admissions and discharge some children. Before the year ended Federation made a hard decision: it ordered the school to abolish its expensive private educational program and allow the city to educate the children. When he learned of the decision, Dr. Ludwig Bernstein resigned in protest.[35] With its most remarkable feature gone, the school lost a good deal of its reputation and luster. Its primacy had lasted just six short years.

The HOA, meanwhile, was planning to move for the third time in sixty years and reestablish itself on the cottage plan in the Bronx.

Decade of Promise and Disappointment

12

For the HOA the twenties seemed to promise a future just as bright as that which then beckoned to all America in the prosperous years after World War I. Nineteen twenty, indeed, was another landmark for the asylum, a moment when a number of new summits were reached. In the size and scope of its facilities and services the HOA surpassed every child-caring institution in the nation, if not the world. Besides the main building on Amsterdam Avenue, these now included two after-care annexes, the Corner House for boys and the Friendly Home for girls; two camps it leased in the Palisades Interstate Park (which made it the only orphanage in the nation with its own camps); and the one-hundred-acre site it had bought in the Bronx, where it was planning to move as soon as it obtained the funds for construction. In addition, it still owned its old site at East 77th Street, now being used as a high school, which it leased to the board of education for about $9,000 a year.[1] Almost all of its new facilities had been acquired in the previous decade and they gave the HOA the image, incongruous for an orphanage, of a sprawling corporate enterprise.

Lionel J. Simmonds, acting superintendent during Lowenstein's war service abroad, was completing his first year as superintendent in 1920. His achievement represented the ultimate triumph of Baar's system: an orphan was running the orphanage. Simmonds's career suggests that he had been waiting in the wings many years for this moment. His parents were British Jews who had come to New York City from Brighton, England in 1891. The following year his father died and his mother placed him in the HOA. Simmonds thrived in his new surroundings. He was appointed a monitor, attended City College on an HOA scholarship while working as a governor, and, after graduation, became a schoolteacher. Then, while holding down two jobs—schoolteacher and HOA governor—he also studied for his master's degree in education at Columbia University and became drillmaster of the cadet corps, with the title of colonel. In 1905 and 1906, he led it to first-place honors in a number of public exhibitions. As a result, he acquired the lifelong nickname of "Colonel," though no one dared address him with that title. In 1907 Lowenstein named him as assistant superintendent. A year later he married a former resident, Clara Gottfried; they lived in the HOA for 33 years and raised two children there, a boy and a girl.[2]

Also in 1920 the HOA's seventh and eighth graders found themselves attending P.S. 5 in Harlem, making it the first racially integrated school in the city. Not intended as an experiment in integration, the move represented a neighborly accommodation by the HOA to help the school resolve an enrollment problem. P.S. 5's all-black classes were only 75 percent full, raising the possibility that the school could be closed if the remaining 25 percent were not found in the district. So the school persuaded the HOA to provide the needed pupils. According to one alumnus who was transferred to P.S. 5, both groups got on well together and there were few incidents. The arrangement ended after a few years and the school was closed.[3]

For the HOA's trustees, 1920 began with high expectations and ended in profound disappointment. The expectations were based on a near certainty that construction on the new home would begin sometime that year. A year earlier, the HOA had announced its building plans with a broadside of publicity. The plans called for a mixed setting of both cottages and institutional-style facilities rather than the purely cottage-type home Lowenstein had originally conceived. A contradictory mix, it reflected the trustees' continuing bias in favor of institutional care. Pride, too, was involved, for the last thing the trustees wanted was an exact replica of Pleasantville. To imitate their upstart rival would have been the clearest confession of declining status. Yet they agreed to include some cottages lest they be accused of being unprogressive.

If there was one word that precisely summed up the plans, it was *grandiose*—a term not generally applied to orphanages no matter how grand. Needless to say, the new HOA was to be bigger, better, and more expensive than any home anywhere in America. Its projected cost, as first estimated in 1917, when the plans were conceived, was $4 million. This figure didn't include the property, already paid for, which cost $350,000. At $4.3 million, the new home would cost almost eight times the amount spent on the Amsterdam Avenue building in the 1880s.

In 1917 prices, the money would have paid for an enormous

number of buildings and facilities—twenty-four according to the announced plans plus several more shown in the architect's drawing. Ten were to be cottages housing thirty children apiece. As at
Pleasantville, each cottage would be self-contained and be supervised by a house mother. The majority of children, though, would
be living in four three-story buildings called pavilions. The pavilions—apparently "dormitory" wasn't used because it suggested institutional living—would have a capacity of eight hundred children, or
two hundred in each. They were to be linked to a central administration building containing cooking and dining facilities, offices, and
a large assembly hall. Ancillary facilities included a synagogue and
living quarters for administrative staff; a residence for staff workers;
a residence for general workers; a reception house; two hospitals,
one for general and one for contagious patients; a school building designed in cooperation with the board of education; a gymnasium; a
laundry; a powerhouse; a greenhouse; a garage; and a special cottage
for the superintendent. Despite the large number of buildings, there
would still be a great deal of open space on the site, enough to provide
a huge campus and a large central playing field as well. No fences
were to be erected; instead, trees would ring the HOA on all sides.[4]

Although the trustees never said so openly, their plans made it
clear that they intended the new HOA to strengthen their shaky primacy over Pleasantville. In this game of philanthropic one-upman-
ship, they regarded their choice of Edenwald, located in the northeast
corner of the Bronx less than a mile from Westchester, as a point in
their favor. What now seemed obvious to many was that the HSGS
had blundered in choosing a rural setting so far from the city. For
one thing, it imposed an expensive commuting burden on staff, the
children's parents, and the children themselves, almost all of whom
returned to the city after their discharge. And the notion that the
country was inherently superior to the city for the care of children
was now seen for the myth it was. Finally, Pleasantville had actually
lost more than it had gained in giving up the extensive services of the
city in exchange for the overrated advantages of rural Westchester. In
choosing a countrified setting just inside city limits, the HOA had
got the best of both worlds—and trumped its rival.

If all went well, the trustees would have their new home ready
by the spring of 1922, just in time for the HOA's centennial celebration. Early in 1920, this still seemed possible for they had found an
eager buyer for the Amsterdam Avenue site—the New York Yankees
baseball team. For many years the Yankees had been using the Polo
Grounds, home of the Giants, and they now wanted a stadium of

their own. Jacob Ruppert, the team's owner, considered the HOA location ideal because, among other things, it could be reached by the Broadway subway on one side and the Amsterdam Avenue trolley on the other.

Negotiations between the HOA and Yankees representatives proceeded quietly all through the spring of 1920. In September the press reported "a definite announcement" was soon expected verifying the sale. The only hitch, according to the stories, was the "uncertainty of building conditions" on the Edenwald property, a matter that wasn't explained further. Nor was it explained why the talks had dragged on so long. The deal seemed settled, at last, on January 30, 1921, when the *New York Times* ran a front-page story announcing the purchase of the HOA lot. Told entirely from the Yankees' side, the story said that they had a year's option on the property and planned to start construction in 1922, with completion scheduled for the following year, in time for the baseball season. Once again, however, the story spoke of a "hitch," and a strange one at that—the HOA had to find new quarters. This was obviously untrue. The real hitch was that the HOA didn't have the money to begin building, and they may have kept this fact from the Yankees all during the negotiations.

The next day, "a flat contradiction" developed, according to the *New York Times*. It reported that the HOA had totally repudiated its previous day's story by denying that negotiations were pending, an option was outstanding, or a sale had been completed. Yet the same story noted that the Yankees' engineering company had insisted that a contract had been signed and that building plans had been drawn. Neither the HOA nor the Yankees ever offered any public statement afterward to explain what had happened. In view of what is known about the HOA's money-raising problems, however, it seems highly likely that it had misled the Yankees. Although no prices were ever mentioned, the Amsterdam Avenue property could have been sold for close to $1 million, money the trustees badly needed for their home in the Bronx. What they were hoping to do, it now appears, was to keep the Yankees dangling until they could obtain the necessary building funds from Federation. But the money wasn't forthcoming from Federation or anyone else, and the Yankees refused to be put off. When the HOA deal fell through, Ruppert looked for another site and eventually chose the Bronx plot, across the river from the Polo Grounds, on which Yankee Stadium was built.

The HOA, on the other hand, never moved again. Its trustees must have sensed, even while negotiating with the Yankees, that they would never receive any money from Federation. They might have guessed this from Federation's behavior in 1917, just after it was organized. In February that year, the trustees sent the new agency a letter advising them of their building plans. Federation duly noted it—and did nothing. Nor would it do anything afterward. It had more or less come to the conclusion in 1917 that Jewish child-care agencies presented the worst mess of all and should be merged as soon as possible for the sake of better care, less waste, and higher efficiency. With that goal in mind, Federation could hardly look kindly upon any plans for expansion. As it turned out, the Federation was absolutely right, but it would take more than twenty years to achieve its goal.

Under Federation's constitution, no member agency had the right to conduct its own building fund campaign, so the HOA waited patiently after 1917 went by, fairly certain the money would come. But within two years, though, many other institutions affiliated with the Federation began asking for funds either to build new facilities or to renovate old ones. Their combined requests totaled about $9 million, considerably more than Federation had in its meager treasury. Rather than refuse them outright (and perhaps prompt some to revive the separate money-raising efforts each had carried on before Federation), it agreed in 1919 to the formation of the United Building Fund Campaign.

Like its needy member agencies, the HOA expected a good deal from the campaign, which accounted for its optimism early in 1920. That optimism soured into disappointment when, for a number of reasons, the campaign was only moderately successful, raising about $6.5 million. The HOA's share came to about $1 million; Federation advised it to obtain the balance needed for building by dipping into its own assets. But now circumstances beyond its control contrived to lock the HOA into a financial bind. Because building costs had risen 50 percent since the end of the war, the new home would cost $6 million, $2 million higher than the 1917 estimate. Even if the HOA took the $1 million offered by Federation and added all of its assets (which it wasn't prepared to do), there would be a gap of over $2 million—a gap that was widening.[5] One alternative was to eliminate some of the least necessary yet desirable facilities included in the plans. Such a curtailment, though, would have also meant yielding the HOA's primacy to Pleasantville, a step the trustees would never have countenanced. Thus, for the first time in its long history, the HOA found itself short of funds and unable to obtain any.

Ironically, it was in 1922, when the HOA celebrated its centennial, that it finally abandoned its plans of starting anew in the Bronx. That year the Bureau of Jewish Social Research published the re-

sults of a study of three institutions—the HOA, Pleasantville, and
the Hebrew Home for Infants—undertaken for Federation's child-
care committee. The study, besides emphasizing the importance of
keeping dependent children out of institutions and at home, where
possible, made four recommendations: the immediate creation of a
central clearing bureau to determine the kind of care a child needed;
the extension of foster home care to include children up to ten years
of age; the creation of a central boarding-out bureau; and the creation
of a joint board with the ultimate goal of promoting a merger of all
Jewish child-care agencies, particularly the HOA and Pleasantville.

The second study of its kind, its findings were identical to those
of the first study, made in 1919. Understandably, the two major institutions involved saw the recommendations of both studies as the
official formula for their mutual extinction and neither would agree
to any of them. Still, there were objective members of both homes
who would have admitted—unofficially, of course—that Federation
was right.

The situation that the child-care committee's recommendations
was intended to correct was chaotic at best and scandalous at worst.
For the truth was that while Jewish children generally received superb
care *after* they were admitted to a facility, the process they went
through *before* placement was, to say the least, humiliating. At the
time, most children were committed to institutions through two
public agencies: the Department of Welfare, for destitute children,
and the Children's Court, for neglected children. Delinquents were
an exception, for the law required that they be sent to a reformatory.

The placement process involved a form of roulette played for the
benefit of the Jewish asylums. It was held in a Department of Welfare
office that maintained a blackboard covered with the names of all
the Jewish homes and, next to each name, that day's tally of empty
beds. A child was committed on the basis of age, available vacancy,
and chance. If under five, the child would be sent to the Home for
Hebrew Infants if it had a vacancy. Older children, on the other hand,
could be sent to the HOA, BHOA, or Pleasantville, depending on
which home had the most empty beds at the moment. No attempt
was made to keep families together; brothers and sisters were placed
in different homes if the blackboard roulette that morning decreed
their separation.

This system, incidentally, was set up at the insistence of the Jewish
agencies, who were in fierce competition with each other for children. The city paid a per capita subsidy for each child, and every home
needed the money. Since a home's expenses were more or less fixed,

a low vacancy rate was the key to a reduction in the per capita cost. And the blackboard roulette guaranteed that no institution would be favored over another.

Children committed by public agencies were likely to be almost total enigmas to the homes receiving them. Little was given to them beyond the name, age, health, and economic status of each child placed. No additional material was included because the public agencies focused only on identifying information. Their scanty files contained nothing about the history, personality, or relationships of the child involved. Yet the homes, curiously enough, made no demand for more vital information. They simply accepted all committed children and checked them only for health. Obviously the main thing was to get the bodies and the money.

When the supply of commitments slackened and the vacancies began mounting, the asylums resorted to the most despicable practice of all: they removed children from foster homes to fill the empty beds. Those sent back to the homes were chosen arbitrarily, without regard to their needs, adjustment, or length of stay simply because they were needed to lower the per capita cost. Although foster children were also subsidized, the money went to the foster parents. An empty foster home bed meant a loss only to the foster parents, not to the homes. Thus, the boarding-out systems were converted into feeder pipelines for their respective asylums.

What was even worse was that only the so-called average children were removed from foster homes. Retarded or physically handicapped children, for instance, were often left in foster homes because the asylums were not equipped to deal with their special needs. Despite a good deal of adverse criticism, the feeder pipeline practice continued for many years. One reason for its use was that those in charge of the boarding-out departments were totally subservient to the wishes of their respective institutions. More important, though, was the fact that neither the HOA nor Pleasantville were firmly convinced that foster homes were superior.[6] The idea persisted that only a great institution could provide children with all the religious, medical, vocational, and disciplinary benefits that would mold them into exemplary citizens. How could any foster parent offer the same advantages, the same moral training, as a perfectly organized asylum?

Though unwilling to accept the findings of the two studies, both the HOA and Pleasantville were compelled to follow one of its recommendations. In 1922 the Department of Welfare, weary of the blackboard roulette game, told the Jewish community in the strongest possible language to establish a central clearing bureau for the commitment of all its children. Bowing to the department's demand, the homes set up the Jewish Children's Clearing Bureau, the first such agency of its kind in the city. Nor was this its only distinction. The new bureau was staffed not only with the usual wealthy business leaders but professionals and women, two groups never before represented on charitable agencies. In addition, both groups were given an equal voice in policy-making, a right previously denied them.

As a mixed body, the clearing bureau might well have dissolved in anarchy brought on by the infighting of the various asylum representatives. Instead, it soon developed into an autonomous unit—an independence that came about largely because the professionals, who tended to be more loyal to their profession than to the institutions they represented, led the way in working out a new approach to the admission process.

Under that approach, per capita cost was subordinated to a higher priority—the needs of the children. No longer was it a question of what home had the most empty beds, but rather if the placement was necessary. If a thorough study determined that the child was better off at home, then plans were arranged to that end. If placement was considered necessary, the bureau tried to determine the child's special needs and which agency was best equipped to provide them. Wherever possible the bureau tried to keep children out of the asylums, and it adopted the policy that foster homes should be the placement of choice for children from three to ten. As a result of this policy, combined with the prosperity of the twenties, the boarding-out systems expanded while the institutional populations declined.[7]

Having abandoned its dream of moving to the Bronx, the HOA was for the moment at a loss to determine what it should do. In practical terms, it came down to the question of how to use the money it received from Federation. That question preoccupied the trustees until 1923, when they decided to spend about $800,000 for an extensive renovation program. Over forty years old now, the building had been declared a fire hazard because of its wooden staircases. To comply with the fire laws, the building was fireproofed. A new powerhouse was built to replace the old one. Two lockers per child were installed, one in the dormitories, for the children's clothing, and another in the basement playrooms, for their personal effects. The dormitory lockers, placed at right angles to the walls, created alcoves for groups of eight to ten children, thus giving them, for the first time, a form of privacy. Their installation changed forever the old barracks look—precisely aligned ranks of beds in a long open room—that visitors had often criticized. In the dining room the long tables seating six-teen were removed and replaced by shorter tables seating eight. The job was done by 1925 and it was the last improvement the old asylum would ever receive.[8]

It was in 1925, too, that the last wedding ever to be held in the HOA took place. The bride and groom were Jenny Bloom and Robert Greene, both of whom had grown up under Lowenstein's administra-tion. Now a secretary for Federation, Bloom had persuaded Lowen-stein to perform the wedding ceremony at the HOA. In addition to the wedding ritual, the guests were treated to a trumpet solo by the bride's brother, Benny, a trumpet player in Paul Whiteman's or-chestra who had also been a cornetist in the HOA band. A story about the unusual wedding appeared in most of the city's newspapers.[9] The Greenes later lost their business in the Great Depression and were unable to care for their two children. They finally brought their chil-dren to the HOA—perhaps the first time children of alumni were brought there. But the children stayed only a week in the Reception House and were transferred to the Brooklyn HOA. Simmonds, who had known their parents, felt it was better for them to grow up in another asylum.[10]

With the renovation completed, the HOA now faced the even big-ger question of what to do with the Edenwald property. Eight years after it had been bought it was still lying unused in the Bronx. Even-tually an idea emerged: to turn it into a special residence for the HOA's retarded children. At the time there were no Jewish institu-tions or agencies for the developmentally disabled in the state (or anywhere else, for that matter) and the HOA didn't want to send them to public institutions. One approach that had been tried was to hold special classes for such children during the summer, but the results had been poor. Now, with Federation's approval, the HOA planned to use Edenwald as a special home.

In May 1925 the Edenwald School for Girls was opened with fif-teen retarded girls between the ages of fifteen and sixteen. Four re-cently hired staff members were waiting for them—a house mother, a vocational teacher, a handyman to teach farming, and a housekeeper to teach cooking and laundering. Neither the children nor the staff knew what to expect from the experiment, for training the retarded was an unknown field.

Before the year ended, though, the HOA had learned enough to know that it had failed. The girls chosen for the project were too old to be easily trained, so the next group of girls was no older than twelve.[11] This time the experiment was a good deal more successful, establishing some guidelines for training the retarded. After six months, the HOA, pleased with the group's progress, transferred a second group in the same age level. In 1929 the project was expanded to include boys. The man appointed to run the boys' school was a young psychologist named Myron Blanchard. A young social worker, Augusta Berdansky, assumed responsibility for the girls' school. Blanchard and Berdansky proved to be the ideal persons to run what seems to have been the first private school for the retarded in the United States. Under their combined administration Edenwald became the model of what a child-care institution should be.

It is hard to imagine a setting more suited for the care of children than the huge former estate they now called home. By a happy irony, Edenwald was aptly named: it was truly a Garden of Eden for its residents. On the grounds were three buildings used as living quarters, shops, classes, and offices, a greenhouse, a farm, a swimming pool, and lots of fields and woods for sports, picnicking, and roaming. There were no gates or fences anywhere and none were ever needed.

Life at Edenwald was totally different from what it was at the HOA. Fortunately, neither Blanchard nor Berdansky were instructed to turn their respective schools into a replica of the parent institution. Indeed, they received almost no instructions at all from Simmonds, the trustees, or anyone else, because no one really knew enough to offer valid advice. They were on their own, free to do what their professional consciences decreed. So they helped turn Edenwald into an enormous extended family, which they governed with few rules, some structure, and a good deal of affection.

A permissive, unregimented, informal style reigned at Edenwald. The boys slept in one building, the girls in another, but both sexes mingled freely without the close supervision that existed in the HOA. They lived in small rooms in groups of six to ten, with various ages mixed together. No bell system existed to wake up the children and shepherd them from one activity to another. The staff performed this function, sometimes assisted by older children. Yet the helpful older children were not monitors; the monitorial system was never instituted at Edenwald. Corporal punishment was not permitted, so the HOA-style beatings administered in cold blood and group punishments were outlawed at long last by at least part of the HOA.

Edenwald's goal was simple and pragmatic: to train its children to earn their own living. To accomplish that end, Blanchard set up a unique vocational offering for the boys. Instead of assigning them to trades, he allowed them to choose their own from a large sampling—carpentry, electrical wiring, barbering, shoe repair, cement work, gardening, chicken farming, vegetable farming, and house painting. Unfortunately the range available to the girls was considerably smaller because the administration assumed most would get married. Moreover, children were paid for the work they did, about one or two dollars a week. One year the children put all their skills at the service of a single enterprise and built a house.

Edenwald's children were highly productive and their efforts helped reduce its expenses. In the summer, for example, they lived on the chickens, eggs, and vegetables produced by their own farmers. And they sent small harvests of corn, carrots, and lettuce to the HOA. All the maintenance on the premises was done with the assistance of the children.

The staff engaged to train and care for the children was fairly large for a home with less than a hundred children. It included, beside Blanchard and Berdansky, one senior and one junior counselor for each side, a psychologist, a caseworker, a chef, an engineer, a porter, a seamstress, a carpentry teacher, and a number of part-time vocational teachers. In addition, there was an educational section consisting of teachers assigned by the board of education. Not knowing what was expected of them, the teachers allowed themselves to be used as Edenwald saw fit.

Although a few HOA counselors were sent to Edenwald at first, Blanchard and Berdansky soon acquired their own staff and trained them in their own fashion. Their instructions were to use patience, encouragement, repetition, and approval—lots of approval. No punishments were prescribed for children who misbehaved. In such instances, their counselor would try to talk out the problem behavior between them. If this failed, the caseworker took over. Actually, instances of misbehavior were uncommon. Rather than impose HOA-style discipline, Blanchard and Berdansky encouraged the children to employ self-discipline. For a time, the children disciplined themselves through their own "courts," which heard "cases" and dispensed "penalties." But the practice was stopped when staff found that the boys were imposing "sentences" far too severe for the offenses involved.[12]

The staff that Blanchard and Berdansky eventually assembled included some remarkably talented people, and their experience at Edenwald would later enrich the social work profession. For example, one counselor was a young German Jewish refugee named Werner W. Boehm, who had been hired by Simmonds. A lawyer in Germany, Boehm apparently intended to work at Edenwald until he was able to resume his law career, but he became so fascinated by his work with the children that he went into social work instead. Boehm became dean of the social work school at Rutgers University in the seventies and a leading professional in the field.[13] Another young counselor at the time was Jacob L. Trobe, a recent college graduate. Impressed by Edenwald, he continued in social work after he left it. Trobe, now retired, was once executive director of the Jewish Child Care Association of New York. A third staff member, Emil Kaney, became a psychiatrist. Blanchard himself has been the recipient of numerous honors. He was elected president of the Manhattan Chapter of the National Association of Social Workers in 1969–70 and was president of the National Association of Jewish Institutional Workers while he worked at Edenwald.

One thing the staff learned about the children was that the intelligence testing they had received in the HOA was not as accurate or as valid as had been supposed. When the children were retested after living in Edenwald a few years, some scored higher than they had originally. The new scores were attributed only partly to errors in testing. Other grounds seemed more valid: some children had obviously improved while others had tested poorly because of their emotional stress during admission. The quality of tests available was another factor, for the science of testing was still in its infancy in the twenties and thirties. This may help explain why some children who tested below normal are working in the business and professional worlds.

Though it did nothing to advertise itself, Edenwald's fame grew and spread during the thirties. Other American schools or institutions came there for consultation and guidance. So did foreign visitors, including a delegation from the Soviet Union. Blanchard and Berdansky saw to it that the visitors did not intrude upon the lives of the children. At least one doctoral student in social work wrote a dissertation on Edenwald and its success in training children to earn a living, though exactly how many Edenwald alumni are now self-supporting is unknown.[14]

What is known, though, is that the relatively few children who lived there—about two hundred altogether—also loved it. Although it is easy to find HOA alumni who hated the asylum, the same cannot be said for Edenwald. Its alumni are unanimous in praise of their former home. "Edenwald was heaven," one man remarked long after he left it and noted that he had been homesick for it many years after his discharge. His feeling of homesickness for Edenwald rather than for his own home is revealing. The children were allowed to spend every weekend at home with their parents if they wished. Many did so and found themselves feeling out of place; they longed to return to Edenwald.[15]

In 1942, after seventeen years in business, Edenwald was discontinued as a school for the retarded and subsequently reopened as a residential treatment center for mentally ill children. Blanchard went off to direct a YMHA in Brooklyn and Berdansky joined Pleasantville. One of the most astonishing experiments in the care of children had come to an end. But Edenwald still lives in the memories of its alumni as the dream home of their childhood. A woman who was placed there in its last years as a school remembered it in these glowing terms:

> I loved Edenwald such as I've never loved any place before or since. It was a time for me that was free of stress and poverty, tension and filth. It was a way of life I never knew existed.
>
> At Edenwald, not with shame and ridicule but with understanding and kindness, the lice were cleaned out of my hair and eventually my bed-wetting stopped.
>
> The staff, which consisted of a director, assistant director, counselor, social worker, cook and teacher were all one happy family.
>
> Coming from the slums of the lower East Side, I sometimes felt I was dreaming while running barefoot through the grass on Edenwald's beautiful grounds, or picking all kinds of berries, working in my own victory garden, or splashing in the pool in the summer, ice skating there in the winter, playing ball on the field, having two boys fighting over me.
>
> . . . I have no recollections of any bad experiences. The sun always seemed to be shining, laughter came easy, close friendships developed where thoughts and dreams were shared.
>
> . . . There wasn't anything about Edenwald I did not like. All the staff was wonderful. When I went back home to my family on the weekends, I could not wait to come back. Edenwald was a great experience for me . . . the happiest time of my life. I loved Edenwald so much that I was absolutely devastated when it closed.[16]

What is ironic about the HOA's extraordinary experiment at Edenwald is that it was set up as an afterthought, a way of using property that might otherwise have been wasted. The HOA had really intended to establish a superasylum on the site, a grandiose institution that would be a monument to child care. But the real monument proved to be Edenwald.

Exit the
Hebrew Orphan Asylum,
Enter "The Academy"   13

As the first former resident ever to become superintendent, Simmonds seemed determined to go much further than any of his predecessors had in improving the life of the children. His approach toward this goal, though, was slightly different from theirs, perhaps because he had lived almost his entire life in the HOA. While they had focused on individualizing the children, he worked on deinstitutionalizing the asylum. In doing so, he was rejecting much of what he had been taught under Dr. Baar. To the revered doctor, whose memory had been honored by a bronze bust placed in the lobby during Lowenstein's regime, the world outside the gates had to be held at bay, lest it intrude upon the children's lives and inevitably taint them. But Simmonds's reforms and innovations reflected a benign view of that world. Indeed, they were aimed at letting the outside world in by removing the barriers that separated the HOA from the community. An institutional man all his life, he apparently wanted only to change its image—to convert it from a military school to a private boarding school, or, in short, an orphanage purged of its nineteenth-century practices. And so there were changes, many more than any previous superintendent had ever attempted. The twenties proved to be the last decade when anything really new was tried at the HOA.

Since images are invariably associated with names, Simmonds early in his administration decided on the step, more symbolic than real, to substitute the name the *Academy* for the Hebrew Orphan Asylum. Officially, the institution remained the Hebrew Orphan Asylum—only an act of the state legislature could legally change its name—but the children were encouraged to refer to their home as the Academy. To validate its new image, two alma maters were written—"H.O.A. Alma Mater" and "Stand, Academy!" The idea behind the change was, obviously, to avoid using the terms *orphan asylum* or *orphanage,* both considered stigmatic. In practice, though, the children rarely used the word *academy* among themselves. It was more useful outside if they were asked where they lived, a question everyone dreaded. Being able to answer "At the Academy" was a relief, provided the questioner didn't pursue the matter.

Another change, also involving names, was that of replacing "governor" and "governess" with "counselor." More counselors were hired so that each dormitory had four, or about one to every twenty children. As its name suggested, counselors were called on to be more than drill-sergeant types, though not quite social workers. They were now required to prepare personality reports on the children twice a year, and they attended monthly staff meetings to discuss behavior problems. The man and woman in charge were given the title of dean.

Visiting practices were liberalized. Parents were allowed to visit their children almost any time so long as they did not interfere with the child's responsibilities, such as attending school. And children were permitted to visit their parents every Sunday if they wished, provided they obtained approval in advance.[1] Relations between the sexes were relaxed to a degree that would have outraged Dr. Baar. Boys were permitted to visit their sisters on the girls' side, although the reverse was forbidden. Girls came to the boys' side only to use the library, the trustees' room, or to attend confirmation class, the only coed religious school class, held on Saturday morning. Weekly dances were introduced for the first time, and a special dance party, called the Masquerade, was held on New Year's Eve for the older children. As might be expected, the dances were tame affairs, chaperoned by both deans and a squad of counselors. All insisted on an arm's length dancing hold that guaranteed at least "six inches of daylight" between partners. The rule had a noticeably dampening impact on romantic foxtrots that cried out for dreamy hugging and cheek-to-cheek closeness. The hallway outside the dining room developed into a public lover's lane after supper almost every night. No counselors were around because those who supervised supper had gone to eat their meal while those who had finished supper on the earlier shift did not return to the dining room area. Taking advantage of this momentary gap in supervision, boys and girls would linger together in the hallway, chat, and hold hands. Hand-holding was the only intimacy practiced, although some couples who sought privacy elsewhere often went much further.[2]

The meals served in the twenties would have been considered banquets by Simmonds's contemporaries. Salads appeared on dining room tables for the first time, though few children enjoyed them because they didn't fill the stomach. Rolls were transformed from "bricks" into long, crispy, tasty buns the boys tried to steal when the bakers left them out to cool. There was more variety in the meats, with liver and frankfurters being served almost every week. Everybody hated the liver, which was broiled or fried. No matter how it was cooked, it was hard to slice and even harder to chew. The frankfurters, though, were popular. The boys loved to wave them at the girls' tables and shout lewd remarks. Beverages, formerly restricted to coffee and cocoa, now included tea, cider (in season), orangeade, and punch, which everybody called cherry water. Several times a week desserts appeared on the menu, the favorite being apple and raisin pie at the Saturday lunch.

During the twenties the chef tried something new and exotic in desserts: Jell-O meringue pie. Although baked well, it apparently didn't catch on with the children. Whenever the pie was served, pieces of it were found all over the asylum that night—plastered on walls, hanging from ceilings, heaped in dark corners. Some unlucky children discovered blobs of it between the sheets at bedtime. Eventually, the chef got the message and Jell-O meringue pie vanished forever from the menu.[3]

In the thirties, the most popular meal was served on Friday nights and consisted of fried filet of sole, mashed potatoes, peas, cherry water, and cheese pie. Coming after the hour-long Friday night service, the first weekend meal was always greeted with an explosion of joy. Most of the expected pleasure from the meal was associated with the cheese pie, everybody's favorite dessert. On the boys' side it had the status of currency; bets were often made with cheese pie as the stake.

Although life in the HOA was still largely regimented, the children of the twenties and thirties had more leisure time than any previous generations. They were free two afternoons a week, about three-quarters of an hour after supper on weekday nights, Saturday afternoon and evening, and almost all of Sunday. During the summer school vacation, the children were kept busy with arts and crafts classes in the morning and sports and games in the afternoon and evening. It was an easy time for children and staff alike because about a third of the population was away at camp.[4]

To help the children use their free time as productively as possible the HOA provided them with an enormous variety of extracurricular activities—as much or more than any public or private high school could possibly offer. Almost any activity that could attract a membership was encouraged and supported. On April 1, 1919, three boys brought out a one-page edition of a new publication they called the *Rising Bell*, named for the first morning bell. Originally intended as a newsy and amusing bulletin, it developed within a few years into something bigger and more ambitious: a general-interest magazine with literary leanings that published short stories, essays, articles, and poems mixed with news, humor, drawings, cartoons, photographs, puzzles, and contests. It also became what one editor called "the mouth-piece of the children." Appearing irregularly, though mostly quarterly, its editions sometimes ran to fifty-four pages and it accepted advertising. The printing club produced it in the HOA's print shop.

In 1921, entering the Columbia Scholastic Press Association's annual contest for the first time, the *Rising Bell* won fourth place in the private school category. This was an enormous triumph since its rivals were such prep schools as Groton, Phillips, Andover, and Lawrenceville. The magazine's prospects for achieving even higher ratings improved perceptibly in the midtwenties when Mildred "Ma" Stember became its staff adviser. She had been promoted to librarian a few years earlier after serving since 1910 as the counselor of M-6, the youngest boys' dormitory. Under Ma Stember's guidance, the *Rising Bell* won the second place silver medallion for three consecutive years—1928, 1929, and 1930—competing in the vocational, technical, and trade school category this time. Finally, in 1932, the HOA won the first place gold medallion, a stunning victory. Two years later, the *Rising Bell* discontinued publication and was never revived except for a special souvenir issue that appeared in June 1941, a few months before the home closed.[5]

Around 1936 a mimeographed publication named the *Newman News* appeared. More gossipy than literary—it was Walter Winchell's heyday—the new three-page sheet had no staff adviser and no regular editor. In addition, the items and opinions it published frequently got it into hot water with the administration. Once an editor was publicly slapped in the face by the boys' dean in the dining room for what it had said about him in the latest issue.[6]

One of the first Boy Scout troops in the city was started in the HOA in 1919. First known as Troop 701, it later became Troop 705. There was also a nature club whose supply of specimens usually increased during the summer vacation, when the boys brought back turtles, snakes, frogs, toads, and insects captured at camp. A photography club, complete with its own darkroom, was started in the thirties.

Not all clubs operated in the open and had official approval. One that flourished briefly around 1920 was a secret group known as the

Skull and Bones. It chose the clock-tower room as its meeting place because it was the highest room in the HOA. Not an easy place to locate and reach, members had to be guided there through a maze of entrances, passages, and stairways. The final route lay up a wall ladder and through a hatch, which opened into a tall, narrow, and musty room. The clock stood in a small wooden hut in the room, which became visible only after a crawl around a huge tank. The first time the boys met there they found, to their chagrin, that the walls were covered with graffiti. They couldn't believe that others had been there first. After a counselor caught the boys on one of their climbs up to the room, the club was disbanded.[7]

Most of the extracurricular activity, though, was centered around music and athletics. Of the two, music was the most popular, at least in the twenties, when the HOA supported an enormous number of musical organizations. These included, apart from the band and field music, an orchestra, a glee club, and the synagogue choir. In addition, some of the most gifted children were receiving private piano and violin lessons. A clarinetist in the band, Sidney Kyle, won the first scholarship to the Juilliard Music School.[8]

The instructors for these organizations were all first-rate musicians. Carl Binhak, who taught the glee club and orchestra from 1904 to 1930, when he died, came from the Metropolitan Opera. Emil Reichardt, who led the band from 1908 to 1923, was also a Metropolitan Opera alumnus and taught a number of professional bands. Reichardt is said to have trained over seven hundred boys during his fifteen years at the HOA, including most of those who became regimental bandmasters in World War I. Leo Braun, choir instructor in the thirties, had been the Metropolitan's expert on Wagnerian opera in the early 1900s. He was also the voice teacher for a number of opera singers, including Jan Peerce.

When Reichardt retired in 1923, he was succeeded by James F. Knox, a professional bandmaster who had been born and trained in Scotland. A former member of John Phillip Sousa's band, Knox taught at least eleven other mens' and boys' bands in the metropolitan area. He took charge of the HOA band early in 1924, a year after Reichardt had left. In that interim, the band had lost so many of its older members that it had ceased to exist as a unit. Nor had there been any training during that interval. At the time Knox was engaged, however, the Guggenheims, who sponsored the Goldman Band Concerts in Central Park, announced the first annual boys' band contest, scheduled for June of that year. Edwin Franko Goldman was named to judge it.

The HOA decided to enter the contest even though it meant that Knox would have only three months to organize and train an entirely new band. He accepted the challenge and soon had the new players performing as well as their predecessors. But there was one curious aspect to his efforts—he was also training the HOA's chief rival, the Brooklyn HOA band. In fact, he had been training the BHOA boys before he was hired by the HOA. Now he had the two best boys' bands in the city and he was working hard with both for the same goal, which only one could hope to achieve. Did he personally favor one band over another? If he did, was this favoritism reflected in the way he trained each band? A taciturn Scot, Knox never revealed his feelings as he shuttled between the two HOAs.

At the contest, Goldman obviously had a hard time deciding which HOA deserved to be first. Both had performed extremely well and no other band had approached them in quality. Because he was himself an HOA graduate, the band expected him to be loyal to his alma mater. But Goldman, who may have anticipated charges of favoritism toward his old home, gave first place to the BHOA, second place to the HOA. The only spectator unaffected by the decision was Knox, who couldn't lose no matter who won. Contest protocol called for the instructor of every award-winning band to accept the prize for his unit. Up stepped Knox, smiling, to accept the trophy for the BHOA; a moment later, still smiling, he returned to the judge's table to accept the trophy for the HOA.

To the boys in the band, accustomed to winning, second place was a humiliating defeat. All that year and into 1925 they worked hard to make sure it wouldn't happen again. Knox, who continued training both bands, kept commuting regularly between the two rivals. In June, the contest went on again, and again it was a very tight decision. But now the results were reversed, with the HOA first and the BHOA second. As he had the previous year, Knox went up twice in succession to the judge's table. And he would go to the table frequently in the years that followed for the HOA band went on winning first place. When the silver loving cups began piling up, Simmonds had a large trophy case set up near the lobby to display them as well as other trophies won in athletics.[9]

Contests aside, the HOA band in the twenties was the busiest musical organization of its kind in the metropolitan area. Demand for its services accelerated during the decade, so that every weekend found them performing somewhere in the city. One frequent source of invitations was city hall, for the HOA band had become—unofficially, of course—the city's "official" band. Whenever there was a civic occasion that required music, the HOA band invariably provided it. Actually, this practice had started during the war, when the HOA had offered its band for use at patriotic occasions. After the war, the practice was continued since there were no municipal bands available for this purpose. So when Douglas Fairbanks and Mary Pickford returned from their honeymoon in Europe in 1923, the HOA band was on the pier to welcome them home. They also took part in the triumphal ticker-tape parade up Broadway in 1927 that honored Charles Lindbergh after his solo flight to Paris.

The most unusual engagement the band ever accepted involved them, unwittingly, in politics. In October 1928, a Catholic Church in Hoboken, New Jersey, invited the HOA band to participate in the city's Columbus Day parade. Upon arriving at the parade's starting point, the boys were surprised to find the BHOA band already there; indeed, the surprise was mutual. Naturally, questions were asked and the HOA boys learned that the same church had also invited the BHOA boys. Both groups were informed they would be marching as a single unit of 120 musicians. Even though the bands had never performed together, the prospect was hardly daunting since they had the same instructor.

As the joint HOA-BHOA band paraded through Hoboken, its members noticed that billboards along the route all contained the same message, "Vote for Al Smith." It was a presidential election year and Governor Al Smith of New York, a Democrat and the first Catholic ever to seek that office, was running against Herbert Hoover. Although the boys probably didn't know it, Hoboken was Irish and Catholic and overwhelmingly pro-Smith.

Another thing the bands noticed was that the parade seemed endless. Indeed it was turning out to be the longest parade either unit had ever been in. One problem this created was that all felt pressured by the need to relieve themselves. But none of the usual marching delays were long enough and none of the stopping points offered respectable cover. Finally, during one long pause, many broke ranks to unburden themselves behind a billboard. Returning to their places, they looked back at the billboard, which read "Vote for Hoover."

As they approached the viewing stands, outside police headquarters, the boys saw the mayor of Hoboken, the police and fire chiefs and—to their amazement—James F. Knox, their director. He had not been expected at the parade. Delighted by his presence, the boys deliberately delayed the parade by standing in place and playing three Sousa marches.

Some days later the two bands learned why they had been invited.

Unknown to them, Knox was also the director of the Hoboken Police Band, but he knew it couldn't perform at the level of either orphanage band. So he got the church to invite them both and had finagled it all without letting on to either orphanage.[10]

Not every band engagement involved parading; at least a third called for concertizing. At one time or another the band had performed on every radio station in the city. In 1929 Station WOR hired the band to give half-hour concerts on Saturday nights. Its announcer always made the boys swell with pride when he introduced them as "the best boys' band in the world."

Nor was the statement hyperbole. The training and experience HOA musicians received enabled them to step into well-paying band jobs shortly after their discharge. For example, Leonard Portnoy, once the best clarinet player in the city, was a member of the Hippodrome Orchestra, which happened to be led by another alumnus, Charles Stein. There were alumni musicians in the bands led by Ben Bernie, Meyer Davis, Paul Whiteman, and many less well known groups. One former band member conducted the National Farm School Band.[11]

In the midtwenties, however, a new kind of band appeared in the HOA that briefly threatened the popularity of the older one. It was a harmonica band, organized in 1924 by an alumnus named Charles Snow. He got the idea for it at the boys' camp that summer after noting the delighted response to his harmonica performances at campfire entertainments. That fall he obtained Simmonds's approval to organize a harmonica band. About thirty boys joined and were given one-octave Marine Band harmonicas donated by M. Hohner Co., a German firm that then produced the world's best harmonicas. Although none of the boys had had any previous training in music, they learned quickly under Snow's guidance. The sound of harmonicas was soon being heard all over the HOA as the boys practiced two nights a week as a group and privately, in the dormitories and anywhere else, when they had a spare moment. After a few months of intensive rehearsals the band was concert ready and began performing at various institutions and on the radio.

To Snow, however, these engagements were simply warm-ups for a bigger goal he had in mind: winning the annual Greater New York City Amateur Harmonica Band Contest on the Central Park Mall in May 1925. Since the Guggenheim boys' band contest would be held in June, Snow hoped his boys would bring home a victory first, as a prelude to a second triumph by the band. With that goal in mind, his harmonica players practiced hard all winter. Their efforts, besides improving their skill at ensemble playing, produced one unexpected result—some girls who heard them asked to form a harmonica band of their own. When Snow agreed to teach them, a group of eight girls started practicing together. But their interest was short-lived and they broke up within a few months.

In May, Snow's boys arrived in Central Park to find themselves in competition with four other groups. One of the judges was a young professional harmonica player, then appearing as a soloist in the Broadway musical *Sunny*, named Borrah Minnevitch. First place was won by a band from P.S. 61, in the Bronx, while the HOA placed second. In the soloist's contest, the HOA's best player, a boy named Louis Delin, came in fourth.[12]

The next year, when Snow learned that Minnevitch was to appear at a Sunday benefit at Carnegie Hall, he went there with a few HOA harmonica boys. Minnevitch gave a brief concert and then announced that he had a surprise for the audience. The curtains then parted to reveal about thirty boys seated on stage, all holding harmonicas. Dressed in semiformal clothes, like serious musicians, the group performed "Deep River." It received an ovation, leading to calls for an encore, a response that left Minnevitch both pleased and embarrassed. He was embarrassed because "Deep River" was the only selection they had rehearsed. Not long afterward Snow and some HOA boys, Delin among them, became friends with Minnevitch.

Convinced by his Carnegie Hall debut—the first harmonica band to perform there—that there was a place for a harmonica act in vaudeville, Minnevitch worked up some more numbers for his band and in 1927 got some bookings for it in the city. He called his thirty-two players the Symphonic Harmonica Ensemble—a pretentious billing the band tried to live up to by playing the classics. Minnevitch was apparently trying to do for the harmonica what Edwin Franko Goldman had done for brass: make it respectable for concert halls. But the effort failed—serious music bored vaudeville audiences—forcing Minnevitch to drop the act.

That same year, though, a publicity stunt at the HOA may have helped give him the idea for another kind of band. A *Daily News* photographer shot Louis Delin holding three small boys, one on each arm and the third straddling his shoulders. All were in World War I uniforms and all were playing harmonicas. Wire services picked up the picture and it appeared in hundreds of newspapers all over America. Its publication, in turn, stimulated a good deal of interest in harmonica playing among thousands of boys who found the handy little instrument irresistible. A few weeks later, Minnevitch visited the HOA, met Snow and Delin, and was introduced to some players.

Because of the harmonica's growing popularity, Snow in 1928 decided to go into vaudeville himself, forming a troupe that included many HOA boys. His act showed that he had learned a good deal from Minnevitch's previous failed attempt. Calling his boys the Broadway Pirates, Snow costumed them accordingly and gave them some shtick to perform between serious musical numbers. Booked by the Paramount circuit, the act opened in New York to good notices, and then went on a cross-country tour that lasted six months. As it happened, 1928 was to be the last great year of vaudeville, and the boys who toured with Snow now look back on it, their first experience in show business, as one of the happiest periods in their lives.

Snow's departure proved almost fatal for the HOA Harmonica Band, depriving it of its instructor and best players at one stroke. Before leaving, though, he managed to find a new instructor, Sam H. Perry, musical director for the Hohner Co. An Austrian, Perry was a pianist, composer, and member of the Royal Academy of Music in Vienna. Unfortunately for the band, he didn't stay long; that year he was named musical director of Universal Pictures and went to Hollywood. Nor did his successor Jimmy Smith, an HOA alumnus who had played cornet in the band—remain more than a few months at the job. When he left, no instructor could be found to lead the harmonica band and it soon fell apart.

Snow's Broadway Pirates disbanded after their national tour and many of them, including Snow himself, joined another new harmonica troupe called the New York Newsboys Harmonica Band, led by a player named Charles Bennington. Bennington's boys dressed in ragamuffin style, with caps, knickers, patched pants, bright striped shirts, and overalls. Their pay was ten dollars a week, a good salary at the time, especially for the HOA boys. Bennington's only competition in vaudeville was a new Borrah Minnevitch act known as the Harmonica Rascals. Its featured performer was midget-sized Johnny Puleo, whom Minnevitch chose for his comic talent. Two HOA alumni from the Snow troupe were invited to join it, Louis Delin and Ben Dansky. With Puleo as a comic foil for Minnevitch, supported by a lot of funny stage bits, the Rascals soon became the most popular harmonica act in show business in the thirties, and the only act of its kind to appear in the movies. In the midthirties, Minnevitch went into business for himself and became rich selling a line of harmonicas under his own name, publishing harmonica lessons, and promoting the growth of amateur harmonica bands. At the height of the harmonica craze almost every city in America had several bands.[13] It was the harmonica's golden age and it owed a large part of its success to the HOA boys who were among its first professional performers.

The twenties were also golden years for the HOA, a time when everything seemed to be going well. In 1925, for example, an HOA girl named Fannie Johannes Dubofsky won a free trip to France as a member of the Thomas Jefferson Pilgrimage. The pilgrimage was a feature of the Jefferson Centennial Commemoration, organized to raise $500,000 to buy Monticello from its private owner and convert it into a national monument. A Cornell University scholarship student, Fannie was one of 130 young women entered in a special voting contest. Contributors paid a dime for a vote, which they could then cast for their candidate. Fannie received 50,110 votes, placing her twenty-second on the winner's list. Almost all her votes came from HOA trustees, employees, and children, who scrounged up dimes wherever they could to support her.

On July 4th, Fannie and fifty-six other winners sailed from New York on a luxury liner, bound for Cherbourg. In Paris the group stayed at a first-class hotel one block from the Champs Elysees. The young women spent two weeks touring Paris and other cities. They were official guests of the French government at the Bastille Day ceremonies and were received the following day by the president of France. When the official tour ended, they returned to Paris to enjoy their final week as they wished. Fannie was back in the States on August 9. Before she left for Cornell in September, she wrote a three-page memoir for the *Rising Bell* titled "So This Is Paris!" In it, she thanked the board of trustees and Lionel J. Simmonds for sponsoring her candidacy and "all the boys and girls for their earnest efforts in putting me over the top."[14]

For the Seligman Solomon Society, the HOA's alumni organization, the twenties were its heyday. In 1922, its thirty-fifth anniversary year, it celebrated this milestone in a palace of status, prestige, and elegance that clearly proclaimed how far its members had come since their orphan days—the Waldorf-Astoria. And what had earlier been a simple dinner meeting with some speeches and a concert by the HOA band had now grown into the "Annual Entertainment and Ball." The format for the Waldorf-Astoria meetings seldom varied. Dinner was always a ten-course banquet, washed down with wine and champagne. When it ended, the entertainment began—a five- or six-act vaudeville show presented by first-rate performers from the Keith circuit. By custom, the HOA band opened the show with one or two concert pieces and the alma mater and closed it with a Sousa march and the "Star Spangled Banner." Dancing followed, with music provided by Solly Cohen and his Supreme Society Orchestra, who were simply HOA alumni.

The society's anniversary meetings were held at the Waldorf-Astoria for five years, from 1922 to 1926. In 1927, the event was moved to the Astor, another fine hotel but not comparable to the Waldorf-Astoria. Why the change was made is not known, though the meetings held at the Astor were scaled-down affairs with no professional entertainment and slimmer banquets, so presumably the annual galas had become too expensive. Although it would not be apparent for some years, the change, combined with a restrictive admissions policy toward new members, signaled the beginning of a slow, though consistent decline for the alumni organization.[15]

In the summer of 1927 some HOA children found themselves unexpectedly and happily performing in a movie. Harold Lloyd was working on *Speedy*, his last silent film and the only one he made in New York. He decided to shoot some scenes at the HOA. Where he got the idea is not known, but it might have come from Babe Ruth, who had been hired to do a cameo role—playing himself, of course. Having grown up in an orphanage, Ruth was always partial toward orphans wherever he played and it seems certain that he knew about the HOA. He was already a Yankee in the early 1920s, when the team considered buying the HOA site for its new stadium. He may even have visited the neighborhood to see what the team's proposed new home looked like.

How many scenes were shot in the HOA is not clear, though they appear only in the final reel. About twenty boys were used as extras in the movie and one of them, Sig Morgenstern, recalled getting an autographed baseball from Babe Ruth, as did many others. *Speedy* was released in 1928, but the movie was never shown in the HOA. Nor have any alumni reported having seen it, including those who were extras in it. Decades later, when he was chief film editor at the NBC Film Center, Sig Morgenstern got to meet Harold Lloyd again when he was a guest on the "Tonight Show."[16]

Of all the new ideas that were tried during Simmonds's first decade as superintendent, the most original was the Godmothers Association, organized in 1920. The idea behind it was that a child needed an adult friend outside his or her own family circle to discuss intimate concerns without fear of embarrassment or disapproval. No adults in the HOA were available to assume this role. Indeed, HOA children had no adults either in the asylum or outside to whom they could relate on a personal basis. Thus, they were likely to develop a distorted view of all adults, seeing them only as disciplinarians, teachers, or uninvolved workers. To correct this negative view, one member's wife, Regina Sternbach, developed the plan for the Godmothers Association, a society of clubs led by women who would take on the role of confidant for a small number of children. Every club was to have six to ten members, with one or two women as godmothers. The clubs were to meet once or twice a week in the home of one godmother and so give the children a taste of family life. Godmothers were expected to relate to their children on a double level. First, they were encouraged to form a trusting relationship with every child, if possible, and provide her or him with the acceptance, advice, comfort, and attention not possible at the HOA. And second, they were also seen as leaders who would use the club as a vehicle for introducing their children as a group to recreational activities with a cultural content. Sternbach also expected—or hoped—that the clubs would continue even after the children left the HOA.

But entrusting groups of emotionally deprived children to untrained, well-to-do, high-minded women could have led to problems, chiefly excessive benevolence. There was a feeling that the "Jewish mother" syndrome might prevail, causing the godmothers to overwhelm the children with food, presents, and smothering affection. To prevent the organization from turning into a "present-giving, stomach-filling, appetite-satisfying" caricature of its real purpose and to protect the children from the "effusiveness of quasi-amateur social workers," a number of rules were established, including limiting the size of clubs and stressing cultural activities. Godmothers also had to attend lectures in child care to further educate them. They could not be entrusted with the care of individual children, except in special cases, nor could they give presents to either children or their parents unless they obtained the superintendent's approval to do so.

Within a few weeks there were thirty-six girls' clubs, led by forty godmothers, with a total membership of 240. Each club's members were about the same age. Godmothers were soon escorting their clubs to museums, concert halls, art galleries, theaters, and parks. In the summer some clubs spent weekends in the home of their godmothers. The HOA did not have to wait long to learn what the girls thought of the new program. They loved it—that was obvious from the start. Godmothers who came to pick up their clubs in the main lobby were invariably greeted with shrieks of joy by members waiting impatiently for their arrival. For the girls, their godmothers were their link and guide to the outside world, a world they often knew less about than the boys, who, for various reasons, ventured outside more frequently.

The Godmothers Association proved to be one of the most successful ideas the HOA ever attempted. The most amazing thing about it, moreover, is that one of its clubs is still functioning, more than sixty-five years later. Named the Sunbeam Club, it was formed around 1922 or 1923 with eleven members and two godmothers. But the godmothers selected remained with the club for only a week and were replaced by one woman, Corinne Judson, whose husband, Abe, happily assumed the role of godfather.

In the twenties the Judsons lived close to the HOA, in Washington Heights. This made it easier for Corinne to collect her girls for their weekly meetings at her home. Actually, once the club got going, the Judsons allowed them to visit almost any night, so long as it didn't interfere with HOA routine. Because the Judsons always made them feel welcome, the girls visited frequently and stayed as long as they could. For all of them these visits were, as one club member described those days, "their first contact with a family in a warm and cozy atmosphere."

Corinne and Abe, who had no children of their own during their first years with the club, treated the HOA girls as if they were adopted daughters. Corinne took them on all sorts of trips—to the Statue of Liberty, to the Indian Museum nearby, to picnics in Long Beach. And there were always parties in the home, practically one a week. Every member's birthday was celebrated, every holiday, Jewish or otherwise, provided an excuse for festivities. At Halloween Corinne's brother, Ralph Newman, would come to the house to help string up the jellied apples and rig the games. A young bachelor, Ralph was a favorite of the girls and they all had a crush on him. "We would all have liked to marry him," one club member recalls.

The Judsons' interest in their girls was as devoted as those of real parents. Whenever one of them was involved in a special activity at the HOA, Corinne and Abe were there to see them. And both would turn up at the HOA if requested, to provide moral support for any member who needed it at some special event in her life. Even at the birth of their daughter, Corinne, the Judsons kept the club going.

With the girls' club doing well, Abe decided that a boys' club might be a good idea, too. He got the HOA to help him organize one but it didn't last long. The boys didn't seem to enjoy it as much as the girls did. After they were discharged, the boys dropped out of it.

But the girls stayed. To them, Corinne and Abe had been transformed from godparents to foster parents: the club and its sponsors had merged to become one extended family. Although the days of parties and outings were over for the club after its members were discharged, they never lost contact with the Judsons. So long as the girls remained in New York, the weekly meetings continued and the club sustained itself. Then, one by one, the girls left the city. In the process, most experienced misfortunes of one kind or another, and through it all, Corinne and Abe were always available for comfort, advice, and—most important of all—immediate and direct assistance. As one member put it, "they were endlessly faithful and always there when we needed them."

When one member got married, it was Corinne who gave her away. She provided a "beautiful wedding" for another member and also helped her get started in her career as a health and physical education teacher. And when the teacher had her first baby, it was Corinne who came to stay with her, buy the layette, and do the cooking.

By the fifties, there were only three club members left in the city; the rest had scattered throughout the United States. Still, the members never lost contact with the Judsons, though now letters and telephone calls sustained the relationship. No matter what happened to one of "their girls," the Judsons were always among the first to learn about it—and offer help if it was needed. As in the past, they never failed to remember the birthdays and anniversaries of their dispersed "family" members and even kept track of their children and grandchildren. If an out-of-town member came to the city for a visit, it usually led to a club meeting at the Judsons.

They moved to Miami Beach after Abe retired from business some years ago. It is now home base for the club, which has eight members left out of the original eleven. One of them lives near the Judsons, and she and her husband visit them frequently. They are also visited by the New York members and by one from as far away as California.

In the spring of 1976, four members were planning to spend the first Passover Seder night at the Judson home, but it was called off because Abe became seriously ill and had to be hospitalized. His illness sent a tremor of anxiety through all the club members, who learned about it by mail and telephone almost immediately. At the hospital, Abe was visited by members from New York and Florida and the get-well cards and messages flowed in from Sunbeam members everywhere.

Fortunately, Abe recovered and lived for another five years. He died in April 1981. Now Corinne alone has been leading the Sunbeam

Club.[17] By any standard, the extraordinary quality and longevity of the relationship that developed between the girls of the Sunbeam Club and the Judsons must be regarded as one of the most enduring successes ever produced by the HOA. It must also rank as one of the most heartwarming achievements in the history of child care in America.

Early in 1928 a new building began rising on the 138th Street side
of the HOA that would become the children's favorite facility: a
gymnasium. It was a gift from the Warner brothers, the motion picture producers who had revolutionized the industry the year before
by turning out the first talkie, *The Jazz Singer*. The gymnasium
was intended as a memorial to their two dead brothers, Milton and
Samuel, by the surviving three, Harry, Albert, and Jack. Although
Harry is said to have originated the idea for donating the building,
some sources credit the superintendent with having fed it to him.
According to the story, Harry was visiting Simmonds in his office
one day and asked him what the children needed to make their life
happier. Neither the visit nor the question was unusual. For years the
Warners, who were frequent visitors to the home, had been furnish-
ing it with free movies and a projectionist. Simmonds recommended
a gymnasium, so Harry got started on it at once.

The Warner Gymnasium, which cost $125,000, was dedicated on
September 30, 1928. Harry and Jack Warner were present for the ceremony, held inside the new building and attended by the children and
many guests. In gratitude for the gift, the HOA honored Harry with
its equivalent of knighthood—membership on the board of trustees.
The gym made the HOA equal to any high school or college with
its facilities for basketball, boxing, acrobatics, gymnastics, and body-
building. On the roof was a fenced-in tennis court. When not being
used for athletics, the gym served as an entertainment center, for it
had a large stage and could easily be converted into a theater, movie
house, or auditorium for meetings and dances. With a single philanthropic gesture, the Warner brothers had transformed the athletic,
social, cultural, and recreational life of the children.

The Warners' generosity didn't end with the gym. A few years later they started the practice of giving a gift to each child during Chanukah. Every child could choose the gift in advance from a list of such items as roller skates, Parker fountain pen, chromatic harmonica, chemical set, and crystal set, among others. Warner family children distributed the gifts in the trustees' room on the first night of Chanukah. Later that night, the home presented an entertainment, dedicated to the Warner family, called the Chanukah Show. Harry or Jack or sometimes both would attend the performance.[1] Their presence usually made the children in the show work harder, spurred by the fantasy that Harry or Jack might "discover" them and offer a Hollywood contract. It never happened.

The Warner Gymnasium helped bring about the apotheosis of athletics in the HOA. It was a process that started when Simmonds became superintendent. Under his administration, the HOA organized an athletics program that was as good as—in some ways, better than—that of any high school in the city. It sponsored varsity and junior varsity baseball, football, and basketball teams and provided all their members with uniforms. As in the past, the HOA continued playing other orphanage teams, but they acquired such a reputation that high schools all over the city were eager to play them. Since HOA teams had no official standing, high schools competed against them chiefly for the practice it provided. Visiting baseball and football teams got a stiff workout during these games. The worst part was getting used to the playing field, which was grassless, gravelly, and level only in patches. But HOA boys had been using it for half a century and were inured to its rocky hazards.

In some instances, visiting high school teams had HOA varsity players on their rosters. This proved awkward for the boys involved. Which alma mater would they play for? In the midtwenties, one star HOA basketball player, John Karetsky, resolved the problem with Solomonic judgment: he played the first half with the HOA team and the second half with his high school team.[2]

The passion for athletics in the twenties reflected the national obsession with it outside the HOA's gates. New heroes were being created in the arenas and stadiums of America and some of them, particularly in boxing, were Jewish. And the HOA would acquire its own ring hero a year before the Warner Gym was built. On December 16, 1927, Izzy Schwartz, who had been in the HOA from 1911 to 1917, won the flyweight championship of the world by defeating Newsboy Brown in fifteen rounds in Madison Square Garden. No one who knew Schwartz as a boy could have predicted such a triumph, for he had seldom boxed while in the HOA. After his discharge he enlisted in the army, where an incident occurred that changed his life: he struck a fellow soldier who had made an anti-Semitic remark. As punishment, his company commander ordered him to enter a boxing tourney on the post. To his surprise and the company's as well, he won the bout even though he had had no previous boxing experience. He fought regularly after that, became an amateur boxer when his enlistment expired, and turned professional in 1922. In the next five years he fought over a hundred bouts and won almost all of them.[3] Schwartz became a familiar figure on the boys' side during those years, for he sometimes trained in the old basement gym and at Camp Wakitan. The day he visited the HOA after his victory over Newsboy Brown he was idolized as a conquering hero. Although he lost the title the next year and retired from boxing, he remained a hero to the HOA for years afterward. Influenced partly by his example, a number of boys went into boxing in the thirties but none achieved Schwartz's success. One HOA alumnus, however, has acquired stature in the boxing world in a related field. Hank Kaplan became the official historian for the Veteran Boxers Association. Now living in Miami, Kaplan is regarded as one of the world's leading authorities on the history of the sport.

For the HOA, the biggest athletic event of the year was its annual Thanksgiving Day football game with the Brooklyn HOA. The BHOA was the HOA's chief rival in sports, music, and almost everything else. Though smaller than its Manhattan peer, the Brooklyn home invariably produced teams that were hard to beat. Both sides viewed the annual football game, played in Lewisohn Stadium opposite the HOA, as the most important athletic contest in the world. The night before the game both asylums held rallies. After the turkey dinner, the entire HOA would cross Amsterdam Avenue en masse and sit in the stadium. At about the same time, a large contingent of BHOA children would arrive and take up seats on the right side of the field. Both sides greeted each other with a loud, prolonged outburst of boos, whistles, and obscene epithets.

During the game cheerleaders for each side whipped up their respective supporters. Sometimes the HOA band paraded before the game and during the halves. And the game itself was always a grueling one, as if both sides felt an obligation to be as tough as possible. At times, fights would break out between players on the field or between spectators in the stands. When the game ended, the winning side often tore down the goal posts. Although the HOA usually won, the winning margin was frequently low because the Brooklyn boys were never a pushover. One team that was always easy to beat, though, was Pleasantville, which the HOA also played in Lewisohn Stadium. Pleasantville produced weak football teams, and the HOA would show its disdain for them by sending in its second-string players.

Some alumni today view the heavy emphasis on athletics under Simmonds as having had a hidden motive—to exhaust the boys and take their minds off the girls. This seems unlikely. Simmonds probably went along with it for a number of good reasons, the most important being that it was a healthy way to keep the boys out of mischief. Maybe he had never forgotten the old days when the boys had to make their own baseballs and bats and wanted to change all that forever. Whatever the reason, the HOA certainly looked more like "The Academy" when the playing field was filled with boys batting and catching balls.

Apart from its effect on HOA athletics, the Warner Gym also helped to improve life in the neighborhood. Indeed, it functioned as the community's unofficial social and athletic center because the HOA allowed outside groups to use it. Children from a nearby orphanage, the Sheltering Arms, were permitted to see the Friday night movie. This was the second movie of the week, intended for the older children; it was always an adult film that had ended its first run of the neighborhood houses. The first movie, shown on Wednesday night, was always a cowboy feature for the younger children. On both nights, however, some neighborhood children would sneak into the gym after the lights went out, stand near the doors while they watched the movie, and quietly leave when it ended, before the lights went on. Obviously HOA school friends had told them about the weekly movies. Admission to neighborhood theaters was ten or fifteen cents so many families during the depression could not afford it. And so, ironically, their children were seeing movies free in an orphanage. In the midthirties, *Treasure Island* was previewed in the gym, to get the reaction of HOA children. They loved it, but they were easy to please, so their response didn't carry much weight. As the children left the gym, they were rewarded with pirate "treasure"—chocolate doubloons dispensed by men in pirate costume.

By far the biggest group that benefitted from the HOA's good neighbor policy was the Roman Catholic Church of the Annunciation, about eight blocks south of the HOA. As a church history published in 1939 noted, "The parish uses the auditorium of the Hebrew Orphan Asylum as a gym and a hall for dancing. This goes to prove the unity that exists in this parish and the spirit of comradeship that is present . . . among the people of different religious beliefs. Because of this cooperation among the neighbors, Manhattanville is a better and finer place in which to live."[4] In a way it could be said that the HOA was repaying the parish for the consideration they had shown decades earlier when the asylum had decided to establish itself in their midst. The land on which the HOA stood was bought from two parish members, John and Daniel Devlin. Many workers in the HOA were Irish people who lived in the neighborhood and their loyalty to the home was often equal to that of most alumni. Irish children frequently came to play in the HOA after school; its gym and field were the only facilities of their kind available in the area.

Despite the good times the gymnasium brought, the lives of the HOA children were still not completely happy. Though Simmonds had removed the statue of Dr. Baar from the main lobby, there was still a lot of Baar in Simmonds that would never be extinguished. Corporal punishment in all of its variations, plus some new ones, was still practiced in the dormitories. And even though Simmonds had provided more counselors for the children, he did not abolish the monitorial system. It was an obvious step, clearly consistent with all the reforms he had introduced, yet he never took it. Simmonds himself often dealt out corporal punishment—perhaps the first superintendent since the pre-Baar days to do so.

Many alumni suggest that he was far gentler in the twenties than he was in the thirties, when he was often brutal. But he seldom beat anyone in cold blood; he had to work himself up into a temper before he started swinging. One alumnus recalls him beating "the living daylight out of an older boy" in the synagogue. To him, it was the "most brutal beating I had ever witnessed and it is undoubtedly my most vivid experience of the HOA."[5] The synagogue was Simmonds's favorite choice for public beatings and he used it chiefly when some particularly outrageous piece of mischief infuriated him. He would then assemble the children to make an example of the guilty ones. Such an incident occurred on a Saturday afternoon in the thirties, when four boys were lined up on the altar of the synagogue. They had been caught stealing stamps from a neighborhood coin and stamp store. Simmonds began his demonstration by working up his anger to the boiling point. He referred to the boys sarcastically as the "four must-get-theirs," a pun he seemed to enjoy and repeated many times. Then he proceeded to beat each boy in turn until he began to cry. The second and third boys caught on quickly and were crying after the first few blows. But the fourth was stubborn; he took the hardest slaps Simmonds could deliver and yet wouldn't cry. It became a contest of wills, with Simmonds swinging hard roundhouse blows to the boy's face, making it turn a deep red. But he refused to cry. Finally, Simmonds had to stop; he was breathing hard, exhausted, arm-weary. He dismissed the children. As they filed out they saw three boys on the altar sniffling while the fourth, whose face had become puffy, was still dry-eyed and determined.[6]

Ironically, the various relaxations in discipline introduced by Adler, Coffee, and Lowenstein had generated a need for new controls to maintain obedience. It had been easy to shout commands during Baar's regime because the children were always silent. When they were permitted to be as noisy as they liked, however, getting them to shut up so that they could hear commands became a problem. Early in Lowenstein's administration someone invented the great silencer, the cry of *"All Still."* When shouted by a counselor or monitor, every child in the dormitory was expected to stop moving and talking at once—in short, freeze like a human statue. Anyone who disobeyed was punished on the spot. But the cry sometimes couldn't be heard, especially in a noisy dormitory. Usually bawled out in barracks-room style, it sounded like *"Awwll Steeeeel!"* Inevitably some didn't hear it and were beaten as a result.

Nor had punishments changed, either in kind or degree. Group punishment still prevailed. If boys who talked after lights out didn't own up to it—no one ever did and no one ever snitched on the guilty ones—an entire dormitory might be ordered out of bed for a "standing lesson" called by a monitor or counselor. Such lessons usually lasted an hour, sometimes more. One ingenious variation required everybody to stand holding their pillow in their hands. If any one's arms drooped or if they dropped the pillow, they were beaten. The girls had standing lessons, too, which were seldom held longer than half an hour, sometimes required them to hold their hands on their heads, and only occasionally involved holding a pillow.

Beatings also inspired creative variations. For example, one counselor who was an alumnus and a college student held weekly paddling sessions on Thursday night. Boys singled for punishment were called up, ordered to "assume the angle" over a bed in the monitors' alcove, and solidly whacked across the buttocks with a fraternity paddle. The number of strokes varied with the infraction involved. It always made a great night's entertainment for the entire dormitory. Whether it improved discipline is questionable. One practice some male monitors favored was to order the entire dormitory to form a line so that each boy could be slapped in turn. Quite often the first boy slapped was slapped again accidentally when he reappeared at the head of the line and wasn't recognized by the monitor. When that happened, he would usually tell the boy, "That's one for next time."[7]

Since no published rules existed, monitors and counselors were free to make up their own and the punishments that went with them. No controls were ever kept on who was being punished, for what offense and for how long. One female graduate always remembered, for example, the Saturday afternoon she spent in a locked classroom because her counselor caught her making a banana sandwich at lunch. The banana sandwich was an HOA invention apparently conceived by some hungry child who presumably wanted to make two dry slices of bread more palatable. Boys made them regularly whenever bananas were served for dessert and were never punished for it. At Passover they made sandwiches out of anything they could place between two matzos.

Counselors in the twenties and thirties were almost evenly divided between HOA alumni and outsiders. Male counselors were mostly students, many of them athletes, who were regarded as more suitable models for the boys. They were generally younger and seldom stayed as long as the female counselors, who were older and often made a career of their jobs. Among the outsiders hired as counselors in the twenties were three college students who would later become famous. One was J. Edward Bromberg, then attending City College. Alumni recall that he had "a genuine interest" in the boys, and one remembered having had "lots of fun together" with him.[8] After graduating, Bromberg left the HOA and became a well-known actor on Broadway and in Hollywood in the thirties and forties. But his leftist views caused him to be blacklisted during the fifties and he died a broken man. Another outsider, and one of the few gentiles hired, was Francis Steegmuller. A Columbia graduate student in literature at the time, Steegmuller worked in the HOA during the summer of 1927. He took the job to earn the money to pay the fees toward his master's degree. That fall, a few months after he left the HOA, his first biography, *O Rare Ben Johnson,* was published under the pseudonym of Byron Steel. Steegmuller has since established a reputation as one of the most gifted biographers in America. In 1971 he won the National Book Award for his biography of Jean Cocteau.[9]

One outsider who worked as a camp counselor in the late twenties and early thirties was a tall, gravelly voiced Syracuse University student whose full name was Sheldon Leonard Bershad but whom everybody called Lenny. Unlike Bromberg, whom he knew, Lenny hadn't intended to become an actor. But he fell into a stage career by chance and did surprisingly well at it in the late thirties, playing mostly gangster roles on Broadway and later in Hollywood. The stage name he chose was Sheldon Leonard. In the sixties, he became the most successful television producer in the industry. Among the many shows he produced was "I Spy," which helped launch Bill Cosby's career.

None of the outsiders, though, produced as much excitement in the twenties as a former British Army officer named Major Bruce May. There had never been nor would there ever be another counselor like him in the history of the HOA. Of average height, slim build, with a thin face and a pencil-line moustache, the major was very British, very very military. He never relaxed his military bearing, as if he were always on the parade ground. Rumor had it that he charmed a trustee during a transatlantic voyage (he was clever at presenting amateur theatricals) who interceded with Simmonds to get him the job. An Anglophile, Simmonds was apparently delighted to have such a dashing representative of British culture available on the premises.

Major May's assignment varied a bit from that of the other counselors. He was in charge of after-school gym activities and drilled the cadets when their regular instructor was away. At drill he was the epitome of British military style: he wore an officer's uniform, cavalry boots, and carried a swagger stick. His orders were delivered in clipped British cadence, not always understood by the cadets. One expression he used invariably produced snickers among the boys— calling the courtyard the "quadrangle."

When he had been the in the HOA about a year or so, some band instruments disappeared from the band room. It was assumed that a boy was responsible. Major May created an uproar when he accused an alumnus who frequently visited the HOA of having stolen them. He even claimed that he had caught the boy at it and chased him— a story the boy vehemently denied. Then one day Major May and all the remaining band instruments disappeared simultaneously. It was now clear that the major was the thief. In the next few weeks a good deal more was learned about the "major." He had never been an officer but was an enlisted man. And his name was probably an alias. It was assumed that he had stolen the instruments to pawn them for passage money back to England. At any rate, no one ever saw or heard of him again.

Yet the mystery of "Major May" and the stolen instruments still intrigues alumni from the twenties. As late as 1975, one twenties' alumnus who had gone to England wrote back to an HOA friend, "Again working with Scotland Yard trying to solve the mystery of 'Major' May and the disappearance of the band instruments." He has become an HOA legend.[10]

The twenties were probably the happiest years for the children since the HOA opened, a decade when the outside world did not appear threatening because of war or depression. Life inside was also the freest it had ever been. Admissions had been declining as prosperity eased the poverty in many Jewish households. That prosperity had affected the HOA, for the boys were given suits with Norfolk jackets and long pants, which they dressed up with white shirts and bow ties; the girls looked similarly fashionable in long, stylish dresses. No orphanage children in America wore the kind of clothes they had and none enjoyed the middle-class life they led. Nor would it all end with the crash of 1929.

The Great Depression of the thirties had an immediate impact on the HOA: its population rose alarmingly. From 1,410 in 1930 it went to 1,635 in 1931 and to 1,800 in 1932, the year Franklin D. Roosevelt was elected president. The 1,800, which included boarding-out children, was the highest figure in the HOA's history. Of this number, 63 percent had both parents, 33 percent had one parent, and only 4 percent were full orphans. The reasons for the growth in admissions, according to a *Times* story on the HOA published on March 21 that year, were the same as those which filled children's institutions all over the nation: mental deterioration or collapse on the part of breadwinners, desertions, breakdown in family morale caused by economic conditions, parental disinterest, and neglect or improper guardianship. In New York City as elsewhere family life was disintegrating rapidly, with the children as the chief victims. Thousands of them, in fact, were already flocking to New York City and roaming its streets. Most were youths from sixteen to twenty years old—a new generation of street arabs.

President Roosevelt's administration would enact within a few years the social legislation that foreshadowed the end of all orphanages in America. Part of that legislation would be included in the Social Security Act of 1935 and its various public assistance titles, particularly the Aid to Dependent Children program. But their impact on children's institutions would not be felt for a number of years. One event of that first momentous year of 1933, however, made Roosevelt a household word in the HOA. In August Eleanor Roosevelt, for reasons known only to her, visited the HOA's girls camp, Wehaha. While there, she awarded the letter *N*, for proficiency in nature, to Jennie Glazer, who was eighteen. Both were photographed and the picture appeared in the *Times* and many other newspapers.[11]

The HOA grew so crowded during the early thirties that many more children had to be boarded out, including a six-year-old boy named Arthur Buchwald. Buchwald was a half orphan; his mother had died when he was six. Unable to care for the family, his father placed him in one home after another, and eventually, Buchwald and his three older sisters wound up in the HOA. His first view of the big red stone building on Amsterdam Avenue did not impress him favorably. The asylum, he recalled decades afterward, "for all its glory did not look like the Fontainebleu. The architecture, if my memory serves me right, was early Sing Sing."

Buchwald and his sisters stayed in the Reception House for six weeks. Then the family was split: his sisters went to the main building and he was boarded out. For the next eleven years he lived in three different foster homes in Queens. He never visited the HOA itself except to receive medical care or clothing, but he did go to camp every summer, where he lived with HOA boys for about a month. Though pleasant, camp had its perils. "My nose used to bleed a lot because HOA kids didn't like the foster home boys." Two boys from his Hollis neighborhood spent their summers at an adjacent camp, but they didn't know he came from the HOA; he lived in "deathly fear" of being discovered by them in a chance encounter. "I spent half my summers ducking behind trees, and hiding in the bottom of canoes, so my terrible secret wouldn't be found out."

Buchwald was never officially discharged from the HOA. Nor did he finish high school. In October 1942, when he was seventeen, he ran away from his last foster home and enlisted in the Marines. After the war he attended college, went to Paris, where he became a columnist for the *Paris Herald*, and continued his career as a syndicated columnist in the United States when the *Herald-Tribune* closed. He is a member of the HOA Association, the alumni group, and has helped them in various ways. On April 16, 1972, when the Jewish Child Care Association, the HOA's successor agency, held its sesquicentennial celebration, Buchwald was the guest of honor. Only then did he get to see a picture of himself taken by another HOA boy at Camp Wakitan in August 1938. It shows him standing at the edge of the diving board, a slender muscular boy smiling faintly at the camera.[12]

At the celebration, Buchwald jokingly told how, as a "confused, lonely and terribly insecure" foster child of seven, he made the decision to "become a humorist." What he meant was that humor had become a strategy of survival for him, a defense against the awesome authority of the adult world. His views seem to support the popular theory that an unhappy childhood is often the stepping stone to a career in comedy. The HOA, after all, produced two great humorists, Julius Tannen and Art Buchwald. Art was awarded the 1981 Pulitzer Prize for political commentary, an honor that was long overdue.

Buchwald's fear of being unmasked as an orphanage boy was common among all HOA children, and presumably all orphanage children anywhere as well. Even though they no longer wore a uniform that clearly defined their status, they still feared the humiliation that could come with accidental discovery of their "terrible secret." HOA children attending J.H.S. 43 on 129th Street and Amsterdam Avenue couldn't conceal it and didn't try to. Those in high school were generally more successful at it. If two or more went to the same high school, they could talk about their home openly without arousing curiosity by referring to it as the "Academy" or the "HOA." But in the thirties, the boys became even more laconic and reduced the code name to its ultimate brevity: the "H." No eavesdropper could possibly guess what *"H"* alone stood for. On the other hand, it probably aroused an inordinate curiosity as to what it meant.

What HOA children hated most was to be found out by their institutional peers, the children of other asylums. If an HOA child could spot another asylum child first—or vice versa—the discoverer could make the discovered feel inferior. As a rule, though, HOA children met other orphanage children only on various "Orphans Day" outings arranged for them by charitable organizations. It was on one such excursion, in fact, that an HOA boy finessed another orphanage boy by a spontaneous turn of phrase that converted a potential put-down into a moment of pure triumph. The incident occurred during the summer, when a large group of HOA boys shared a Hudson Day Liner cruise to Indian Point with hundreds of other orphanage children. All were guests on an annual Orphans Day Outing. The HOA boys wore their usual summer outfit, red jerseys bearing the initials HOA, and khaki shorts, called "flappers." During the cruise, another orphanage boy approached an HOA boy and asked him what the initials on his jersey stood for. It was the dreaded question. For a long, dead moment the HOA boy said nothing, not knowing how to answer. He wasn't afraid of "Hebrew" but he would not admit to "Orphan Asylum." Then inspiration struck. Putting words together carefully, he replied, "Hudson Outdoor Association." "Oh," said the other boy and walked away. But the brief meeting had been overheard by some HOA friends and they quickly spread the new phrase around when they got back to the asylum. By bedtime that night, it was being repeated everywhere. A great new euphemism had been coined. From then on "Hudson Outdoor Association" became the standard cover-up for "Hebrew Orphan Asylum."[13]

Apart from a huge increase in admissions, the depression produced few changes in the HOA. One early casualty was the cadet corps, which was abolished in 1931. Its termination probably owed less to the depression than to other causes—the biggest, perhaps, being the antiwar movement of the late twenties. Militarism of any kind became very unpopular then, and the cadets suffered from the general low esteem in which martial organizations were regarded. Cadet exhibitions had gone out of style and the cadets themselves were in demand only for patriotic parades. The HOA was pleased to see the corps go because it saved the expenses of an instructor, uniforms, and military hardware. Nor did the boys object to its demise; most of them hated the drilling anyway. And so, after sixty-five years, the cadet corps, another of Dr. Baar's cherished projects, became a victim of history. The blue banner won by the cadets at the Washington Centennial Parade of 1889 still hung from a dining room wall, but it meant nothing to the children of the twenties and thirties.

Some of the clubs started in the twenties—the orchestra and glee club, for example—were eliminated to save money. The boys' Norfolk jackets were replaced by less elegant double-breasted suits and the girls' long dresses by more prosaic fashions. On the whole, though, the losses were minor, for the HOA continued to keep Edenwald, its two summer camps, and its two after-care facilities. Moreover, with the advent of the Works Progress Administration, a lot of activities were reinstated, paid for now by the federal government. At the HOA's request, the WPA provided the children with arts and crafts teachers, athletic instructors, and concert artists who performed twice a month in the synagogue. In 1939, a WPA artist began painting a mural on the walls of the main entrance lobby. In the summer, the WPA Caravan Theatre, housed in a trailer, gave performances on the field at night to which neighborhood people were invited. Because of its many contributions, the WPA became a potent cultural force in the lives of HOA children.

It was in the thirties also that ominous world events began to intrude on the children's relatively sheltered existence. Eight HOA alumni joined the Abraham Lincoln Brigade, went to Spain, and fought for the Loyalist government in the Spanish Civil War. A few were captured and imprisoned by General Franco's forces. In response to a request by the mother of one prisoner, Leo Grachow, Simmonds attempted to enlist the help of Secretary of State Cordell Hull. When he had proof that six alumni had died, Simmonds told the children about their deaths during an emotional Saturday service. One alumnus, Arch Kessner, was the last American to die in the Spanish Civil War, according to the Abraham Lincoln Brigade. Ironically, he was killed the day before American volunteers were scheduled to be evacuated.[14] The six are still buried in Spain, though no one knows where.

Hitler's rise to power in 1933 created a new group of children in need. In 1940 the HOA began accepting German Jewish children for admission. Most would never again see the parents they had left behind in Germany.

The depression was, in general, a period of retrenchment rather than innovation for the home. By 1936 it was caring for nearly twenty-five hundred children, about one thousand in the main building and in Edenwald and fifteen hundred in foster homes. With so many needing just the basic necessities, it might have seemed far-fetched to pursue the ideal of individualizing all of them. Yet the HOA tried to do it as best it could. An attempt was made, for example, to give the children a semblance of self-government with the formation of the Academy Council, a body of boys and girls who met with the deans to suggest ideas for improving the life of the children. No major changes came about through their efforts, yet their presence was a step in the right direction. More casework was tried with the children and their parents, reflecting the professional approach then becoming dominant in the HOA. And despite the general shortage of funds, Simmonds found the means to provide spending money for deserving children. Allowances of up to five dollars a month were given to boys and girls who had a perfect grade point average in high school and a similar amount went to those who were captains of various groups, activities, or facilities, such as the band, drum corps, library, choir, dormitories, tailor and shoe shops, and the dean's office. In handling these duties, the boys were acquiring work experience and a sense of responsibility. It was also leadership training that would prove invaluable after their discharge.

The generation of children that grew up during the depression years was clearly different in many respects from its predecessors. Most of them had parents, so they didn't see the HOA as the only refuge from the streets, as previous residents had. In some cases, single working parents paid the HOA to board their children because they were unable to care for them. A few orphans were left with estates that paid for part or all of their keep.

No matter what caused them to be placed in the HOA, the children of the thirties were likely to view it as a benevolent prison, relieved only by the three weeks spent at camp every summer. To many, those three glorious weeks redeemed the other eleven months in the HOA. No day in their lives was more exciting than the day they left for camp. Although it meant five hours of travel—taking the subway to a downtown Manhattan dock, crossing the Hudson by ferry, a train ride afterward, a three-mile hike over a hilly path known as the Indian Trail and, finally, ending with a rowboat ride across a lake—nobody complained. Camp was the great escape, a place where no one yelled "All Still," bugle calls replaced bells, and there were no monitors on your back. Of course, there were rules to follow but no one punished you if you ignored them. Camp was only for swimming, boating, canoeing, sunbathing, baseball, basketball, overnight hikes, sitting around a campfire listening to a horror story, pancakes on Sunday morning, hearing a real Indian sing tribal songs, becoming aware of how bright the stars shone at night. Returning to the HOA from camp was the lowest point of the year, especially after everyone heard the first "All Still."

The chief reason camp was such an exciting experience was that it was run by an exceptional leader named Murray Sprung. An outsider and a former HOA counselor, his goal was to make camping a progressive, democratic, and educational holiday from the HOA. In pursuing that goal he was innovative, hiring Indians from upstate New York reservations as counselors and arranging four-day canoe and kayak trips up the Hudson River. Monitors had no power in camp and corporal punishment was forbidden. Sprung himself never struck anyone. In addition, he proved to be a spellbinding storyteller at campfires. Understandably, he acquired the honored nickname "Pop" because of his warm, fatherly way with children. Today, because alumni remember camp as the happiest experience of their childhood, "Pop" Sprung has become the most revered and beloved figure from their past. He has been frequently honored at testimonial dinners, and in 1987 he was elected president of the alumni association.

The depression children were probably more rebellious than previous generations. In the thirties, fights between older boys and younger counselors broke out from time to time—something inconceivable in earlier administrations. One counselor was beaten in a fight with a boy and lost face so completely that he was never the same. Even the deans were publicly defied on certain occasions. More boys were willing to take chances in committing such high sins as smoking and gambling, and almost everyone would leave the HOA without permission fairly regularly.

There were more runaways than ever. Many had only a vague idea of where they were going and why they were doing it. They saved a few dollars to take with them and carried even fewer belongings. Most seemed to head for New Jersey, where an alert policeman would spot them, learn they were runaways, and call the HOA. At that point the home's private detective would be sent to bring them back. Punishment usually followed. The most unusual "runaways" in the thirties were two boys who never left the HOA. They climbed up a ladder into a crawl space and stayed in it for three days. Friends who knew they were there brought them food and water. During meal-times and late at night they would descend and use the toilet. Their absence made the HOA frantic because no one knew where they had gone. When they finally came down from their roost, they were marched to Simmonds's office. Their punishment: baldy haircuts. Considering the trouble they had caused, it was relatively mild.

Despite the anti-authority mood of the thirties, the HOA didn't collapse, or even come near it. The rebels were always a minority; most children were obedient. Still, it was during those years that the last official attempt to abolish corporal punishment was made—an attempt that was doomed, ironically by the children themselves.

Merger at Last   15

The new boys' dean, Dr. Moses Chaim Shelesnyak, was introduced by Simmonds himself at a special night meeting held in the synagogue. Many children knew him because he had been working in the HOA for a year on a study sponsored by a Rockefeller Foundation Fellowship. The study dealt with "adjustment during adolescence" and represented "an attempt to correlate emotional adjustments, growth in general, and cardiovascular stability." Dr. Shelesnyak did most of his work at Columbia University, where he had earned his doctorate in endocrine and reproductive physiology. In addition, Simmonds let him use a small room in the HOA as a laboratory. Although he was falling behind in the project, he still felt he could manage the new job and continue working on the project—a judgment he would later regret.[1]

Such a direct study of the children was unusual; most studies were based on their case records. The children of the HOA were probably the most studied group of children in the United States. Scientists and scholars came to evaluate their intelligence, physical condition, emotional stability, and sexual maturity. Simmonds usually gave the researchers access to the records, provided their confidentiality was observed. In the twenties, studies made by a Jewish research agency of the HOA and other Jewish asylums in the city suggested that institutional care was superior to foster home care. Columbia University tested the manual dexterity of stutterers in the early thirties. A study made of 250 HOA girls in 1934 found that they matured faster than girls elsewhere, though they could not explain it.

At the meeting the new dean—who preferred to be called Doc Shelly—made an electrifying speech. He planned to abolish corporal punishment and eliminate a lot of the regimentation as well. Persuasion and discussion were to take the place of force and he asked the boys' counselors to cooperate with him. Though he said nothing about abolishing the monitorial system, he still launched the last great experiment in discipline at the HOA.

There was something paradoxical about Simmonds sponsoring a scientist with no experience in administration, education, or social work as the person to introduce a system of rational discipline. Still, Simmonds agreed to it because he apparently liked Doc Shelly's ideas on child care, which were similar to those of Maurice Bernstein, the assistant superintendent and an HOA graduate himself. Bernstein, who had gone to college and social work school after leaving the home, had returned to become a counselor and then Simmonds's assistant. He was the only professional member of the staff and strongly opposed to the HOA's archaic disciplinary system. Like many thinkers of his generation, he believed in self-discipline rather than imposed discipline. Doc Shelly held the same ideas, though as a scholar and a scientist he had never been involved in the care of children.

Under Doc Shelly a period of permissiveness lasting almost two years was to reign on the boys' side. Boys could leave the building almost anytime without permission. Older boys were allowed to go out after the Friday night movie to have a snack. Corporal punishment declined a good deal, although it didn't disappear entirely. Some monitors and counselors practiced it now and then, but Doc Shelly never heard about it because of the tradition against complaining. Despite the looser discipline, the boys' side didn't collapse in anarchy, as many boys and counselors thought it would.

In the first few months Doc Shelly was tested a good deal. The reaction to his pronouncement had been mixed—the younger boys joyful, the older ones skeptical, even contemptuous. He was going to "use psychology on us," many noted sneeringly. Everybody agreed with his ideas in principle, though few thought they would work in practice. As a result, he met with a great deal of resistance, particularly from the monitors and counselors, whose absolute authority had been abolished.

Doc Shelly himself was generally well liked. A slender man of average height, he wore glasses, and talked quietly, rarely raising his voice. His manner was professorial rather than authoritative. What came across in his talks with the boys was a genuine concern with their needs, a feeling of compassion, a humane outlook. The younger boys flocked to him wherever he appeared and seldom tested him. The older boys, though, saw him as soft and weak, an academic who had no business being dean. Now and then, they would openly insult him, hoping he would lose his temper. For a long time he reacted coolly to this behavior. Then, one day, when an older boy became insolent, Doc Shelly lost his temper and slapped him. Within moments the news was flashed around the HOA. The implication was that he was really "like everyone else," that his anti-corporal punishment stance was just a pose. Actually, it was an isolated incident, which he seems to have deeply regretted afterward. He never did it again. Still, the boys were influencing him, and it occasionally cropped up in the language he used. Once, finding a washroom very dirty, he blurted out, "This place looks like a shithouse!" Coming from him, the obscenity was startling. That remark, too, flew around the HOA.[2]

Doc Shelly never punished anyone in the old, established style. One alumnus, who recalled him with a good deal of affection as "the only person on the entire staff whose first interest was his job," had an encounter with him that he never forgot. One Friday night after the movie he and a few other boys had gone out to have a snack. They also bought cigarettes and began smoking them on the way back to the HOA. Unexpectedly, they ran into Doc Shelly. They promptly threw their butts into the gutter—but not soon enough. Doc Shelly took them all up to his room.

None knew what to expect. Smoking cigarettes had always been one of the major sins in the HOA, second only to stealing, with gambling third. Those who smoked did so in out-of-the-way places, like the basement toilets. Anyone caught at it was subjected to severe punishment, usually beatings followed by restrictive penalties. But Doc Shelly just talked to them. First, he asked them how much money they had. Then he pointed out that they were spending at least half their meager allowances on cigarettes. Furthermore, cigarettes were not acceptable socially at their age and could probably harm them physically. "He spoke to us in about the same way that I would speak to my own son under the same circumstances," the alumnus noted. "It was the first time that I had ever been 'punished' in this intelligent manner." After his talk, he sent them back to their dormitory.[3]

In 1939, Doc Shelly resigned the dean's job to take another fellowship in endocrinology and pediatrics. He had already found that he couldn't manage his research and his administrative responsibilities at the same time. In fact, he had been devoting so much time and energy to administration that his project suffered and could not be completed. He had grown weary, too, of trying to inculcate a new philosophy of discipline among staff and boys who weren't taking him seriously. For the truth was that although the boys hated the discipline and the injustices it produced, they seemed lost without it. To the counselors, corporal punishment was immediate, effective, certain. Persuasion was a chancy thing, not to say time-consuming, compared with simple force. The monitors were unhappy because they had a vested interest in corporal punishment. There was no point in being a monitor unless you had the power that went with it—the power to beat up the kids you supervised. Doc Shelly, though, was telling them that this power was wrong, that it invariably led to abuses. But he had a lot of history and tradition to undo, and his goals couldn't be accomplished easily.

Part of Doc Shelly's difficulties could be ascribed to his own lack of experience. What he knew about children he had learned mostly from books. He seems to have assumed that his rational ideas about discipline were self-evident and would achieve instantaneous acceptance. Moreover, he was thrust upon the HOA without any preparation or planning. No allowance seems to have been made for a period of adjustment, a transitional phase that would have permitted the changeover to have taken place gradually.[4]

The man who replaced him as dean was a former home boy with a reputation for being tough. Although he took no public stand for or against corporal punishment, he acted as if he favored it. The counselors and monitors obviously felt better about him than they had about Doc Shelly; they were now free to use their hands as they had in the past.

Yet the gentle scientist's influence had a residual impact on the boys. His ideas didn't quite leave with him; a lot of boys had absorbed them and felt his loss. An incident that seemed to reflect this took place one morning before breakfast about a year or so later, in M-2, the second oldest boys' dormitory. About 6:30, when most boys were dressed, a counselor entered the dormitory to march them to the dining room. In one alcove he found a boy still asleep in bed—an indication of the monitor's laxness. Angered, he overturned the bed, yanked the sleepy boy to his feet, and began slapping him very hard. Few paid much attention. But when he lifted the loudly weeping boy by an arm and leg and was about to batter his head against an upturned bedpost, an amazing revolt took place. He felt a tap on his shoulder and turned around to find the entire dormitory gathered in the alcove—all eighty boys. Most were crowded behind him, others were standing on beds and perched on lockers. "Drop him," he was ordered by the boy who had tapped him on the shoulder. For a moment the counselor was stunned, not knowing what to do. If he refused, eighty boys stood ready to jump him and he knew he couldn't count on the monitors to back him. Then he was literally saved by the bell—the breakfast marching bell. It gave him an excuse to get out of the crisis with the least loss of face. Dropping the boy, he ordered everybody to line up and march downstairs. He never struck another boy again, nor did any other counselor when news of the incident got around. Thus ended corporal punishment in the HOA, and without any official proclamation, as there had been so often in the past. It had taken a revolt of the boys themselves to accomplish it unofficially. Yet the revolt was practically meaningless, for it had come too late to do much good.[5]

Change came so slowly to the HOA that Baar alumni could return and not feel strange. Its problems were essentially the same, even decades later. One of the biggest problems, as always, was sex and its role in the life of the children. Sexual abuse was prevalent, though there were never any reported inquisitions as during the Adler and Coffee regimes. Either the children involved were more successful in keeping their behavior secret or the administration didn't take it seriously.

Yet, in the thirties it became easier for boys and girls to meet openly in some social situations and clandestinely when the couples involved could arrange it. Some couples are said to have arranged rendezvous after lights out on the playing field, where the night watchman never went. One of the more ingenious choices for such a meeting was the synagogue. It had two sets of doors, one facing the main lobby and the other opposite the dining room, neither of which was ever locked. A couple wishing to be alone would enter separately from either end when no one was around and slide under the benches. Such trysts were easier to arrange on the weekends, especially on Sunday afternoon and early evening because most children were away visiting their parents and counselors were scarce. Occasionally there was gossip about a pregnant girl being sent home or to reform school. And there are some alumni today who brag of having had sex regularly. A great many boys and girls did meet in the HOA, fall in love and get married. One of them was Lionel Simmonds himself, who met his wife, Clara, during the Baar years, when the girls were making up the boys' beds and leaving notes under their pillows.

Sexual misconduct became a real and public issue in the thirties with the arrival of one of the most exciting outsiders ever to appear in the HOA. He was middle-aged, wore a Ronald Colman moustache, dressed like a Broadway sport, and radiated charm, joie de vivre, and success. His name was Harry Revel, a Hollywood songwriter whose partner was Mack Gordon. Gordon and Revel had become famous writing songs for Hollywood musicals. Revel seemed to adore the children and was unbelievably generous with them. He invited June

Preisser, a Hollywood starlet who had played a minor role in an Andy Hardy movie, to visit the HOA and perform for the children. She sang and danced and was mobbed when she agreed to sign autographs. He would take a dozen children at a time to dinner or he would escort similar groups to the movies or the theater. Whenever he arrived at the HOA, children would collect around him as if he were Daddy Warbucks, hoping to get invited to one of his treats. No one since Seligman Solomon had engaged in the kind of personal philanthropy he was showering on the children.

Then, as momentously as he had entered their lives, Harry was gone, never to be seen again inside the HOA. No reason was given publicly for his unexplained departure, but privately everybody soon learned the story. A few weeks before he vanished, he had begun inviting some boys alone to his hotel near Times Square. Some boys talked and the word reached Simmonds; Harry became persona non grata at the HOA.[6]

One innovation in the twenties became a liability in the thirties. The installation of lockers, though greatly appreciated by the children, led to the locker inspection. The locker inspection was the home's response to stealing. Stealing had always been prevalent, though on a minor scale because there was no way to conceal stolen property except in the pockets of the thief. Ironically, the installation of lockers made stealing more feasible, converting a nuisance into an enduring plague. Whether locked up or unguarded, valuable or trivial, anything that could be carried off, no matter who owned it, was fair game. Newcomers quickly learned, for example, not to leave anything valuable under their pillow, especially money. Boys about to be discharged frequently stole bedding, silver, dishes, and clothing to take home with them. The clothing was stolen either from other boys' dormitory lockers or from the tailor shop. Although always locked after working hours, the tailor shop was easily raided on a Sunday afternoon by forcing a window. Bakers had to keep a sharp eye on any products they left out to cool because children would snatch some away in a twinkling and dash off. A nickel candy machine on the main floor near the superintendent's office was so routinely emptied of its Hershey bars (despite a sawtooth metal guard designed to stop prying fingers) that it was soon removed. Books were spirited out of the library right under the watchful librarian's nose. Neighborhood stores were hit regularly. Almost every Saturday afternoon a boy carrying an empty shopping bag would leave the HOA to make the rounds of local stores and return by suppertime with a full bag.

Not all the loot he brought back was useful or saleable; some items were stolen just to confirm his prowess.

Most of the stolen property usually wound up in the basement locker, which was reasonably safe because it was secured with a combination lock. Although basement lockers were not invulnerable and were sometimes raided, they were still safer than dormitory lockers, which were intended chiefly for clothing and were never locked. The HOA presumably conceived of the locker inspection to recover stolen goods and perhaps discourage stealing. It failed on both counts.

Locker inspections were usually called when some outrageously heinous theft of HOA or other property occurred. They were always held on a Saturday night, with counselors in charge. Only rarely were stolen goods ever found this way because the thief or thieves invariably outwitted the administration. As soon as the locker inspection was called or even earlier in some cases, the children would stash the booty in their dormitory lockers, which were temporarily safe since everybody was tied up by the locker inspection downstairs. Some even managed during the inspection to transfer their stuff to a friend whose locker had already been inspected. This wasn't hard to do, for the counselors, never enthusiastic about working on Saturday night, performed their task perfunctorily. Locker inspections became less frequent in the late thirties, probably because they were considered futile exercises. By then, the HOA may have recognized that stealing was not an aberration that could be corrected, but an established way of life.

Like the locker inspection, the bedwetters' alcove was viewed as the answer to a problem that appeared unsolvable. Until the lockers arrived and caused every dormitory to be divided into eight alcoves, bedwetters had not been segregated. Instead, they slept scattered among the other children. Their condition damaged the floor under their beds and created a difficult cleaning problem every morning. That seems to have led someone in authority to suggest isolating them in a separate alcove. Although it made the daily clean-up easier, it did little else for the bedwetters. Every morning, while those in other alcoves were washing and dressing, the bedwetters were unhappily removing their wet bedding—sheets, blankets, and rubber sheets—and hanging it out to dry on the fire escape. They also had to clean up the puddle under their beds.

No one looking on ever made fun of them as they went about these messy tasks; indeed, everyone felt sorry for them. Although bedwetters had always been punished for their failing, the HOA's psychiatrist had managed to abolish the punitive approach in favor of weekly counseling sessions. One alumnus who went to these sessions recalled, "We all loved the psychiatrist and so each week our charts showed an improvement. This went on until they checked our beds and discovered that the puddles were still there under them and that the holes in the bedsprings were rusty and getting larger. My very worst experience as a bedwetter came when the dormitory captain decided to make every bedwetter box another boy for three rounds. Needless to say, I was boxing every morning."[7] In this instance, the captain was acting on his own authority and against the policy of the home, but clearly the separate alcove was no improvement. It was not the kind of special attention they needed to help them overcome their problem. Instead, it was a wounding stigma that hurt them even more.

Late in 1939 Simmonds announced during a Saturday service that the HOA would be closing in the near future. He was as much shaken by the news he had to tell as the children were in receiving it. Although he could not offer a closing date Simmonds indicated that it was a certainty, a matter of a few years at most. What had happened, though he didn't explain to the children, was that the long-awaited merger between the HOA and Pleasantville had finally been achieved. Federation's long campaign to unify the two biggest Jewish asylums in the city had finally accomplished its goal. Although it had been self-evident since 1917 that it was the only logical, efficient, and sensible thing to do, it had taken about twenty-two years of ceaseless effort to bring the two homes together. The story of that effort suggests an epic rivalry between two kingdoms rather than between two child-care agencies. For example, after the first two studies in 1919 and 1921 by the Bureau of Jewish Social Research had recommended merger, they were followed by two more studies, in 1926 and 1930, also recommending merger. Neither home would accept the results, nor would they agree to any understanding that linked them in any way. Once committees representing the asylums agreed, as a start, to merge their boarding-out bureaus; each board of trustees refused to ratify the agreement.

Both sides had the same reasons for rejecting merger. Each felt proud of its own name and accomplishments. Each board distrusted the other board, so neither would accept a nominee of the other as president. Each feared that merger might result in bigger deficits rather than in increased assets. Each thought it might be subordinated to the other and thus disappear. And, of course, there were conflicting personalities. By 1937, after twenty years of struggle, the situation had produced, as Pleasantville president Herman Block put it, "a 100% *battling* average."[8]

Less than a year later, though, things seemed to have taken a more promising turn. It had now become clear to both asylums, despite their long history of independence, that merger was inevitable and simply a matter of time. For one thing, the new federal Aid to Dependent Children program, an important part of President Roosevelt's social legislation, was making it possible for widowed, deserted, and divorced mothers to care for their children at home. The idea behind the program was, of course, to keep dependent children out of institutions. As a result, Jewish homes in the city, like others elsewhere, were beginning to experience a falling pressure in admissions. In addition, a consensus had finally grown among the boards that institutional care, no matter how good, was a doomed system. The first Jewish institution to act on this view was the BHOA. Its board was persuaded to do so by its director, Aaron L. Jacoby, an HOA alumnus. Early in 1939, the BHOA gradually moved its children out. Most went into foster homes, some were transferred to the HOA, and a few went home to their parents. By July, the Brooklyn home proudly became "the institution that emptied itself." Then, renaming itself the Children's Service Bureau, it remained in business solely as a foster home program.[9] To the HOA and Pleasantville, the BHOA's closing was more than a straw in the wind, it was an unmistakable omen of the future.

Both institutions' boards were in agreement, finally, that foster home care was the superior system. Now the only real issue that stood in the way of a merger was how to negotiate it without either side losing face. Relations between the two homes were still formal though growing more cordial. Indeed, their respective presidents, I. Howard Lehman of the HOA and Herman Block of Pleasantville, were meeting regularly for lunch and talking merger. But both knew that they were not the ones to arrange it. A mediator was needed to work out the plans so that neither side would feel that it was being swallowed by the other.

Lehman and Block agreed on Dr. Maurice Hexter, whose diplomatic and administrative credentials were impressive. He had spent fourteen years as the executive director of Jewish charities in Milwaukee, Cincinnati, and Boston. In the preceding ten years he had been in Palestine, where he had administered the Palestine Emergency Fund and dealt regularly with the Palestine Royal Commission and the British Cabinet. With nearly twenty-five years of national and international experience behind him, Dr. Hexter was, to say the least, overqualified for the job of negotiating the merger of two orphanages. But the HOA and Pleasantville thought that only a man of Dr. Hexter's stature could manage it with the finesse and expertise both sides considered indispensable.[10]

Apart from Simmonds and his closest aides, no one in the HOA knew about the negotiations. Outside the HOA, negotiations between the two asylums were proceeding more smoothly than either side had anticipated—a tribute to Dr. Hexter's skill. The only hitch was finding a name for the new agency. Neither home wanted a name suggesting that it had been swallowed by the other. One compromise offered was an amalgam of both names, the Hebrew Orphan Guardian Society. Then someone pointed out that the resulting acronym would then be HOGS. How would it look to have Jewish children seen with such initials on their clothes? HOGS was promptly killed and the negotiators tried harder. The name they finally agreed upon was the New York Association for Jewish Children. Though not entirely satisfying it was acceptable for the moment. I. Howard Lehman was elected its first president and Herman Block its first vice-president— a choice that reflected the HOA's primacy as the first Jewish orphanage in the nation. Four organizations were represented in the new agency; the HOA, Pleasantville and its after-care unit, Fellowship House, and the Jewish Children's Clearing Bureau. Simmonds was named director of institutions and Maurice Bernstein, his assistant, was named director of the HOA. Bernstein thus became the second HOA alumnus to be placed in charge of the asylum.

The final agreement between the two homes was ratified in the spring of 1939. Enabling legislation authorizing the formation of the new agency was signed by Governor Lehman the same year. On January 1, 1940, the new agency became officially operative. It was the biggest private child-care agency in the world, caring for 3,471 children—2,084 in foster homes, 302 at Pleasantville, 607 in the HOA, 90 at Edenwald, and 388 at Fellowship House.[11]

NYAJC's first goal was the termination of obsolete services; the first of these was, of course, the HOA. No one knew for sure how long it would take to empty the huge home because no one had taken the time earlier to survey the families to learn which were willing and able to care for their children. A study found that at least 30 percent of the children could be sent home almost at once, and they were. The major reason their families could take them back was that the economic climate had improved. Though far from over, the depression was easing, largely because America was gearing up its defense efforts and more jobs were available.

Throughout 1940, the last full year the HOA would be in operation, more children were discharged—most to foster homes, some to the Corner House and the Friendly Home, a few to Pleasantville. With so many children leaving, a lot of activities had to be discontinued, including the band and the drum corps. The best boys' band in the city would be heard no more. Some athletics programs had to be curtailed or dropped. Yet, while their world was withering away around them, the basketball team scored the greatest triumph in its history. In the 1939-40 season, it became the unofficial city champion for the first time by defeating every high school team, all twenty-five of them. Its sole loss, in its twenty-sixth game, was to the Long Island University junior varsity. But even that defeat represented a small victory, for in 1941 that LIU team won the national basketball championship.[12]

By the spring of 1941, the HOA was becoming a ghost asylum. Only three full dormitories were in use, two on the boys' side and one on the girls' side, occupied almost entirely by children finishing high school. Seven dormitories were empty, filled only with the beds and lockers of their former occupants. Discipline was minimal and supervision became more lenient. If a boy went out to buy a nickel's worth of "yesterday's cake" at the Knoblowitz bakery on 140th Street and Amsterdam Avenue—a tradition with HOA children for at least twenty years—no counselor made a fuss about it. The last Prize Day was held in early June and the last confirmation class to graduate from religious school went through its exercises in the synagogue a few weeks later. Since many children had also graduated from high school at the same time, more of them were discharged afterward. That summer the remaining children took their last trip to camp. In the fall the huge building was practically empty, except for fourteen retarded children, who were sent to state institutions.[13]

On September 20, 1941, the last day the HOA was officially open, its graduates held a farewell dinner in the dining room. Nearly a thousand alumni attended, including persons who had grown up under every regime from the Baar days to Simmonds's long reign. A twenty-page souvenir booklet was published for the occasion, containing a photograph of the HOA, a brief history, a listing of its achievements and contributions, and the evening's program. Guest speakers at the dinner included Aaron L. Jacoby as toastmaster; Samuel Strasbourger, the last president of the HOA; I. Howard Lehman, the first president of the NYAJC; William Hodson, commissioner of the Department of Welfare; Solomon Lowenstein; and Lionel J. Simmonds.

When the dinner and speeches were done, everybody sang the

HOA alma mater and "Auld Lang Syne." Then all left the dining room and went to the Warner Gym for entertainment and dancing. Since the band was no longer available to provide entertainment, some former choir members performed—a baritone soloist and a group calling itself the Academy Quartette. They were accompanied on the piano by Leo Braun, the former choirmaster. The mood was both nostalgic and mournful, as if a great institution was passing into history. The HOA had been in existence for nearly eighty-three years and it had cared for about thirty-five thousand children. Its closing marked the end of institutional care for Jewish children in New York City.

Although the HOA was officially closed, it was not completely empty. P.S. 192 remained open for neighborhood children. The local draft board soon arrived on the premises and established its office in the Reception House. In the main building some administrative activities were still being carried out. One was the after-care department, left behind temporarily to serve the children in foster homes. Some employees of the cashier's office were still working there. The head porter, Phil Riley, lived in the porter's quarters and assumed the additional duty of night watchman. Occupying a room connected to the superintendent's apartment was the last former resident and former counselor still living in the HOA, David Shorr. A New York University student who would graduate in January, he had been granted a deferment until then. Finally, there was Simmonds himself, who would remain for another six weeks. On November 1, he and his wife left for Florida for a long vacation, after which they would start a new life in an apartment near Columbia University. That day he was given an emotional and tearful farewell by the remaining staff and David Shorr. "*Where are all our boys and girls?*" he cried, shaken by the momentous event about to occur. He had lived in the HOA since 1892, entering as a half orphan and, through his own efforts, rising to become superintendent. Now he was, in effect, discharging himself from the only home he had ever known.

Five weeks later came the attack on Pearl Harbor. On February 1, 1942, David Shorr enlisted in the United States Coast Guard. No longer an orphanage, the two-block square complex of four buildings—asylum, Reception House, Warner Gym, and power plant—became the responsibility of Phil Riley.[14]

The Luckiest Orphans 16

For about a year and a half the great asylum remained empty, used only by children attending P.S. 192 and members of the local draft board in the Reception House. Early in that period, employees of the aftercare and cashiers departments were gradually relocated to the offices of the New York Association for Jewish Children. The HOA's sole resident was Phil Riley, who maintained the premises with the help of a small crew. After Simmonds's departure, Riley became "drunk with authority," David Shorr recalled decades later. Carrying a huge ring of keys, he would lock the main gate and front door every night. It was the first time since the building had opened that both had been locked. Shorr also remembered going through the long dark halls at night with a flashlight and coming upon Riley "stalking around checking things." Riley was behaving imperiously, like the lord of a manor.[1]

Late in 1942 the HOA was sold to the city for $1.5 million. But the city never used it. Instead, it turned the building over to the army, which renamed it Army Hall and converted it into a barracks for soldiers studying at City College under the Army Specialized Training Program (ASTP). Ironically, one HOA graduate accepted by the program was sent to City College and wound up back in the HOA, this time as a GI. Happy to be there, Ralph Henry was even happier to be assigned to a former girls' dormitory. Living in it was disappointing, though, since it was the same as a boys dormitory, except that the toilet lacked urinals. Wondering what changes Army Hall had made in the building, he found that the unkindest fate of all had befallen the superintendent's apartment: it was being used as a prophylaxis station.[2]

Hundreds of alumni served in the armed forces and the merchant marine during World War II. Few had trouble adjusting to military life; indeed, most found the services a far less rigorous experience than the HOA. Alumni were involved in almost every major action of the war and a number played key roles in some of its most dramatic moments. Samuel Ledwith, a marine sergeant, and Daniel Fruchter, an army artilleryman, were at Pearl Harbor when the Japanese attacked. Ledwith later took part in the Iwo Jimo landing, the Okinawa landing, and the shelling of the Japanese coast. He was on the carrier *Bennington* in Tokyo Bay when General MacArthur formally accepted the Japanese surrender on the *U.S.S. Missouri*. Despite orders against it, he and seven other Marines entered Tokyo before General MacArthur got there. A dormitory captain in the HOA, Ledwith earned three ribbons and six combat stars.[3] Daniel Fruchter was at Schoffield Barracks having what he thought would be his last breakfast before returning to the States—his enlistment was up on December 8—when he heard loud, thumping noises coming from Wheeler Field and all over the base. Along with other soldiers he ran out of the barracks to find Japanese planes bombing and strafing the area. That night, Fruchter and another soldier went to the top of the crater overlooking Pearl Harbor and saw the base and its ships still burning and smoking. "It was a sight beyond description," he remembered, "all we could do was weep." Today Fruchter is chair of the New York State branch of the Pearl Harbor Survivors Association; previously he had served as head of the organization's New York City chapter. In the HOA, he had been an Eagle Scout and leader of its troop.[4]

Abe Korman, a soldier in the Phillipines, was captured by the Japanese, survived the infamous Death March on Bataan, and remained a prisoner until the islands were liberated.[5] Abe Simon and Lt. Philip Werfel, both in the navy, took part in the Normandy invasion on D day.[6] Leo W. Schwarz won a battlefield commission while with General Patton's army in Normandy.[7] During the hedgerow fighting in France, Ernie Pyle, the famous war correspondent, met Lt. Eddie Sasson, a graves registration officer, and mentioned him in a dispatch.[8] Five days later Sasson was dead.[9] When General Patton slapped a soldier in a hospital bed in Sicily, the chief eyewitness to the event, lying in the next bed, was Jerry Fraiden.[10] A former member of the choir and the drama club, David Gaber appeared in the stage and screen versions of Moss Hart's *Winged Victory*. Before being chosen for the air corps drama, Gaber had been entertaining troops at a base near Wichita Falls, Texas.[11] Morris Delfin regularly made the run to Murmansk, in the Soviet Arctic, as a member of the merchant marine without being torpedoed. But his luck changed when a ship he was on in the Pacific sank. He saved himself by swimming to an empty raft to find that he had to fight off a horde of monkeys (part of the cargo) who were trying to climb aboard.[12] The first United States soldier to hear of the German surrender offer, on May 4, 1945, was Seymour Sandler, a telegrapher at General Eisenhower's headquarters.[13] One alumnus who served in the Pacific claimed to have been the real-life model for Goldstein in Norman Mailer's *The Naked and the Dead*. Not true, Mailer said.[14]

Back in New York, a new alumni organization called the Academy Alumni Association (AAA) maintained contact with hundreds of members by sending them letters, a bulletin, and packages. It also acted as a clearinghouse for alumni seeking the addresses of friends and news about those who had become casualties. The new organization had been organized in 1939 by graduates of the twenties and thirties because the Seligman Solomon Society (SSS) had not accepted new members for twenty years. But the need for another organization did not become compelling until everybody realized that the HOA was closing. Unlike the SSS, the new organization had an open membership policy, which helped it grow quickly.

Although there was no HOA to return to, as there had been after World War I, the AAA helped ease the loneliness felt by most alumni. In February 1946 it held a grand reunion ball in the Warner Gym, attended by hundreds of alumni, many still in uniform. Two months later it sponsored the first alumni Seder, led by Lionel J. Simmonds, and that fall organized a Labor Day weekend at Camp Wakitan.[15]

Simmonds's career as a child welfare expert, considered over after the HOA closed, was unexpectedly revived. When the city decided in 1946 to open its first public shelter for dependent children of all faiths, the Children's Center, he became its first director. Some of the counselors Simmonds hired, needless to say, were HOA alumni.[16]

Another change overtook the old HOA after the GI Bill of Rights was passed. Shortly afterward it became an annex of City College and was reconverted from a barracks into low-cost housing and classrooms for student veterans. Among its first new residents were two former HOA residents, Abe Simon and Jack Carl. Simon didn't stay long, but Carl, who for a time shared the superintendent's apartment with five other roommates, remained until 1950, when he graduated. In doing so, he fulfilled a long-held childhood dream. As a boy he had developed an attachment for City College that was all-consuming. Carl became the official mascot for all its teams—baseball, basketball, football, and lacrosse.[17] This enabled him to attend all their local games and, with HOA approval, most of their out-of-town games as well. Because he spent so much time on campus, he became a familiar and popular figure there. Carl expected to attend City College after graduating from high school, but the closing of the HOA and the war combined to prevent it. After the war, the GI Bill and the HOA's new role as affordable student housing made it possible for him to enroll as a student. Carl thus became the last alumnus to live in the HOA.[18] Such a distinction would not have seemed worth cherishing at the time. In the past twenty years, though, as the HOA has faded into near legendary status, it has assumed a certain nostalgic cachet.

During the war years, the population of the neighborhood changed as many large families moved in. P.S. 192 became overcrowded and needed more classroom space, so the board of education built a new school at the western end of the field and had it connected to the Warner Gym. Given a new name, the Jacob H. Schiff School, in honor of the HOA's most famous benefactor, it opened in 1952. Even this proved insufficient after a few years, so a Quonset hut structure was installed near it containing additional classrooms.

In 1955, when the number of student veterans needing housing declined, the city turned the building over to the Parks Department, which planned to build a park and playground there. It decided to demolish every building except the Warner Gym. Only one person had to be dispossessed to begin demolition—Phil Riley. For fourteen years he had patroled the vast empty building alone, zealously protecting it against all intruders. Only in New York could a Jewish orphanage end its existence being guarded by a fiercely devoted Irish custodian. No one knows how he reacted to the eviction order, where he went to live afterward, and what happened to him. Presumably, like Simmonds before him, he made a tearful departure, orphaned finally by the death of an orphanage that had been as much a home for him as it had been for the children.

The demolition of the HOA took a full year, from December 1955 to November 1956, one of the longest jobs on record.[19] That left the Warner Gym as the only surviving asylum facility on the premises, although it is not the oldest HOA building left in the city. That distinction belongs to the original building at 303 West 29th Street (formerly 1 Lamartine Place) where the HOA opened in 1860. Decades ago, it was converted to a rooming house and, in the eighties, became a cooperative.[20]

Five years after it became the successor agency for all the Jewish orphanages in the city, the New York Association for Jewish Children in 1945 changed its name to something shorter and more precise: the Jewish Child Care Association (JCCA). It continued to absorb more agencies and develop new facilities, including an innovative one called a residential treatment center, a group home for emotionally troubled children. In many respects, the new facility was an updated version of Edenwald.

But while the JCCA grew bigger, it didn't sacrifice its high quality of care in the process. This was acknowledged in a series of *New York Herald-Tribune* articles on foster care in February 1965. One article warned, "If you're going to need foster care in New York, be sure and be born Jewish." It then went on to praise JCCA's "all-encompassing services" that care for children from infancy to the age of twenty-one.[21] Written when Jewish children were still the majority under care, this situation was permanently reversed in the seventies. Today it is not only the oldest but still the foremost Jewish residential child-care agency in the city and the nation. It cares for about ten thousand children and family members with a staff of about eight hundred employees. Its facilities include eight group residences, one youth residence, a foster home division, three institutions, a family day-care service, six residences for the retarded, two group day-care programs, and an adoption service. The majority of children accepted for care are emotionally troubled adolescents from single-parent homes. Ninety percent or more of JCCA's funding comes from government sources.[22] Although it accepts contributions from private courses, it does not engage in direct fund-raising. Non-Jewish children now comprise about 85 percent of the caseload.

Like the HOA it replaced, JCCA continues to spend more for services than any other private child-care agency. *Money* magazine in December 1989 ranked JCCA as the second most cost-effective social service agency in the United States. It spent 102 percent of its income on programs, thus incurring a deficit that was offset by private funds. Thus, the care the HOA gave its children has become, through its successor JCCA, the standard for all social services in the nation.

In the early fifties, efforts began to merge the AAA and the SSS. Both were aware of the poignant fact that the closing of the HOA foreshadowed the inevitable shrinkage and not too distant demise of their membership. Since the recruitment of new members was no longer possible, a merger offered the possibility of creating a larger organization whose combined resources could keep the alumni bond strong for many more years.

Although both sides professed to favor the merger, their initial steps toward it were a low-key reprise of the merger between the HOA and Pleasantville. The usual stumbling blocks—choosing a name for the new organization, deciding between amalgamation or integration, guaranteeing the SSS's burial benefits—delayed its union for years. Each side had a membership committee that met separately and then jointly to make its members familiar with its counterparts. At SSS meetings some officers held out for the integration of AAA members; that is, accepting them on an individual basis. The AAA moved slowly and cautiously, feeling that pressure would create new problems. Despite the meetings and the time-consuming discussions, nothing was happening.

Finally, in 1956, the AAA named a merger committee of just two members to meet formally with a similar SSS committee to work out a plan. The upshot of their talks, held frequently and amicably that year, was an agreement on the following terms: amalgamation, all AAA members accepted en masse; first president and first treasurer of new group must be SSS members; SSS burial benefits to be guaranteed; and a new name, the H.O.A. Association, Inc. Both sides agreed to the terms early in 1957 and the new organization was born. Arthur J. Raumann, an insurance executive, was named the first president, and Al Lang, an accountant, the first treasurer.[23] The SSS had lasted seventy years, the AAA only eighteen. The merger guaranteed that alumni would hold their "family" together at least to the end of the century.

Lionel J. Simmonds died on November 12, 1961, in Scarsdale, at the age of 79. His final residence was a measure of how far he had gone in his lifetime, from an orphanage to residence in one of the most affluent towns in America. About three years earlier, on May 28, 1958, he and his wife, Clara, had been given a testimonial dinner in honor of their golden wedding anniversary. A six-page souvenir booklet consisting almost entirely of photographs of HOA personalities and scenes from asylum life from the 1890s to 1941 was published for the occasion. It had a double title, "This Was Your Life," referring to Simmonds's career, and "This Was Our Life," showing how "our images of HOA life are inextricably woven out of the warp and woof of Mr. Simmonds's life," for "in honoring Lionel and Clara . . . we are honoring ourselves." The program that night was a "Remembrance of Things Past." Alumni who grew up with Simmonds as well as many who had followed him in the next five decades told humorous or touching stories about him in the style of the then-popular television show of the same name. One of the guests that night was David Shorr, a stock broker and the only alumnus present when Simmonds bid a tearful farewell to the HOA in 1942.

Two of the HOA's most faithful alumni are a couple who never lived there, John and Eleanor Murray, both of Irish descent. John's family moved to West 135th Street, a block from the HOA, in 1930. He made his first venture inside the home in 1932 and found it more attractive than forbidding. The boys were friendly and welcomed him to their games. After school and on weekends, he would join them in baseball or football, played basketball in the Warner Gym, and watched HOA teams play outside teams. Almost overnight, the HOA became his second home. While playing baseball there in 1937, he hit a line drive to left center field that seemed a sure double. But a girl playing centerfield made a great running catch, depriving him of a hit. That was how he came to meet Eleanor, who would become his girlfriend and later his wife. Like him, Eleanor loved athletics and had also discovered the HOA simply by walking inside its gates.

"The HOA became part of our lives," John recalled many years later. Some of their closest friends were boys and girls from the home. Eleanor endeared herself to the girls by buying candy for them and passing it to them over the fence. (Girls seldom sneaked out of the building the way the boys did, so Eleanor's help was appreciated.) Today, John and Eleanor feel that "the happiest years of our lives were from 1932 to 1941," when they were involved in the life of the home. Indeed, they regard the HOA today as a kind of childhood shrine and they continue to visit a small part of the girls' playground on West 136th Street where a few trees from the old HOA days are still standing. "The trees are a living memorial to all the thousands of children who resided there," John wrote to the *Rising Bell*, the alumni newsletter. "If I concentrate sometimes, I can see and hear them all." At a meeting in September 1985, the association named them honorary alumni and presented them with a special certificate of membership "for their lifetime attachment to the HOA and for the enduring friendships they made with the children who lived there from 1932 to 1941."[24]

In 1987 the H.O.A. Association, Inc. celebrated its one hundredth anniversary, making it the oldest functioning orphanage alumni organization in the United States, if not the world. Congratulatory messages were sent to the association from President Reagan, Governor Cuomo, and Mayor Koch. Member of Congress Charles Rangel of Manhattan, whose district includes the HOA, inserted a notice of the association's anniversary in the *Congressional Record*.[25]

The following year the association, with the approval and cooperation of the Jacob H. Schiff School, unveiled a plaque memorializing the HOA on a wall of the Warner Gym. Taking part in the ceremony that afternoon, April 17, 1988, were the district commissioner of education, the principal, some teachers, parents of students, and

HOA alumni. The association's plan to install the plaque had the unintended though happy effect of restoring the Warner Gym. It had been closed six years earlier because a leaky roof had badly damaged the floor, causing many boards to warp. Using the unveiling of the plaque as justification, the principal persuaded the board of education to repair the floor and renovate other parts of the gym as well. Since then, the gym has been used not only for athletics but for other activities, such as art shows, dance classes, and exhibitions.[26]

On April 30, 1989, the date of the Washington Bicentennial celebration, fourteen alumni marched in the parade. They carried two blue and white pennants with the words, "HOA Association," two large mounted photographs—one of the HOA and the other showing the cadets corps—and a large blue banner displaying the HOA logo and the following words in white lettering:

> In Honored Memory of
> The Hebrew Orphan Asylum Cadets
> First Place Winner, Marching Contest
> Washington Centennial Parade, 1889

The HOA unit was the only orphanage alumni organization represented in the parade and the only Jewish unit as well. This was true of the cadets that had marched in the centennial in 1889. Thus, twice in a century, HOA people were the sole representatives of the city's Jewish community in an important historical parade. To honor the event, the *Rising Bell* published a special edition headed, "The Last HOA Parade."[27]

Although the HOA has been closed for over fifty years, its history didn't automatically end with its demise. The lives of alumni offer strong evidence that the HOA had a lasting effect. Many have done remarkably well since their discharge. Their careers argue against Charles Loring Brace's thesis that orphanage life inevitably turns its inmates into robots or zombies whose spirits are crushed and who are incapable of having a normal life.

Heading the list, of course, is Art Buchwald, the only alumnus who is also a national celebrity. How does he feel about the HOA? In a message to the association's one hundredth anniversary celebration, Art summed it up in one measured sentence: "It [the association] is probably one of the most successful organizations in existence because it glues together people who have experienced a unique childhood—not necessarily good and not necessarily bad—but unique."[28]

Norman Rales (with his sons Steven and Mitchell) owns Danaher, a conglomerate that combines real estate and various manufacturing enterprises, chiefly auto parts and hand tools. A few years ago Dana-her became a Fortune 500 company. Rales has homes in Maryland and Florida and commutes between them on his own jet. He supports association activities and sponsors the annual alumni reunion in Florida every January.[29] He is also a generous contributor to Jewish philanthropies in south Florida.

The owner of the world's largest privately owned tanker fleet is Captain Leo V. Berger, a former boarding out boy from the thirties. An HOA scholarship supported him while he attended Cornell University. Later, deciding on a maritime career, he graduated from the Kings Point Merchant Marine Academy with a third mate's license. After years as a captain of tankers, he began buying them. A few years ago, he honored his HOA childhood by donating $500,000 to an Israeli orphanage, Boys Town in Jerusalem.[30]

Another scholarship boy, Aaron L. Jacoby, won first prize in a national speech contest for college students while a senior at New York University. The gift of oratory it demonstrated became the key to his highly successful career. One of the HOA's golden boys, Jacoby was talented, versatile, ambitious, and outstanding in many fields. Public service, though, was his chief interest. At twenty-four, he became superintendent of the Brooklyn HOA. While still working in that position, he was elected registrar and then sheriff of Kings County (Brooklyn) and subsequently named chief clerk of Brooklyn's Surrogate Court. Governor Harriman later named him to the state Public Service Commission; he also served on the state parole board and the New York City Parole Commission. When his political career faded, he became the vice-president of one bank, president of another bank, both in Brooklyn, and was appointed to the board of directors of Penn-Texas (now Colt Industries) and later elected its chair. But the assignment he treasured most was being chosen to introduce President Franklin D. Roosevelt at Ebbets Field, in Brooklyn, in 1940, the first campaign stop in his bid for a third term. Roosevelt had heard of his reputation as a speaker and insisted that Jacoby, instead of other bigger politicians who also coveted the role, be given that honor.[31]

Louis Nierenberg yearned to become a doctor while in the HOA but never made it. Still, he managed to become skilled at surgery of another kind after he began working in the fur industry. He invented and patented a new method of cutting ermine, squirrel, and weasel skins that made seams almost invisible. The Soviet Union learned of it and invited him there to teach the technique to its furriers. Nierenberg also invented the first synthetic furs with a realistic look. His innovations made him rich and a leader in the fur business.[32]

Two alumni from the thirties have achieved world-class status in science—Dr. Herman Schwartz and Nathan Mantel. Dr. Schwartz was a founding member of the Nature Club, an event that proved to be the major inspiration for his career. After graduating from Cornell University, he became an assistant professor in botany at the University of California at Berkeley. Then, temporarily forsaking botany, he attended Harvard Medical School on an HOA scholarship, graduating with honors, and became an oncologist at Kaiser Permanente Hospital in San Francisco. But while practicing medicine he resumed working at his botanical interests. Dr. Schwartz soon found himself drawn to the study of a large family of plants, known as *Euphorbia,* which includes about two thousand species world-wide, mostly in Africa. Dr. Schwartz now owns the world's largest collection of *Euphorbia* and is considered the world's leading authority on the subject. He is now engaged in a monumental personal publishing project describing and illustrating all the known species of *Euphorbia.* Five volumes, all illustrated with superb photographs, have been published so far. In 1989 the British Book Publishing Association awarded him a prize for having published the most valuable and beautiful specialized books in the previous year. He also publishes the *Euphorbia Journal,* perhaps the only scientific journal in the world published by an individual. Today, he continues simultaneously to teach at the University of California Medical School, practice at Kaiser Permanente Hospital, and pursue his *Euphorbia* projects.[33]

Nathan Mantel is a pioneer and world-class authority in a new field, biometrics, the statistical study of biological data. A former boarding-out boy whose sister grew up in the main building, he received an HOA scholarship in 1935 to attend City College, where he majored in statistics. In 1947, after many minor jobs in and out of his chosen field, he got his first big break: a position as statistician with the National Cancer Institute in Washington, D.C. While working there he earned his master's degree in statistics. By the time he retired from the National Cancer Institute in 1974, he had acquired a reputation as one of the leading biometricians in the nation. He is a fellow of four major societies, including the Royal Statistical Society of England, and is past president of the Biometrics Society. He has received numerous awards and honors, including membership (by special election) in the International Statistical Institute. He is an editor or board member of six journals. So far, he has published 367 articles in American and foreign journals, mostly on cancer statistics, his specialty. He has held teaching positions in twelve universities and institutes, among them posts in China, Israel, and England.[34]

Some alumni have made a name for themselves in the liberal arts. Alice Herzig, for example, achieved national recognition as an educator in nursing. She entered the HOA during World War I and stayed ten years. During that time her mother worked as a cook in the isolation hospital atop the reception house. What Herzig saw in the hospital when visiting her mother may have influenced her choice of a career. At any rate, Herzig decided on a nursing career after leaving the HOA and pursued it with iron-willed determination. Entirely on her own, without a scholarship from the HOA, she earned four degrees: a bachelor's from Hunter College, a nursing degree from Mount Sinai Hospital Nursing School, a master's in teaching from Teachers College of Columbia University and a master's in public health from the University of Minnesota. In 1945 she joined the United States Public Health Service and progressed steadily upward through the ranks. Eventually, she was promoted to colonel in the agency's commissioned corps. At the time she retired in 1971 she was chief of nurse education and training and had won many citations and awards.[35]

Until he walked into an art class taught by a WPA instructor during the thirties, Harold Tovish had no idea about what career he should follow. What he did in that class, though, changed his life forever. With the instructor's encouragement, he tried sculpting, became absorbed by it, and found his life's work. Today he is a nationally known sculptor whose works are part of the permanent collection of such museums as the Guggenheim and Whitney in New York; the Hirshhorn in Washington, D.C.; the Boston Museum of Fine Arts; the Art Institute of Chicago; the Honolulu Academy of Art; and the Philadelphia Museum of Art. Tovish has won numerous honors, including sculptor in residence at the American Academy in Rome, 1966; a Guggenheim Fellowship, 1967; fellow at the Center for Advanced Visual Arts, MIT, 1967 and 1968; and National Institute of Arts and Letters awards, 1960 and 1971.[36]

Leo V. Schwarz, who was sent to Harvard in the twenties on an HOA scholarship, became a widely known anthologist of Jewish literature. Among his many works are *The Jewish Caravan* (which spawned an imitator, *The Negro Caravan*), and *Great Ages and Ideas of the Jewish People,* still in print in a Modern Library edition.[37]

Before World War I, most HOA musicians who became professionals worked in bands. But this changed in the midtwenties, when the HOA began giving scholarships to Juilliard, the leading music school in the nation. First to receive a Juilliard scholarship was a former band captain, Sidney Kyle. In the fifties he became a clarinetist with the Metropolitan Opera Orchestra.[38] Jimmy Smith, another

Juilliard graduate, joined the New York Philharmonic as a cornetist in 1942 and performed with them for thirty-five years, longer than any other player. Earlier in his career he had performed with the NBC Symphony under Arturo Toscanini, the CBS Symphony, and the Andre Kostelanetz Orchestra. He was also the HOA band's last instructor.[39] When Leopold Stowkowski, conductor of the Philadelphia Symphony, heard trombonist Albert Godlis play at Juilliard, he hired him on the spot. After retiring Godlis freelanced, playing with pit orchestras for Broadway musicals or with pickup bands for radio or television.[40]

A few alumni have had unusual careers that probably never occurred to them when they were growing up. Ray Hollander became a carnival performer with an act called "The Show of Hope." In it he billed himself as "the only handless trick shot artist in the world using a human as a target" and "the only handless airplane pilot in the United States." In the sixties and seventies he was on the road fifty weeks a year touring the midwest and south central states. Hollander had lost one hand and lost the use of the other in an accident in 1941. Instead of being defeated by these disabilities, he overcame them and created an act that exploited them. Calling it "The Show of Hope" conveyed a message to all disabled people: courage and determination can conquer any disability—the least of which is growing up in an orphanage.[41]

Murray Silverman, the original founder of the Nature Club, once ran another kind of show. For about thirty years he operated the Acapulco Safari, which was actually an enlarged version of the Nature Club transplanted to Mexico. It featured the first glass-bottom boat in Mexico, a small zoo, and an aquarium. Nicknamed "Nature Boy" in the HOA because he was always bringing back live specimens from the club's hikes, Silverman had converted a hobby into a thriving livelihood. His safari tours of the region's flora and fauna became famous and attracted such celebrities as Lady Bird Johnson, Johnny Weissmuller, James Roosevelt, Prince Albert of Belgium, and the families of several Mexican presidents. In the seventies one visitor who took the tour without knowing who operated it made him especially happy: he was Maurice Bernstein, the former assistant superintendent of the HOA in the thirties. Both held an emotional reunion over dinner that night. Silverman is retired now and the Mexican government has built a multimillion-dollar aquarium on the site of his old aquarium. It is a major tourist attraction and a tribute to the Nature Club founded in a basement room of the HOA. Silverman has maintained a lifelong friendship with another Nature Club alumnus,

Dr. Herman Schwartz. Their mutual childhood interest in nature, supported by the HOA, has led each to self-fulfillment, though down vastly different paths.[42]

It would be possible to name dozens of others who became doctors, lawyers, dentists, engineers, rabbis, professors, principals, advertisers, publicists, writers, journalists, government officials, army officers, architects, Wall Street brokers, store owners, real estate brokers and insurance executives. Many more, of course, earned a living at various skilled and unskilled occupations. How many were great successes? Limited successes? Total failures? No one knows.

Unfortunately, despite the number of studies made while the children lived in the HOA, follow-up studies made after the HOA closed are rare, so many alumni cannot be traced.

Any consensus on what the HOA meant to its graduates is unlikely. Answers vary considerably depending on who is asked. Those who made a lot of money credit the HOA for their good fortune. Many say that the training they received there, such as the discipline, regimentation, and learning to get along in groups, provided the underlying personal and social structure for their success. But the same "training" is blamed by less fortunate graduates for their personal problems and work failures. Their argument is that the HOA permanently scarred them by squelching their personality, leaving them feeling insecure and inferior. Many alumni will admit to having undergone various forms of psychotherapy, but this group includes the successful as well as the unsuccessful. Alumni have had problems with authority or raising a family or staying married. It is also a fact, though, that children from natural families have similar problems and frequent therapists' offices just as often. Life's casualties are produced under many roofs.

As a rule, those who belong to the alumni association share a generally positive view of the HOA. At meetings, some will offer critical comments about the discipline while others say nothing, perhaps because they have made their private peace with the negative aspects of HOA life. What seems more important to most alumni now are the friendships formed in the home, the sense of kinship that now binds them together. A frequent comment voiced by alumni is that they consider themselves reasonably successful if they have managed to stay out of jail or a mental institution. Some, in fact, have spent time in one or the other.[43]

One fact about HOA life that must be taken into account before making any final judgments about it is that, as in any family, no two children experienced it in exactly the same way. In addition, alumni have selective memories about what they saw and experienced as children. Everyone has some memory blocks. For those who were hurt and humiliated by the brutal discipline, it was clearly the most degrading period of their lives. But not everyone was beaten; the majority were not. Nor was everyone equally sensitive to the harsher, competitive aspects of group living. And implausible as it may sound, some found the HOA an opportunity and thrived on its possibilities. A great deal of what happened to a child depended on a combination of many factors: previous family circumstances, age on admission; the support or lack of it by siblings, if any; first-day experiences; inner resources, character, and personality; ability to make friends; capacity for change; personal ingenuity; and relationships formed with staff or employees. It seems reasonable to argue that although the HOA left many of its alumni with psychological, emotional, and social deficits, a large number in this group, alone or with help, managed to overcome them. Since HOA children at discharge were at the lowest rung of the social and economic ladder, there was nowhere else to go but up. What successes they achieved should be considered in terms of their starting point rather than by the rosier expectations of their more comfortable peers.

Although some calls to revive the orphanage as an answer to the current foster care crisis have been heard recently, they should not be taken seriously. Still, some form of institutional care is needed to deal with the huge number of children involved. The social work profession's dependence on only one form of care in the past fifty years was a smug, narrow, and short-sighted approach. There will never be enough foster homes, let alone good ones, for all the desperate children who need them. And foster homes have been over-idealized. Many former HOA foster home children from the thirties who belong to the alumni association say they would have preferred the main building to the homes they were in. "I always felt like an outsider in all of my foster homes," one woman remembered in a letter to the *Rising Bell*. She always looked forward to receiving new clothes at the HOA during her yearly visit but never got to wear them because "they were promptly confiscated by my foster mother to give to her children."[44] Art Buchwald, who lived in three foster homes in Queens, told Mike Wallace on a "60 Minutes" interview that "neither the child nor the people that take you make an emotional commitment. . . . A foster child senses this very early and he doesn't want to get too close because he knows these people aren't for real."[45] Among the rare foster home placements that did succeed one deserves special mention. In 1926, Jack Gould, then nine and a full orphan, was placed with a Bronx family and felt an instant rapport with them, which the family felt as well. Although Gould wanted to stay with the family, who also wanted to keep him, the HOA, for some unknown reasons, kept removing him and placing him in other foster homes and in Edenwald. Gould ran away from all of them and returned to the home he loved. Eventually, the HOA relented and let him remain there. He was to live with the family for fourteen years, from 1926 until 1940, when he married and left. For nine of those years he was a foster home child, the other five an "adopted" son. Gould considers the foster mother, whom he called "Tante," to be his only real mother and her family to be his only real family. Even after fifty years, he continues to maintain a close relationship with Tante's children and grandchildren and is regarded by them as family.[46]

Determining who will make a good foster parent is a feat beyond the capacity of many social workers, who are easy to fool despite their claimed expertise. The truth is, no one really knows how a foster home will turn out until the first child is placed. Sometimes, as the Gould case demonstrated, social workers don't know they have a good home even when the evidence is overwhelming.

Group homes housing about sixty children are needed as backup for the foster home system to ensure that all needy children receive some form of consistent care. They offer stability, security, and structure, values that should not be minimized at a time when the foster home system has become a huge revolving door. It is possible for group home children to be treated with kindness and respect, receive affection and support from caring adults, and live with each other as a loving extended family. The HOA's Edenwald experiment proved that.

Although is true that a really good foster home would be the best alternative to replace a failing, disorganized, or neglectful natural family, could enough of them be found to care for perhaps half a million or more dependent children nationwide? They are alone because their own families have disintegrated and society's alternatives—foster homes, group homes, and orphanages—are either inadequate or nonexistent. Even worse alternatives—the streets, jail, mental institutions, reformatories—remain. For the children who were fortunate enough to live there, the HOA, despite some obvious shortcomings, was a far better choice.

Today, the alumni association is a national network of siblings that meets regularly, holds annual Seders in New York and Fort Lauderdale, publishes a newsletter, and gathers for an annual reunion in

Florida. Many alumni have had the uncanny experience of meeting a stranger far from home and learning that he or she is also an HOA alum. Whatever their natural families may mean to them, their only real family now consists of the children they grew up with. That is where their roots are; it is the only enduring bond that unites them.

The source of that bond was probably best expressed emotionally by Charles Lehman in the text for the "This Is Your Life/This Was Our Life" booklet:

> All of us have the world's largest collection of boyhood chums and girlhood friends. . . . The HOA was a phenomenon in the growth and development of our country. It was a by-product of vast surges of immigration to the U.S.A. We were what was left of dreams, hopes and aspirations that somehow went astray.
>
> The home taught us to bear it and grin. It gave us comfort and strength "by the numbers." It gave us solace and warmth compounded of a mutual desperation. It filled a void in children hungry for love and affection, even hungrier for some form of basic security. To all of us the HOA was momma and poppa . . . with 1,500 ready-made "cousins."
>
> It shielded us from slum environment, juvenile delinquency, rough-and-tumble street gangs, poverty and deprivation. It fed us, clothed us, fixed our teeth, psychoanalyzed our heads, tested our aptitudes, put us through school, gave us spiritual, moral and cultural guidance.
>
> We were the luckiest orphans in the world. We were the victims of an organized conspiracy aimed at teaching us to forget the past. We built our own world inside the HOA and, looking back, it was a world we remember with genuine affection.

Notes

Abbreviations

AR   Annual Reports of the Hebrew Orphan Asylum
ASM   *Asmonean*
JM   *Jewish Messenger*
NYT   *New York Times*
RB   *Rising Bell*

Chapter 1: E Pluribus Dis-Unum

1. Grinstein, 469.
2. Ibid., 144–45.
3. Congregation Shearith Israel in a letter to the author, 27 June 1970, reported there had been no male burials in 1820, 1821, or 1822.
4. Goldstein, 51–55.
5. Laws of New York, 55th Session, chap. 14, 14–15.
6. Grinstein, 134.
7. Grinstein, 469.
8. Goldberg, 74–250.
9. Grinstein, 146–47.
10. "Anniversary of New York Charities," *ASM*, 16 Nov. 1849.
11. "German Hebrew Benevolent Society," *ASM*, 1 Nov. 1850.
12. Korn, 1–22.
13. "Hebrew Benevolent Society Anniversary," *ASM*, 15 Nov. 1850.
14. Grinstein, 469.
15. "Hospital and Asylum Committee Meeting," *ASM*, 28 Mar. 1851.
16. Grinstein, 277–78.
17. "The Hebrew Benevolent Society," *ASM*, 25 Apr. 1851.
18. "Hebrew Hospital," *ASM*, 13 June 1851.
19. "Young Men's Hebrew Association," *ASM*, 17 Oct. 1851.

20. Isaacs, 109–17; Grinstein, 157.

21. "Jews Hospital and Asylum for Widows and Orphans," *ASM*, 16 Jan. 1852.

22. "9th Anniversary of German Hebrew Benevolent Society," *ASM*, 19 Nov. 1852.

23. "31st Anniversary of Hebrew Benevolent Society," *ASM*, 3 Dec. 1852.

24. Isaacs, 113–16.

25. Kaganoff, 28–30.

26. Isaacs, 113–16.

27. "Samuel Myer Isaacs," *Encyclopedia Judaica*, 4th ed.

28. Editorial, *JM*, 6 Nov. 1857.

29. Editorial, *JM*, 20 Nov. 1857.

30. Editorial, *JM*, 4 Dec. 1857.

31. "Jewish Children in Christian Orphanage," *JM*, 9 Apr. 1858.

32. "Mortara Case," *Encyclopedia Judaica*, 4th ed.

33. Editorial, *JM*, 12, 19 Nov. 1858.

34. "Mortara Protest Meeting," *JM*, 10 Dec. 1858.

35. "Societies Hold Joint Dinner," *JM*, 24 Dec. 1858.

36. "Merger of Societies," *JM*, 8 Apr. 1859.

37. "Joseph Seligman Tribute," *JM*, 23 Dec. 1859.

Chapter 2: The Hero of Lamartine Place

1. "The New Orphan Asylum, *JM*, 6 Apr. 1860.

2. Patterson, 69.

3. "The Orphan Asylum," *JM*, 27 Apr. 1860.

4. *AR*, 1863.

5. Bernard, 10.

6. "The Orphan Asylum," *JM*, 19 Oct. 1860.

7. *AR*, 1863.

8. "An Orphan 50 Years Ago," *American Hebrew*, 8 Apr. 1910.

9. Ibid.

10. Grinstein, 472–78.

11. "An Orphan 50 Years Ago," *American Hebrew*, 8 Apr. 1910.

12. "The Orphan Asylum," *JM*, 2 Nov. 1860.

13. "The Orphan Asylum," *JM*, 23 Nov. 1860.

14. "The Orphan Asylum," *JM*, 16 Nov. 1860. Within two years the membership grew to 235 members and their output increased proportionately, including making all the clothes and bed linens. Their work continued until 1903, when the population of the orphanage rose to about one thousand children and the task became too great. *AR*, 1904.

15. "James Sloan Gibbons," "Abby Hopper Gibbons," National Cyclopedia of American Biography, 1st ed.

16. Morse, 1.

17. Martin, 256; Emerson, 45.
18. Emerson, 261.
19. "Names Drawn in Draft Lottery," *NYT*, 11 July 1863.
20. Richardson, 130–35; Ellis, 299–300.
21. Hale, 272–74; Van Deusen, 298–99.
22. Morse, 2.
23. Ibid., 3.
24. Ellis, 309.
25. Richardson, 136–42.
26. Morse, 4–5; Gibbons, 66.
27. "An Attack on Greeley's Boarding-House," *NYT*, 16 July 1863.
28. Morse, 5; Gibbons, 66; Richardson, 141; Strong, *Diary*, 336.
29. "An Attack on Greeley's Boarding-House," *NYT*, 16 July 1863. Ironically, Wilson's views were exactly those of the rioters. Morse, "Draft Riot," 7.
30. Martin, 256.
31. Morse, 6; Gibbons, 49.
32. Gibbons, 49–50.
33. Gibbons, 51, 67; Morse, 6–7.
34. "Superintendent for Orphan Asylum," *JM*, 21 Aug. 1863.
35. "The Orphan Asylum," *JM*, 16 Oct. 1863. The building still exists and is now numbered 303 West 29th Street.
36. Morse, 6.

Chapter 3: Growing Pains in Yorkville

1. Frankel, 91.
2. "Dedication of the Orphan Asylum," *JM*, 13 Nov. 1863.
3. *AR*, 1864. In 1866 they would open a boarding school for Jewish children and operate it successfully for many years. "Educational Institute and Day School," *JM*, 9 Feb. 1866.
4. "The Orphan Asylum," *JM*, 29 Jan. 1864.
5. Max Grunbaum, "Report to the Board," *Minute Book*, Hebrew Benevolent Society, June 1866, 8.
6. *AR*, 1866.
7. Duffy, 76.
8. Ibid., 536.
9. "Mt. Sinai, JCCA end 100-Year Agreement on Care, *RB*," May 1971.
10. "Abraham Jacobi," *Encyclopedia Judaica*, 4th ed.
11. "The Orphans' Religious Training," *JM*, 5 Oct. 1866.
12. "The Orphan Asylum," *JM*, 12 Oct. 1866.
13. Metropolitan Board of Health Annual Report, 1866, 44.
14. "Louis Schnabel," *Encyclopedia Judaica*, 4th ed.
15. Adler never became a rabbi. Instead, in 1875, he established a new secular faith he called Ethical Culture that would later become the basis for the worldwide humanist movement. Friess, 22–23.

16. *AR*, 1868.

17. *AR*, 1867.

18. "The Orphan Asylum," *JM*, 16 Apr. 1867.

19. *AR*, 1911.

20. "The Orphan Asylum," *JM*, 30 Apr. 1869.

21. *AR*, 1867.

22. Ibid.

23. The 1869 annual report contained some letters from foster families. One proud Georgia farmer wrote that his HOA boy "has demonstrated his bravery, in promptly resenting all insults, such as calling him Yankee, etc., so that now the little boys know they cannot insult him with impunity, as some have felt the result of his gymnastic exercises at the asylum, and believe it wiser not to molest him." But another writer commented that his HOA boy was "rather a little too quiet."

24. *AR*, 1869.

25. *AR*, 1870.

26. "The Orphan Asylum," *JM*, 13 Jan. 1871.

27. Gardner, 204–5.

28. "50th Anniversary of the Hebrew Benevolent Society," *JM*, 12 Apr. 1872.

29. "The Orphan Asylum," *JM*, 3 May 1872.

Chapter 4: The Unhomelike Homes

1. Rothman, 207–35.

2. Brace, 235–36.

3. Bierce, 93.

4. Brace, 241–42.

5. Schneider, 333–34.

6. Richmond, 299–356.

Chapter 5: An Orphan's Lot

1. *AR*, 1872.

2. "The Orphan Asylum," *JM*, 21 June 1872.

3. "The Orphan Asylum," *JM*, 14 Mar. 1873.

4. "The Orphan Asylum/Annual Meeting," *JM*, 12 May 1873.

5. "Report by Commissioner of Charities," *NYT*, 16 Aug. 1874.

6. *AR*, 1874.

7. "Report of the Investigating Committee," *New Era*, Mar. 1875.

8. "The Orphan Asylum," *JM*, 21 June 1872.

9. "The Orphan Asylum," *JM*, 4 July 1873, 8 Aug. 1873; 29 Aug. 1873, 17 Oct. 1873.

10. "Our Leading Charity," *JM*, 24 Apr. 1873.

11. Letters to editor, *JM*, 21 May 1874, 28 June 1874, 14 Aug. 1874.

12. "William F. Havemeyer," *Dictionary of American Biography*, 1st ed.

13. "Charges against Commissioner of Charities," *NYT*, 18 July 1874.

14. "New Charges against Commissioner of Charities," *NYT*, 5 Sept. 1874, 24 Sept. 1874.

15. Their engagement had been approved by the board of governors. They married at the HOA in 1875, the first wedding held there. *Minute Book*, Hebrew Benevolent Society, 21 Mar. 1875.

16. "An Account of the Proceedings of the Investigating Committee," *New Era*, Feb. 1875.

17. "Open Letter to the Board," *JM*, 8 Jan. 1875.

18. "The Orphan Asylum/Report by the Investigating Committee," *JM*, 15 Jan. 1875.

19. "An Account of the Proceedings of the Investigating Committee," *New Era*, Feb. 1875.

20. "Louis Schnabel," *Encyclopedia Judaica*, 4th ed.

21. "The Orphan Asylum," *JM*, 16 Apr. 1875.

22. "Entertaining the Orphans," *JM*, 19 Feb. 1875, Apr. 1875.

23. Box 2, Hebrew Orphan Asylum Collection, American Jewish Historical Society, Waltham, Mass.

Chapter 6: The Right Man in the Right Place

1. "The Orphan Asylum," *JM*, 5 May 1876, 27 Oct. 1876.

2. "The Orphan Asylum," *JM*, 24 Mar. 1876, 31 Mar. 1876.

3. "The Orphan Asylum," *JM*, 29 Dec. 1876.

4. Baar may not have been the first choice for the job. There is evidence to suggest that Meyer Goldman, also of New Orleans, was offered the job two years earlier, but had died on his way. In Aug. of 1874 his ship caught fire while traveling on the Ohio River and sank. Though he was a strong swimmer he drowned because he carried a money belt with $10,000 in gold. Ironically, his grandson, Edwin Franko Goldman, ended up in the HOA thirteen years later. Robert B. Goldman, letter to author, 2 May 1979.

5. Prof. Ebel, Archiv der Georg-August Universität Göttingen, letter to author, 4 Mar. 1958.

6. Meyer B. Cushner, "Dr. Herman [sic] Baar," *Seligman Solomon Society Souvenir Journal*, 1924, 10–13.

7. Ebel, letter to author, 30 Nov. 1957.

8. Dr. Gerhard Ballin, letter to author, 15 Nov. 1975.

9. Ebel, letter to author, 30 Nov. 1957.

10. "Hermann J. Baar," *Universal Jewish Encyclopedia*, 2d ed.

11. Dr. Hermann J. Baar, Obituary, *American Hebrew*, 9 Sept. 1904.

12. B. L. Benas, Presidential Address, Liverpool Jewish Literary Society, 25 Nov. 1906.

13. Historic Society of Lancashire and Cheshire, letter to author, 10 Apr. 1958.

14. Nordlinger, 7.

15. Baar essays reprinted, *JM*, 15 Apr. 1870, 16 June 1870, 8 July 1870, 15 July 1870, 29 July 1870, 12 Aug. 1870, 26 Aug. 1870.

16. Rabbi Julian Feibelman, letter to author, 6 Mar. 1958.

17. Baar essays reprinted, *JM*, 16 June 1871, 7 July 1871.

18. Feibelman, letter.

19. B. L. Benas, Presidential Address, Liverpool Jewish Literary Society, 25 Nov. 1906.

Chapter 7: Behind the Baars

1. "Tales of an Old-Timer," *RB*, 1941.

2. "Compassionate Israel," *NYT*, 4 Feb. 1877.

3. Harry Gottheimer, letter to author, 23 June 1957.

4. "Prize Day at Orphanage," *NYT*, 3 June 1878.

5. *AR*, 1878.

6. *AR*, 1878, 1890.

7. "Hebrew Sheltering Guardian Society," *JM*, 12 Sept. 1879.

8. "The Orphan Asylum," *JM*, 3 Dec. 1880.

9. *AR*, 1880.

10. "The Orphan Asylum," *JM*, 3 Dec. 1880.

11. The high ground at 137th Street and Amsterdam Avenue was the point from which George Washington and his staff directed the battle for the Hollow Way, now 125th Street, on September 16, 1776, during the Battle for Manhattan. Bruce Bliven, letter to author, 13 Dec. 1972.

12. *AR*, 1880.

13. *AR*, 1882.

14. "Cornerstone Ceremonies at New Hebrew Home," *NYT*, 17 May 1883.

15. "Dedication of New Orphan Asylum Building," *JM*, 24 Oct. 1884; *AR*, 1885.

16. Editorial, *JM*, 18 Jan. 1884.

17. "New Hebrew Orphan Asylum Proposed for New Orleans," *JM*, 7 Aug. 1885.

18. Annual Report of the New York State Board of Charities, 1885.

19. Questionnaire responses and follow-up letters: Harry Gottheimer, 23 June, 3 July 1957; Samuel Schwartzberg, 3, 10 July 1957; Jacob Gurkin, 9 September, 10 Oct. 1957; Harold Greenberg, 10, 27 Aug. 1957; Louis Freund, 15 Oct. 1957; Herman Spriter, 16 Nov. 1957; confidential responses received 25 July 1957, 18 Aug. 1957.

Chapter 8: The End of an Era

1. "Centennial Preparations," *NYT*, 24 Oct. 1888, 11 Nov. 1888.
2. Harry Gottheimer, response to questionnaire, 3 July 1957; Louis Freund, response to questionnaire, 15 Oct. 1957; Samuel Schwartzberg, letter to author, 10 July 1957.
3. "Washington Centennial," *NYT, New York Herald, New York Tribune, The Sun,* 2 May 1889.
4. Freund, questionnaire response.
5. *AR*, 1890.
6. "Banner Presented to Orphans," *NYT*, 29 Nov. 1889; *JM*, 29 Nov. 1889.
7. "Sherman's Funeral," *NYT*, 15 Feb. 1891.
8. *AR*, 1891; Freund, questionnaire response.
9. Gottheimer, questionnaire response.
10. Ibid.
11. When the new Brooklyn Hebrew Orphan Asylum was dedicated in May 1892 the HOA band was there, but the Brooklyn HOA soon formed its own band. It would become the second best boys' band in the city and soon took over some of the HOA band's workload. "Brooklyn Orphanage Ceremony," *NYT*, 4 May 1892.
12. "Jesse Seligman Band," *JM*, 12 Oct. 1894.
13. "Jesse Seligman Dies," *JM*, 4 May 1894.
14. "The Orphan Asylum," 5 Apr. 1895; *AR*, 1895, 1896.
15. "Dr. Baar's Birthday Party," *JM*, 10 Apr. 1896.
16. "Memorial to Jesse Seligman," *JM*, 17 Apr. 1896.
17. "Orphan Asylum Adds New Wings," *NYT*, 27 Nov. 1896; "The Orphan Asylum," *JM*, 27 Nov. 1896.
18. "Lehman Gives $100,000 to Orphanage," *NYT*, 17 Feb. 1897.
19. "Dysentery Epidemic in 1898," *RB*, Apr. 1968.
20. Schwartzberg, letter.
21. "Bad Water Kills Orphans," *NYT*, 15 Aug. 1898; *AR*, 1899.
22. Schwartzberg, letter.
23. "Orphan Asylum Sickness," *NYT*, 17 Aug. 1898.
24. *AR*, 1903.
25. "Rev. Dr. Baar to Resign," *NYT*, 21 Dec. 1898.
26. Goldman, 1–25.
27. "*Edwin Franko Goldman and the Goldman Band*," souvenir booklet.
28. Harold Presser, letter to author, 11 Apr. 1974.
29. Julius Tannen, Obituary, *Los Angeles Times*, 4 Jan. 1965; "Julius Tannen Dead," *RB*, Feb. 1965.
30. Louis Freund, interview with author, 11 Nov. 1957.
31. American Ophthalmological Society, letter to author, 20 Aug. 1974.
32. Dr. Hermann J. Baar, Obituary, *NYT*, 5 Sept. 1904.

Chapter 9: From Philanthropy to Social Work

1. *AR*, 1866.
2. *AR*, 1874.
3. "Jacob Schiff," *Encyclopedia Judaica*, 4th ed.
4. Confidential reply to questionnaire, 26 July 1957.
5. "Otto H. Kahn," *Encyclopedia Judaica*, 4th Ed.
6. "Isidor Straus," "Oscar Straus," *Encyclopedia Judaica*, 4th ed.
7. Arthur J. Raumann, letter to author, 8 Nov. 1974.
8. "Seligman Solomon Society," *American Hebrew*, 18 Mar. 1887.
9. "The History of the HOA Association," *RB*, Mar.-Apr., May-June, 1987.
10. "Edward H. Lauterbach," *Encyclopedia Judaica*, 4th ed.; "Souvenir in Commemoration of the Organization of the Hebrew Orphan Asylum of the City of New York 1822–1922."
11. "Louis Strauss Dead at 84." *RB*, June 1968; "Louis Strauss Is Recalled as 'Real Dutch Uncle,'" *RB*, June 1968.

Chapter 10: The Young Reformers

1. "Tales of an Old-Timer," *RB*, Sept. 1941; Harry Gottheimer, letter to the author, 3 July 1957; Jacob Gurhin, letter to the author, 10 Oct. 1957; Samuel Schwartzberg, letter to the author, 10 July 1957.
2. Confidential reply to questionnaire, 11 Oct. 1957.
3. Gurkin, letter.
4. Confidential reply to questionnaire, 9 Sept. 1957.
5. Schwartzberg, letter.
6. Michael Romanoff, Obituary, *NYT*, 2 Sept. 1971.
7. James DeForest, Obituary, *NYT*, 12 Oct. 1932; Schwartzberg letter; *AR*, 1905; Stanley Cobb, letter to author, 20 May 1974.
8. Gurkin, letter.
9. Gottheimer, letter.
10. Schwartzberg, letter.
11. Gurkin, letter.
12. "Louis Stern," *Encyclopedia Judaica*, 4th ed.
13. "Orphans' Wedding," *NYT*, 28 Apr. 1902.
14. *AR*, 1904.
15. Schwartzberg, letter.
16. Schneiderman later became one of the founding staff members of the American Jewish Committee, sponsored by Jacob Schiff. For thirty years he edited the organization's *American Jewish Yearbook*, an annual compendium of social statistics and information about the Jewish community. Harry Schneiderman, interview with author, 5 Jan. 1969.
17. "Tales of an Old-Timer," *RB*, 1941; Herman Spriter, letter to author, 16 Nov. 1957.

18. Confidential reply to questionnaire, 10 Aug. 1957.
19. Confidential reply to questionnaire, 16 Nov. 1957.
20. Dr. Rudolph I. Coffee, Obituary, *NYT,* 12 May 1955.

Chapter 11: Individualizing the Children

1. "Solomon Lowenstein," *Encyclopedia Judaica,* 4th ed.
2. Maurice Bernstein, interview with author, 12 Nov. 1975.
3. Federation, 26–27.
4. *AR,* 1904.
5. *AR,* 1903.
6. Annual Report of the Department of Public Charities of the City of New York, 1903, 24–25.
7. *AR,* 1905.
8. *AR,* 1906.
9. Ibid.
10. Dr. Jacob Goldenkranz, letter to author, 20 Mar. 1974.
11. Sol Modell, letter to author, 12 Dec. 1957.
12. *AR,* 1905.
13. *AR,* 1906,
14. Captain Philip Egner, publicity release, American Society of Composers, Authors, and Publishers, undated.
15. "Lionel J. Simmonds," *Who's Who in American Jewry,* 1938–39.
16. Bernard, 39–50.
17. *Proceedings,* 151.
18. *AR,* 1910; "Hebrew Home Holds 50th Anniversary," *NYT,* 5 Apr. 1910.
19. "Visiting Rabbi Criticizes Jewish Boarding Homes," *NYT,* 3 Feb. 1910.
20. Solomon Lowenstein, "A Study of the Problem of Boarding Out Jewish Children and of Pensioning Widowed Mothers," *Proceedings of the Sixth Biennial Conference of Jewish Charities in the United States, 1910,* 206–11.
21. Bernard, 55–57, 61–65.
22. *AR,* 1911.
23. *AR,* 1905, 1908, 1909; Herman Spriter, response to questionnaire, 16 Nov. 1957.
24. *AR,* 1912, 1913, 1916.
25. Murray Sprung, letter to author, 7 Apr. 1974; *AR,* 1918, 1919, 1922.
26. *AR,* 1922.
27. *AR,* 1916.
28. *AR,* 1918.
29. "Solomon Lowenstein."
30. "Orphans War Record," *NYT,* 14 Feb. 1919; "Hebrew Home Buys Site," *NYT,* 28 Feb. 1919.
31. List of HOA children buried in Salem Fields Cemetery.
32. *AR,* 1922.

33. *AR,* 1903.
34. "Solomon Lowenstein."
35. *AR,* 1910; "Hebrew Home Holds 50th Anniversary," *NYT,* 5 Apr. 1910.

Chapter 12: Decade of Promise and Disappointment

1. *AR,* 1921.
2. "Lionel J. Simmonds," *Who's Who in American Jewry,* 1938–39.
3. Mac Modell, letter to author, 27 Jan. 1958.
4. "Souvenir in Commemoration of the Organization of the Hebrew Orphan Asylum of the City of New York 1822–1922." The inside back cover of this eighty-page booklet contains a foldout diagram of the proposed new buildings.
5. *AR,* 1921.
6. Block, 2–12.
7. Report of the Intake Committee, Jewish Children's Clearing Bureau, undated.
8. HOA Biennial Report, 1925–26, 102d and 103d Annual Meetings. This was the first and apparently the only biennial report ever issued.
9. "Wed in Orphanage That Sheltered Them," *NYT,* 2 Feb. 1925.
10. "Tommy Tucker Unjumbles Confusion over Blooms and Greenes," *RB,* Dec. 1970.
11. HOA Biennial Report, 1925–26.
12. Myron Blanchard, interview with author, 3 Oct. 1974; Augusta Berdansky, interview with author, 8 Nov. 1957.
13. Werner W. Boehm, letter to author, 26 Mar. 1976.
14. Blanchard, interview with author; Berdansky, interview with author.
15. Confidential reply to questionnaire, 27 Nov. 1957.
16. Miriam Steiger Corito, letter to author, 27 Jan. 1976.

Chapter 13: Exit the Hebrew Orphan Asylum,
Enter "The Academy"

1. HOA Biennial Report, 1925–26, 102d and 103d Annual Meetings.
2. Personal observation.
3. "What We Used to Eat," *RB,* Apr. 1931.
4. Personal observation.
5. Columbia Scholastic Press Association, letter to author, 12 Jan. 1957.
6. Personal observation.
7. "The Verdict Was Thumbs Up," *RB,* Nov. 1964.
8. "Sidney Kyle Dead at 79; First to Attend Juilliard," *RB,* Mar.-Apr. 1990.
9. "Golden Age of the Band," *RB,* Nov. 1978, Dec. 1978.

10. "Both HOA and BOHA Bands Represented Catholic Church in 1928 Parade," *RB*, Mar.-Apr. 1986.

11. "Golden Age of the Band," *RB*, Nov. 1978, Dec. 1978.

12. Charles Snow, letter to author, 10 Jan. 1976.

13. Louis Delin, "Harmonica on Stage—Vaudeville," *Harmonica Happenings*, Spring 1972.

14. "Jefferson Pilgrimage Contest," *NYT*, 15 June 1925, 3 July 1925; Fannie Dubofsky, "So This Is Paris," *RB*, Autumn 1925.

15. *Seligman Solomon Society Souvenir Journal*, 1922–26.

16. "Writer Says Harold Lloyd Made Movie at HOA," *RB*, Nov.-Dec. 1988.

17. Abe Judson, Obituary, *RB*, Sept. 1981.

Chapter 14: From the Happy Twenties to the Depressed Thirties

1. Col. Jack L. Warner, letter to author, 5 June 1970; "Warner Gymnasium Dedicated," *NYT*, 1 Oct. 1928.

2. "Our Athletic History," *RB*, Apr. 1929.

3. "New Flyweight King Fit Successor to Throne," *New York Telegram*, 18 Dec. 1927.

4. *The Church of the Annunciation, 1853–1938*, 28.

5. Confidential reply to questionnaire, 23 Nov. 1957.

6. Personal observation.

7. Ibid.

8. Confidential reply to questionnaire, 4 July 1958.

9. Francis Steegmuller, letter to author, 29 May 1979.

10. Related to author by Louis Delin.

11. "Mrs. Roosevelt Visits Orphans Camp," *NYT*, 8 Aug. 1933.

12. The photograph was taken by Aaron Bogen.

13. Ralph Henry, reply to questionnaire, 11 Nov. 1957.

14. Veterans of Abraham Lincoln Brigade, letter to author, 10 Jan. 1987.

Chapter 15: Merger at Last

1. Dr. Moses Chaim Shelesnyak, letter to author, 20 Oct. 1961.

2. Personal observation.

3. Confidential reply to questionnaire, received 4 Apr. 1959.

4. Doc Shelly went on to become a member of the Endocrine and Reproduction Physiology Department at Weizmann Institute of Science in Rehovot, Israel. He has spent many years working on the male contraceptive pill. Shelesnyak, letter to author.

5. Personal observation.

6. Related to author by boys involved.

7. "Harold Greenfield Recalls Unforgettable Years 1921–1928," *RB*, Mar. 1979.

8. Block, 1.
9. BHOA Annual Report, 1944.
10. Bernard, *The Children*, 117–21.
11. "4 Child Aid Groups Join Forces Here," *NYT*, 15 Jan. 1940.
12. "HOA Championship Basketball Team," *RB*, Mar. 1979.
13. Personal observation.
14. "Dave Shorr Says He Was Last Discharged HOA Kid, in 1942," *RB*, Dec. 1981.

Chapter 16: The Luckiest Orphans

1. "Dave Shorr Says He Was Last Discharged HOA Kid, in 1942," *RB*, Dec. 1981.
2. "The Last Discharged HOA Kid," *RB*, Sept. 1981.
3. "Samuel Ledwith Chosen Marine Veteran to Break Ground for Pearl Harbor Museum," *RB*, Mar.-Apr. 1990.
4. "Danny Fruchter Recalls Pearl Harbor Attack," *RB*, Dec. 1981.
5. Related to author by Milton Korman.
6. Personal knowledge.
7. Leo W. Schwarz, Obituary, *NYT*, 2 Dec. 1967.
8. Pyle, 452–53.
9. Related to author by David Shorr.
10. "Jerry Fraiden Dead," *RB*, Nov. 1971.
11. Personal knowledge.
12. Related to author by David Shorr.
13. "Sy Sandler Dead," *RB*, Jan.-Feb. 1987.
14. Norman Mailer, letter to author, 11 Feb. 1958.
15. "History of H.O.A. Association," *RB*, May-June 1987.
16. Personal knowledge.
17. "Dave Shorr Says He Was Last Discharged HOA Kid, in 1942," *RB*, Dec. 1981.
18. "Jack Carl Was Last Grad to Sleep Under HOA Roof," *RB*, Sept.-Oct. 1989.
19. New York City Department of Buildings, letter to author, 1 Oct. 1957.
20. Personal observation.
21. "Children in Limbo," *New York Herald-Tribune*, 10 Feb. 1965.
22. JCCA Annual Report, 1989.
23. "History of H.O.A. Association," *RB*, May-June 1987.
24. "Meet John Patrick Murray," *RB*, Apr. 1985.
25. "Reagan, Cuomo, Koch Send Congratulatory Messages," *RB*, Mar.-Apr. 1987.
26. "HOA Plaque Is Unveiled at Warner Gym," *RB*, May-June 1988.
27. "The Last HOA Parade," *RB*, June 1989.
28. "Art's Message to Dinner," *RB*, Jan. 1988.
29. Personal knowledge.

30. "Leo Berger, Boarding Out Boy, Made Fortune with Tanker Fleet," *RB*, Sept.-Oct. 1987.

31. Aaron L. Jacoby, Obituary, *NYT*, 3 Oct. 1987; "Aaron L. Jacoby Dead," *RB*, Nov.-Dec. 1987.

32. "Louis Nierenberg Dead," *RB*, Oct. 1980.

33. Murray Silverman, letters to author, 20 July, 4 Aug. 1990.

34. "Nathan Mantel, World Class Biometrician," *RB*, May-June 1980.

35. "Alice Herzig Dead at 67," *RB*, May-June 1980.

36. "The Transformations of Harold Tovish," *RB*, May-June 1980.

37. Leo W. Schwarz, Obituary, *NYT*, 2 Dec. 1967.

38. "Sidney Kyle Dead at 79," *RB*, Mar.-Apr. 1990.

39. "Jimmy Smith Retires from Philharmonic," *RB*, Sept. 1977.

40. "Al Godlis Dies," *RB*, Feb. 1978.

41. "Ray Hollander Dead," *RB*, Oct. 1978.

42. "Murray Silverman Operates Acapulco Safari," *RB*, Jan. 1976; Murray Silverman, letter to author, 4 Aug. 1990.

43. One felony offender was, coincidentally, assigned a parole officer who had also been in the HOA, though the parole officer did not tell the parolee.

44. "Should Have Stayed in HOA, Foster Home Girl Writes," *RB*, Sept.-Oct. 1989.

45. Art Buchwald, "Sixty Minutes," 19 Oct. 1980.

46. "Alumnus to Speak on 60-Year Link to Foster Family," *RB*, Nov.-Dec. 1989.

Bibliography

Archival Sources

American Jewish Historical Society, Waltham, Mass.
Human Resources Administration Library, New York City
Jewish Child Care Association, New York City
Jewish Theological Seminary Library, New York City
Library of Congress, Washington, D.C.
New York Historical Society
New York Public Library, Jewish Division

Newspapers, Journals, and Annual Reports

Asmonean, 1849–55
Annual Reports of the Hebrew Orphan Asylum, 1863–1926
Jewish Messenger, 1857–96
New York Times, 1851–1941
Rising Bell, 1919–34; 1964–present
Seligman Solomon Society Souvenir Journal, 1910–37

Questionnaire

A questionnaire was sent to alumni on the mailing list of the H.O.A. Association, Inc. in June 1957. It drew 91 replies, 63 from men and 28 from women.

General Sources

American Jewish Committee. *American Jewish Yearbook*. Philadelphia: Jewish Publication Society, 1899.

Baar, Dr. Hermann. *Addresses on Homely and Religious Subjects*. New York: H.O.A. Industrial School Printing Office, 1880.

———. *Bible Lessons for School and Home*. New York: Bloch, 1902.

Bernard, Jacqueline. *The Children You Gave Us*. New York: Jewish Child Care Association, 1973.

Bierce, Ambrose. *The Devil's Dictionary*. New York: Thomas Y. Crowell, 1979.

Brace, Charles Loring. *The Dangerous Classes of New York and Twenty Years of Work among Them*. New York: Wynkoop and Hollenbeck, 1872.

Block, Herman W. "The New York Child-Care Situation." Paper presented at the annual meeting of the National Council of Federations for Support of Jewish Societies. Philadelphia, Jan. 28, 1937.

Connable, Alfred, and Edward Silverfarb. *Tigers of Tammany*. New York: Rhinehart and Winston, 1962.

Duffy, John. *A History of Public Health in New York City, 1625–1866*. New York: Russell Sage Foundation, 1968.

Ehrlich, Susan. *Ella's Diary*. New York: Pageant Press, 1961.

Ellis, Edward Robb. *The Epic of New York City*. New York: Coward-McCann, 1966.

Emerson, Sarah Hopper. *Life of Abby Hopper Gibbons*. New York: G. P. Putnam, 1897.

Federation of Jewish Philanthropies of New York. *The Golden Heritage*. New York: 1969.

Frankel, Lee K. "Report of the Committee on Dependent Children." In *Trends and Issues in Jewish Social Welfare in the United States, 1899–1958*, edited by Robert Morris and Michael Freund. Philadelphia: Jewish Publication Society, 1966.

Friess, Horace L. *Felix Adler and Ethical Culture*. New York: Columbia University Press, 1981.

Gardner, Ralph D. *Horatio Alger, or the American Hero Era*. Mendota, Ill.: Wayside Press, 1964.

Goldberg, Isaac. *Major Noah: American-Jewish Pioneer*. Philadelphia: Jewish Publication Society, 1944.

Goldman, Edwin Franko. "*Facing the Music*." Ms. 1936. Private collection.

Goldstein, Dr. Israel. *A Century of Judaism in New York*. New York: Congregation B'nai Jeshurun, 1930.

Green, Abel, and Joe Laurie, Jr. *Show Biz*. New York: Henry Holt, 1951.

Grinstein, Hyman B. *The Rise of the Jewish Community of New York, 1654–1860*. Philadelphia: Jewish Publication Society, 1947.

Hale, William Harlan. *Horace Greeley, Voice of the People*, New York: Harper, 1950.

Hellman, George S. "The Story of the Seligmans." Ms. 1945. New York Historical Society Collection.

Isaacs, Myer S. "Sampson Simson," *American Jewish Historical Society Quarterly* 10 (1902).

Kaganoff, Nathan M. "Organized Jewish Welfare Activity in New York City (1848–1860)," *American Jewish Historical Society Quarterly* 56, no. 1 (1966).

Koshel, Jeffrey. "Deinstitutionalization—Dependent and Neglected Children." Washington, D.C.: Urban Institute, 1964.

Korn, Bertam Wallace. *Eventful Years and Experiences*. Cincinnati: American Jewish Archives, 1954.

Letchworth, William P. "Homes of Homeless Children." Report by the Commissioner of the State Board of Charities sent to the Legislature. January 14, 1876.

Martin, Edward Sanford. *Life of Joseph H. Choate*. New York: Charles Scribners Sons, 1921.

McCabe, John. *George M. Cohan The Man Who Owned Broadway*. New York: Doubleday, 1973.

McCague, James. *The Second Rebellion*. New York: Dial Press, 1968.

Morse, Lucy Gibbons. "Personal Recollections of the Draft Riot of 1863." Ms. 1927. New York Historical Society Collection.

Nordlinger, Bernard I. "A History of the Washington Hebrew Congregation," *The Record* 2, no. 4 (Nov. 1969).

Patterson, Samuel White. *Old Chelsea and St. Peter's Church*. New York: Friedele Press, 1935.

Pool, Rev. de Sola, and Tamar Pool. *An Old Faith in a New World*. New York: Columbia University Press, 1955.

Proceedings of the Conference on the Care of Dependent Children. Washington, D.C.: GPO, 1909.

"Proposed Merger of the Child Care Agencies Affiliated with the New York Federation for the Support of Jewish Philanthropies." Typewritten report, 1937.

Pyle, Ernie. *Brave Men*. New York: Henry Holt, 1947.

Richardson, James F. *The New York Police*. New York: Oxford University Press, 1970.

Richmond, Rev. J. F. *New York and Its Institutions*. New York: E. B. Treat, 1871.

Rothman, David J. *The Discovery of the Asylum*. Boston: Little, Brown, 1971.

Schappes, Morris U. *Documentary History of the Jews of the United States, 1654–1875*. New York: Citadel Press, 1950.

Schneider, David M. *The History of Public Welfare in New York State*. Chicago: University of Chicago Press, 1938.

Simmonds, Lionel J. "Edenwald: An Experiment in Education." Paper delivered at the National Conference of Jewish Social Service. New York, 1929.

Simson, Sampson. "Subsistence Account for Service as Acting Assistant Deputy Quartermaster General in the War of 1812 for the period August 11, 1814 to December 13, 1814."

Stein, Herman D. "Jewish Social Work in the United States (1654- 1954)." In *American Jewish Yearbook*, vol. 57. Philadelphia: Jewish Publication Society, 1956.

Strong, George Templeton. *The Diary of George Templeton Strong*, vol. 1. New York: Macmillan, 1952.

United Hebrew Benevolent Association of Boston. Testimonial to the Hebrew Orphan Asylum of New York, June 1891.

Van Duesen, Glyndon G. *Horace Greeley, Nineteenth Century Crusader*. Philadelphia: University of Pennsylvania Press, 1953.

Index

Note on the Author

Hyman Bogen was in the Hebrew Orphan Asylum from 1932 to 1941, when it closed. He received a master's degree in social work at Adelphi University. For thirty years he worked for the Human Resources Administration of the City of New York. In his last eleven years he was the director of the Division of Family Homes for Adults, which placed aged, disabled, or homeless adults in family homes similar to foster homes for children. A retiree, he serves the H.O.A. Association, Inc. as both president and editor of its newsletter, the *Rising Bell*.